I0223065

Digital Development

Praise for this book

'This is a must-read for anyone committed to understanding how information and communication technologies have become integral to global economic, political, and social development. Based upon a collection of case studies, it provides an opportunity to learn from those involved in the practices that are making a difference. These authors have made a positive contribution to our understanding of digital development, offering valuable insights for scholars, policy makers, and practitioners.'

Professor Susan V. Scott, Information Systems and Innovation Faculty,
Department of Management, London School of Economics
and Political Science

'The authors – all leaders in the field of information technology for development – take readers on a journey across a series of in-depth cases, zooming in on stories across geographies and technologies assessing the broad contribution of digitalisation. The lessons are diverse; grounded in the domains of health, maintaining peace, gender violence, refugees and payments. This book is unique in its depth and breadth and is both insightful and inspiring.'

Professor Brian Nicholson, Alliance Manchester Business School,
University of Manchester, UK

'This book makes a unique contribution to the ICTD field of study presenting a compendium of stories about how digital technologies in the hands of citizens can promote socioeconomic development. Apart from providing rich insights about the socially-embedded nature of ICTD interventions, these stories constitute locally-grounded theories of change to guide further research and practice on digital development.'

Shirin Madon, Associate Professor of Information Communication Technologies
and Socioeconomic Development, London School of Economics

Digital Development
Stories of Hope from Health and Social Development

Edited by
Sundeep Sahay, Arunima Mukherjee,
Geoff Walsham and Thomas Hylland Eriksen

Practical
ACTION
PUBLISHING

Practical Action Publishing Ltd
25 Albert Street, Rugby,
Warwickshire, CV21 2SD, UK
www.practicalactionpublishing.org

© Sundeep Sahay, Arunima Mukherjee, Geoff Walsham and
Thomas Hylland Eriksen, 2022

The moral right of the editors to be identified as editors of the work and the
contributors to be identified as contributors of this work have been asserted
under sections 77 and 78 of the Copyright Design and Patents Act 1988.

This open access publication is created under a Creative Commons
Attribution Non-commercial No-derivatives CC BY-NC-ND licence.
This allows the reader to copy and redistribute the material, but appropriate
credit must be given, the material must not be used for commercial purposes,
and if the material is transformed or built upon the modified material may
not be distributed. For further information see https://creativecommons.org/
licenses/by-nc-nd/4.0/legalcode

Product or corporate names may be trademarks or registered trademarks, and
are used only for identification and explanation without intent to infringe.

A catalogue record for this book is available from the British Library.

A catalogue record for this book has been requested from the Library of Congress.

ISBN 978-1-78853-206-8 Paperback
ISBN 978-1-78853-205-1 Hardback
ISBN 978-1-78853-207-5 Electronic book

Citation: Sahay, S., Mukherjee, A., Walsham, G., Hylland Eriksen, T.,
(2022) *Digital Development*, Rugby, UK: Practical Action Publishing
<http://dx.doi.org/10.3362/9781788532075>.

Since 1974, Practical Action Publishing has published and disseminated
books and information in support of international development work
throughout the world. Practical Action Publishing is a trading name of
Practical Action Publishing Ltd (Company Reg. No. 1159018), the wholly
owned publishing company of Practical Action. Practical Action Publishing
trades only in support of its parent charity objectives and any profits are
covenanted back to Practical Action (Charity Reg. No. 247257, Group VAT
Registration No. 880 9924 76).

The views and opinions in this publication are those of the author and do
not represent those of Practical Action Publishing Ltd or its parent charity
Practical Action.

Reasonable efforts have been made to publish reliable data and information,
but the authors and publisher cannot assume responsibility for the validity
of all materials or for the consequences of their use.

Cover photo shows: Community health worker in India
Typeset by vPrompt eServices, India

Contents

List of tables and figures

Foreword

I am pleased to write a short Foreword to this important book. I want to draw the reader's attention to the multiple reasons for reading this book closely.

The first reason is that this book is a hopeful story about both digitality and development. This is noteworthy in an era in which both these phenomena have received considerable negative attention both from academics and from activists. In the case of development, we have a long history of critiques of development, from names as different as James Scott, Arturo Escobar, Ashis Nandy, and James Ferguson. Many of these justified critiques have come from scholars who take culture seriously, are alarmed by top-down initiatives, and tend to be suspicious of technology. This suspicion, which was also echoed by Marxists, environmentalists, and even some major multilateral organizations, needs to be revised and rethought, as this book invites us to do.

The same is true of the subject of digital tools, techniques, and affordances. These have also attracted a lot of criticisms about 'the digital divide', about corporate greed, or about the threats to privacy coming from the state–corporate nexus. Recent alarms about Pegasus, Facebook, and Cambridge Analytica exemplify this view of the dangers of digital connectivity. There are more optimistic views, of course, but the voices of doubt and opposition seem louder and sometimes better argued. Thus, the entire apparatus of ICT, both ideological and machinic, tends to be seen as anti-poor, anti-democratic, and anti-liberal. The chapters of this book, without much fanfare or exaggeration, make it hard to hold on to the more dogmatic forms of critique of digital connectivity.

The second reason for my enthusiasm for this book is a trend in media studies, especially in the United States and in many parts of Europe, which has almost completely severed the topic of communications from the topic of media. The field of communications evolved after World War II, in the context of the Cold War, as an effort to study the impact of communications technology on propaganda, advertising, technology-transfer, and development. It suffered from various limitations of method and theory, but it had the virtue of keeping the whole world in view. Media studies, a product mostly of the 1980s and since, has tended to become a highly discursive Euro-American space, mostly confined to the humanities and critical cultural studies, and is framed by interests in materiality and posthuman forms of agency, as well as by a meta-discourse about algorithms, screens, interphases, and infrastructure. This new brand of media theory makes a direct connection between the critical humanities and the high natural sciences, notably through the discourse of STS (science and technology studies). This direct link allows a dramatic bypass of the social sciences, which are mostly to be found in the now unglamorous space of communication studies. Since interest in ICT belongs to the social sciences, we can safely say the rise of STS has meant the fall of ICT. Along with this fall has come a radical disinterest in political, economy, development, global inequality, planning, policy, and comparative social science as a whole. This is a big loss and the chapters that follow are a welcome reminder that we cannot throw out the baby of ICT with the bathwater of Cold War ideology.

There is a final and even more compelling reason for my enthusiasm. We all know that our world is facing a variety of planetary problems, of which those of migration, epidemic disease, racism, inequality, and climate are the most prominent. It is also evident that though the nation-state is not the best platform for addressing these problems, it remains the major ideological and practical basis of our solutions. It may take many decades for this design to be replaced by a better, more planetary, pan-species and post national architecture. Meanwhile, we do have the many virtues of ICT to deal with the impacts of these huge problems. This book shows vividly the ways in which problems of displacement, poverty, health, finance, and technical apartheid are being combatted by the creative, emancipatory, and inclusive uses of ICT. It is a major invitation to the politics of hope in our times of darkness, division, and despair, when hoping itself is a singular act of courage. I hope this invitation will be accepted by many.

Arjun Appadurai
Berlin
18 November 2021

CHAPTER 1

The hope of ICTs building a better world

Sundeep Sahay, Geoff Walsham,
Thomas Hylland Eriksen, and Arunima Mukherjee

The trial, in spring 2021, of Derek Chauvin for the killing of George Floyd a year earlier was followed closely over television by millions of people the world over. The landmark judgment that convicted Chauvin to 22.5 years in prison was hailed as a harbinger of 'hope' for the bringing in of larger police reforms in the USA. While this judgment might be seen as the cumulative effect of years of struggle by activists and civil society to usher in police reforms, what cannot be ignored was the central role of the video-recording made by a casual bystander using his mobile phone. That video-recording, a crucial piece of evidence, was played in its entirety by the prosecution during the trial opening. It was an up close and personal recording of the full incident, which had unfolded over 9 minutes 29 seconds. In its closing argument, the prosecution urged the jury to 'believe what they saw'. The power of this visual and auditory evidence was rendered indisputable by its high-quality resolution: it captured the intimate details of the voices, Floyd's struggles, the expressions on the police officers' faces – and even Floyd's last breath. The story this video told was reinforced by the images captured by the body-worn cameras of the police officers involved in the incident.

It may be instructive to contrast this with the beating, on 3 March 1991, of Rodney King by four Los Angeles police officers. This incident was also videotaped by George Holliday from his balcony nearby, but it lacked the resolution of the Chauvin video-recording. This enabled the prosecution and the defence to construct contrasting narratives from the same 'murky pixels' (Goodwin, 1994), leading to the initial acquittal of three of the four police officials involved.

These incidents highlight the important role that mobiles can play in law, the unceasing improvements in mobile technology, and that the quotidian use of the mobile has been invested with large-scale societal and institutional implications. While these two examples do not in themselves concern development, they indicate the capability of the new media to set agendas, influence social relationships, and speak truth to power. The evidential contrast between the Rodney King affair and the death of George Floyd shows the massive changes in the realm of information and communications technology in just over a quarter of a century.

We could also speak about response to the COVID-19 pandemic by the Government of India. India has been in the news for reacting poorly, which made starkly visible the shortcomings of its public healthcare system, including poor planning, the insufficiency and inadequacy of the beds in its intensive care units, the ruinous shortfall in medical oxygen, and many other facets (*The Lancet*, 2021). In this chaos, perhaps the one redeeming factor may have gone largely unnoticed: the digital backbone of the response, particularly related to the vaccination rollout. Based on a perspective of over a decade of the Indian public health information mechanisms, there was a welcome change in the digital system, described by Mukherjee (2021) as 'flipping the coin' from the state to the citizen. For the first time, citizens felt a degree of control over the state-initiated digital system, and used it to make different choices, such as when and where to go for their vaccinations. Such a degree of choice was earlier unheard of. The 'citizen-centric' vaccination system – in contrast to the systems of the past, which tended often to be designed for state surveillance and control (Mukherjee, 2017) – arguably contributed to a positive experience for the citizenry. Digital interventions based on a citizen-centric design approach have the potential to strengthen public health systems more broadly and beyond the pandemic, such as in providing immunization and pregnancy care.

The above examples, although from vastly different settings, show that digital technologies can hopefully strengthen the processes of social development. The focus of this book is to understand the nature of this hope, and how these technologies can be materialized to strengthen 'digital development'. The book seeks to propose hope not in terms of grand visions and strategies but through building locally grounded theories of ICT-enabled change. Over the past couple of decades, hope in various forms has been promised by the dramatic changes in the development and use of information and communication technologies (ICTs), making them pervasive in virtually all areas of human activity and in nearly all countries. There was debate, at one time, particularly in the poorer countries, about whether ICTs were relevant, or whether funds should be spent on basic amenities such as water and food. This period of uncertainty was followed by debates on how ICTs could be implemented effectively (Sahay and Avgerou, 2002).

However, often the question of relevance is not *how* ICTs can make the world better, but *if* ICTs can make the world better. Addressing this question requires the need to seriously consider the question of timing and spacing. An example comes from Madon's (2014) long-standing research on primary healthcare in India. During this period, a policy vision was that implementing ICTs at the primary care level would improve accountability of primary healthcare to rural communities. Madon argues that the real question that should have been addressed at policy level was 'whether ICT were good' for achieving the policy goal, or indeed whether another policy instrument was better. In effect, the policy instrument that has made some contribution to improving accountability to rural communities has been the establishment of village health governance structures rather than ICTs. Arguably, the question of whether or not ICTs can make a difference continues to remain relevant because ICT is clearly not relevant all the time and in all spaces. Different initiatives over time have aimed to address improvements in primary healthcare accountability, but in different ways, with or without ICTs and information, and with varying impacts.

This book seeks to extend inquiry into how ICTs can be the harbingers of hope for individuals and organizations seeking to pursue development for a better world. Mobile phones are now nearly omnipresent even among the poor, and are employed across the social strata for very different purposes. The debate needs to shift from whether or not ICTs are good to how ICTs can make the world better.

Theoretical approach

A key aim of the book is to theorize the relation between ICTs and development (ICT4D) from a social sciences perspective. The research field of ICT4D, having originated in the late 1980s, is relatively nascent. Its evolution, however, has been impressive, with increasing diversity of theoretical approaches adopted, and methods, countries, and domains of applications studied. However, two signal criticisms of the research endure. First, while the field is interested in the relationship between technology and development, the very concept of development has been largely under-theorized; it has focused more on ICTs in developing countries rather than ICTs for development. Arguably, the reason for the concept of development to have been largely under-theorized is because the origin of the ICT4D field of study has been in information systems, which itself comes from the parent of computer science. Second, research tends to promote technology-deterministic assumptions that newer and modern technologies will on their own address developmental challenges. As a result, the focus is predominantly on the supply side (provision of more computers, internet, mobile devices, etc.) rather than on the demand side, which indicates how these digital interventions improve the wellbeing of the people and meet their aspirations, in terms of access to health, education, or other things valuable to them.

This book seeks to theoretically advance the ICT4D research domain in the following ways: first, bringing a multidisciplinary focus to bear, spanning information systems, social anthropology, and development (with both a strong developing country and a global component); second, normativizing 'hope for the better' as a key criterion in understanding the relationship between ICT and development, while allowing for different perspectives and understandings of what, indeed, might be 'better' in varying contexts involving different technologies, countries, application domains, and units of analysis. In this sense, what is 'better' is not viewed or treated as an overarching global concept, but is locally situated and a process that unfolds over time.

To avoid the danger of promoting technology-deterministic assumptions, we adopt a socio-technical approach that considers the context and the process, and the relationship between the context and the process (Walsham, 1993). This is operationalized via a three-legged interconnected approach. The first leg concerns the means for creating hope for a better world, which entails considering existing conditions such as available infrastructure, capacity, and problems such as the challenges of health and gender violence. The second concerns the processes by which the means can be converted into hopeful and desirable visions of the future. These processes represent the approaches by which the ICTs are implemented, capabilities strengthened, and the benefits reach the people. The third concerns the ends, the outcomes achieved, which could be in the forms of better health or improved peace.

This meta framework depicted in Figure 1.1 seeks to address two limitations in the current ICT4D research. The first concerns the dominance of research on supply-side dynamics. These supply-side figures are converted into indicators reflecting the technology's coverage per unit population, which are then taken to represent indicators of development. Of course, while the provision of ICTs is a necessary condition for technology-enabled development, it is not by any means a sufficient condition. For that, the technology should begin contributing to situated development processes, such as providing information to health workers who can use it to provide better care to pregnant mothers. To achieve sufficiency, many things need to be in place: means – for example, the necessary infrastructure and human resources; processes – for example, governance and capacity building; and ends – for example, the technology applications for improving development (such as of health, education, and peace).

Secondly, we seek to address the limitations of factors-based theorization and move to a more processual analysis. A factors-based approach to evaluation seeks to develop a snapshot view of ICT implementation, which tends to be limited, by design. Various experiences have taught us that there are many twists and turns in technology adoption and use, and that this process is rife

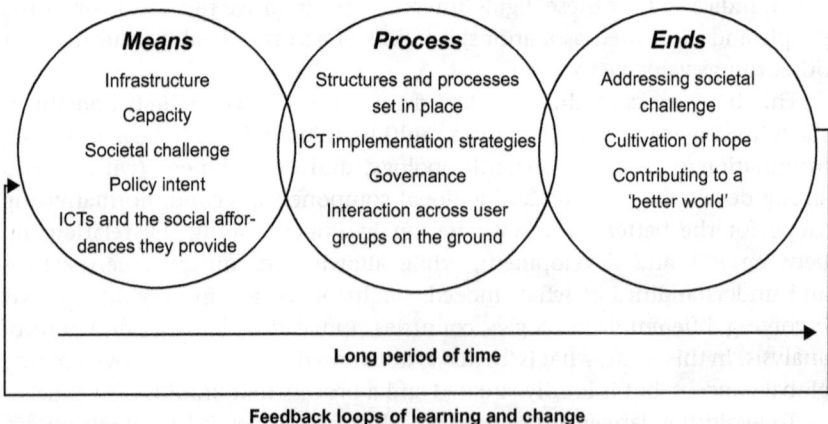

Figure 1.1 Analytical framework of means, process, and ends

with unintended consequences and side-effects. A factors-based approach does not acknowledge that technology-use is a process that involves many small, incremental steps; that each step brings with it changes in and of the networks of people supporting and resisting a technology; and that each step may even bring about changes in the content of the technology. A process perspective, in contrast, helps to see how learning takes place over time, and how people, as reflective and capable agents, learn even from failures and modify their actions to create unexpected outcomes. A process perspective helps also to better account for changing contextual conditions, such as a new political regime or technologies becoming obsolete, all of which goes to enable a more nuanced view of the context–process relationship.

Our theoretical approach is eclectic. Different cases have been analysed using different theoretical means ranging from informatics, development studies, to social anthropology. We believe that stories of hope, as argued by Appadurai (2004), can help develop a culture of aspirations as a form of a 'navigational capacity' that can guide future successes – in our case, of designing, implementing, and using ICT initiatives to strengthen development processes. It is important that contexts of development, often stifled by constraints, possess such a navigational capacity. Appadurai identifies three sets of constraints: 1) social structures that force the poor to subscribe to norms that further diminish their dignity, exacerbate their inequality, and throttle their access to material goods and services; 2) lack of a voice that enables engagement in civic action and prevents the poor from participating in policy decisions that affect their lives; and 3) limitations on opportunities.

We are also inspired by Amartya Sen's *Development as Freedom* (1999), in which he argues for development choices to be made by the citizens and not imposed on them by the state. Within Sen's framework, ICTs can be viewed as both a means and an ends to development, having the potential to enable people to convert their capabilities to functioning, or realized, achievement. In this context, the role of the state is to remove 'major sources of unfreedom' such as lack of roads, schools, and health services. Sen's ideas help to strengthen the demand-side focus of ICT4D initiatives and address some of the supply-side biases in ICT4D research, where development is equated with the mere provision of new technologies.

We are also guided by Manuel Castells' ideas relating to the network society (1996), the need for marginalized groups and regions to strive to be included in these modern global informational networks, or else to run the danger of being further and more systematically marginalized. As Castells describes it, in the past, colonization took place when the colonizers went to other lands; but, in contemporary times, colonization will take place if countries are excluded from global trade, knowledge, and informational networks. However, for these groups to be included, it is not just a matter of 'plug and play' in the network, but 'counter networks' that need to be created through long-term, intensive efforts. Mosse and Sahay (2005) describe how a marginalized region in northern Mozambique had to make long-term and sustained efforts to overcome its inherent limitations of infrastructure, capacity, and high disease burdens in order to join the 'network society' and make the health challenges visible to the authorities. Only through this visibility were advocacy efforts initiated towards addressing these challenges.

ICTs are themselves inscribed with material features that can enable or constrain hope for a better future. ICTs have the potential to provide opportunities to address aspirational constraints, but these opportunities are not uniformly available. For example, social media can serve as a vehicle for the disadvantaged to find a voice in a global setting. However, while specific social media tools such as Facebook or WhatsApp provide particular affordances, they also come with their respective risks and opportunities. The diversity of ICTs in common use at organizational and individual levels is now immense, and ranges from social media to robotics to the Internet of Things. Each requires a different design and implementation approach, and needs to be tailored to particular circumstances. Whether these ICTs bring hope or despair will be contingent on how appropriately they are designed and implemented.

Despite their wide use, the fundamental question remains about whether or not we are actually making a 'better world' with ICTs (Walsham, 2012). Who is benefiting from improved technology? Do the technologies widen or reduce the gap between the advantaged and the disadvantaged? Even in the relatively rich South, questions are being raised about whether the increasing collection and use of data by large technology companies and governments is a new form of what Zuboff (2019) labels 'surveillance capitalism'. There are concerns about the 'dark side of ICTs', such as threats to privacy, the security of personal data, and its misuse for a variety of purposes such as in influencing elections and for committing cybercrime. The phenomenon of fake news is a function of the widespread use of social media and its intermingling with politics and money.

Over the years and in different ways, the authors of this book have been engaged in studying and shaping the relationship between ICTs and society through education, research, and policy-oriented initiatives. A particular focus of their engagement has been on ICT4D, within the broader contexts of globalization and the shaping of social processes in an interconnected world. As social scientists, we are not 'neutral' researchers who are merely studying and reporting on the world, but are, through engaging with it, also participating in shaping it. As Easlea (1981) has argued, there is no such thing as value-free social sciences:

> Values and goals inform all significant social activity. Without values and without goals, human enterprises, if they can be conceived of starting at all, must inevitably peter out into a wasteland of trivialities. Champions of 'value free' enterprises are deceiving themselves. Nowhere, of course, is self-deception greater than in the social sciences. Value free social sciences does not and cannot exist ... (p. 274)

... The fundamental choice confronting social scientists is essentially that between commitment to programmes of 'social engineering' within the established structures of power and control or commitment to programmes of revolutionary political action with the intention of building societies significantly less exploitative and manipulative than existing ones (pp. 153–4).

The aim of this book is to focus on the positive and hopeful implications of ICTs, particularly in low- and middle-income countries (LMICs). Through this book, as engaged social scientists, the aim is to both explore what we consider to be a 'better' ICT-enabled world and, through the empirical analysis of a diversity of cases, inductively infer how this 'better' can be constructed. Walsham (2012) was one of the first in both the ICT4D and mainstream information systems research to have asked: 'Are we making a better world with ICTs?' He emphasized the need for researchers to focus on ethical goals and increase the use of critical-research approaches, while also embracing diversity and multidisciplinary methods. This paper helped raise a conversation between different information systems researchers, which was carried as a research paper in the same issue of the *Journal of Information Technology* (Walsham, 2012a). Inspired by Walsham's question, Sahay (2013), in a plenary talk in Jamaica at the International Federation for Information Processing (IFIP) 9.4 virtual conference on Social Implications of Computers in Developing Countries, further examined the political and contextual conditions that shape the answer to this question, and extended the question to also try to understand 'how this better can be shaped'. Taking a wider social sciences-based perspective, he discussed how different social scientists at different points of history and through the lens of the respective theories and the science of their disciplines, had engaged with making the world better. For example, Marx and Keynes had very particular research-action programmes that they pursued through their writings. Marx loathed capitalist society and looked for possible agents of change who could overthrow the class structure and create a different social order. Keynes, on the other hand, committed himself to the preservation of that very same social order.

Sajda Qureshi, editor of the *Journal of Information Technology for Development*, also discussed research concerning the question of the better world within the ICT4D research domain (Qureshi, 2015). She echoed the concerns of various researchers that the ICT4D field has not done justice to improving the condition of the poor because of its failure to engage with policy issues and the real concerns of users. The guiding academic motivation (particularly in North America) of 'publish or perish' had not helped in making the development world better, and systemic changes in both research and practices were required to bring in more positive change.

This book seeks to further expand on this research agenda – but with a difference. As 'non-neutral' social scientists, we give voice to our concerns of the need for more engagement in shaping ICTs to have more positive outcomes. We specifically engage with 'stories of hope'; to understand, from both theoretical and practical perspectives, what 'better' means; and how 'better' can be achieved.

Empirical basis

This book aspires to develop stories of hope around how ICTs are contributing to making the world better. This helps us go beyond stories of both gloom and doom and of utopia and techno-optimism, and focus on the particular empirical means by which ICT outcomes can be shaped. We analyse in the context of development, defined by the interdisciplinary research field of ICT4D, and with a strong social sciences grounding. We build case studies of interesting stories of ICT initiatives that we believe have had positive impacts on development processes. These case studies are developed drawing on typically long-term engagement with the experiences described. Our selection of cases with 'positive' development outcomes aids in analysing what has made these initiatives succeed. We also seek to highlight the challenges faced, and discuss how they are being sought to be overcome. The inductive and systematic intra- and inter-case analysis helps build a theoretical understanding of 'better', and, practically, how ICTs can contribute to this effort.

This book includes eight case studies representing different forms of technologies (such as mobile phones, early warning systems, and health information systems) being used in varying contexts of development (such as health, epidemic management, gender violence, and conflict mitigation) across different countries (India, Sri Lanka, Kenya, Guatemala, and the global context). These cases cover a range of issues and technologies located in the Global South, all concerning social development processes. While this broad brush is indicative of the primary research interests of the authors around ICT4D, it should not be taken to imply that the rest of the world is of less interest. Indeed, in the later conclusions in the book, we discuss ICT4D's relevance to the wider world and to broader information systems and social sciences research. In some depth, we examine these examples for what we mean by 'better', and whether or not (and how) the benefits anticipated have actually happened. We also analyse the findings for ways that others may find helpful in analysing cases of their own. Most of the cases in this book are long term, spanning up to 10 years, and this temporal perspective helps in understanding not only the dynamics involved but also the extent to which the past shapes the future, analysed through the means, the process, the ends.

The cases have three unifying themes that help in the synthesis of what we have learnt. The first theme concerns the means, the process, and the ends, which are independently analysed for each case using micro-level theoretical concepts such as capabilities, networks, and sustainability, and subsequently synthesized. The analytical focus on the means, or process, or ends varies from case to case. In some cases, we may focus more on the process; on others, the means or the ends. The second theme concerns the role of technology, which we assume has particular inscribed affordances that shape the outcomes in particular ways. The third theme concerns the notions of 'hope' and 'better', with each case having particular implications in terms of better health or improved institutional capabilities of the state, or reduced conflicts.

The structure of the book is straightforward. Following the introductory Chapter 1, Chapters 2–9 are devoted to the detailed case studies. Each chapter has a similar format that provides the context of the development challenge being faced (for example, conflict or pandemics), followed by the introduction to the case (details of where, when, how, and by whom). The case narrative that follows describes the case study and how it unfolded over time. In the analysis section, some theoretical concepts are introduced to aid the analysis. Finally, in the conclusion, we discuss our analysis of what aspect of 'better' has been emphasized by the case, and how ICTs contribute to achieve this state. Chapter 10 synthesizes the findings and presents the theoretical and policy-related implications. Table 1.1 provides a brief overview of the chapters.

Table 1.1 Summary of chapters

Chapter 1: The hope of ICTs building a better world	Introduction to the aims of the book, analytical framework, the structure, and expected contributions.
Chapter 2: Enabling empowerment and platforms for learning: ICTs for strengthening maternal and child health in India	This case concerns a pan-India digital initiative for tracking case-based health data for pregnant mothers and children for immunization. While the visible impact of this project was that of a 'failure', we take a temporal perspective to understand, through the theoretical lens of 'empowerment', the invisible learning that helped create an enabling foundation for future digital health initiatives.
Chapter 3: Empowerment of displaced persons through the smartphone	The spread of the mobile phone/smartphone has been extremely fast and comprehensive in the Global South, resulting in a broad range of new practices, opportunities, and forms of communicating. This chapter analyses how smartphones have helped provide displaced persons with a form of stability over time and space.
Chapter 4: Building resilience to strengthen HIS response to pandemics: Case study from Sri Lanka	This chapter describes the articulation of the information systems response to the COVID-19 pandemic in Sri Lanka. Key to a successful response was a form of socio-technical agility, enabled through a free and open-source digital platform supported by a lean governance structure.
Chapter 5: Enabling sustainability qualifiers of health management information systems: Case study from Odisha, India	Achieving sustainability is an enduring challenge of ICT4D projects. Analysing the evolution of a state health information system over a 10-year period, we identify how the state enabled 'sustainability qualifiers' to build capabilities and infrastructures to help direct information systems in addressing their ongoing health challenges.
Chapter 6: Building citizen trust in public health systems: Hospital information systems in India	The absence of trust between citizens and the state often undermines the efficacy of ICT4D initiatives. In this case, we trace the evolution, over a decade, of an integrated hospital information system across 20+ hospitals in an Indian state, and how, gradually, over time, trust has evolved.

(Continued)

Table 1.1 Continued

Chapter 7: Mobile payments as a means to an end	We trace the growth in use of mobile money within the informal sector in the South, and how this enhanced means of financial transactions has enabled many groups of people to engage in new means of living with more dignity and status in society.
Chapter 8: ICT-enabled counter networks for peace: Mitigating violence in Kenya	This case concerns the process of conflict mitigation in regions of ethnic strife in Kenya. We discuss how ICTs enable the formation of 'counter networks' for invoking peace not only by building social capital but also by mitigating the negative consequences of social capital.
Chapter 9: Enabling spaces for conversation: Engaging with violence against women in Guatemala	Mitigating violence against women is an important normative goal in many developing countries. We focus on the process of using ICTs to build spaces for conversations between the various institutions involved in supporting women who are victims of violence. This helps the building of a shared understanding of the nature of the violence, and enables the formulation of coherent collective action.
Chapter 10: Implications for theory, policy, and practice	This chapter presents a synthesis of the case studies, based on three dimensions: 1) the means-end-process framework; 2) the role of ICTs; and 3) contributions to hope for a better world. Multiple actors – the state, citizens, researchers, and donors – have a stake in ICT4D initiatives. Also outlined here are some of the practical implications for these stakeholders to develop more relevant ICT4D initiatives that can contribute to a better world.

Conclusions

We believe the debates raised in the book will be of direct relevance to those working on ICTs in the Global South: in particular, for those working on topics such as health information systems, peace, gender violence, and other signal issues. We also believe that the book should be of relevance to those working on ICTs more generally, across the domains of research, education, policy, and practice. While the book does not seek to provide prescriptions on how to build and use ICTs, we have tried to synthesize issues of importance that should be considered, beyond just the technical systems.

References

Appadurai, A. (2004) 'The capacity to aspire: culture and the terms of recognition', in V. Rao and M. Walton (eds), *Culture and Public Action*, pp. 59–84, Stanford University Press, Palo Alto, CA.

Castells, M. (1996) *The Rise of the Network Society*, Blackwell Publishers, Oxford; Malden, MA.

Easlea, B. (1981) *Liberation and the Aims of Science*, Scottish Academic Press, Ltd, Edinburgh.

Goodwin, C. (1994) 'Professional vision', *American Anthropologist* 96(3): 606–33.

Lancet (2021) 'Editorial: India's COVID-19 emergency', *The Lancet* 397: 1683 <https://doi.org/10.1016/S0140-6736(21)01243-5>.

Madon, S. (2014) 'Information tools for improving accountability in primary healthcare', in B-S. Gigler and S. Bailur (eds), *Closing the Loop: Can Technology Bridge the Accountability Gap?* World Bank Publications, Washington, DC.

Mosse, E. and Sahay, S. (2005) 'The role of communication practices in the strengthening of counter networks: case experiences from the health sector of Mozambique', *Information Technology for Development* 11(3): 207–25 <https://doi.org/10.1002/itdj.20017>.

Mukherjee, A. (2017) 'Empowerment: the invisible element in ICT4D projects? The case of public health information systems in India and Kenya', unpublished doctoral dissertation, University of Oslo, Norway.

Mukherjee, A. (2021) *'Flipping the Coin' from State Controlled to Citizen Enabling Health Information Systems: A Decade of Reflections from Engagement with Public Health Systems in India*, Working paper, Information Systems Research Group, University of Oslo, Norway.

Qureshi, S. (2015) 'Are we making a better world with information and communication technology for development (ICT4D) research? Findings from the field and theory building', *Information Technology for Development* 21(4): 511–22 <https://doi.org/10.1080/02681102.2015.1080428>.

Sahay, S. (2013) 'Are ICTs contributing to a better world? Experiences from the public health sector in India', Keynote Speaker at the *IFIP 9.4 Conference, Ocho Rios, Jamaica, May 2013*.

Sahay, S. and Avgerou, C. (2002) 'Introducing the special issue on information and communication technologies in developing countries', *The Information Society* 18(2): 73–6 <https://doi.org/10.1080/01972240290075002>.

Sen, A. (1999) *Development as Freedom*, Alfred A. Knopf, New York.

Walsham, G. (1993) *Interpreting Information Systems in Organizations*, John Wiley and Sons, New York.

Walsham, G. (2012) 'Are we making a better world with ICTs? Reflections on a future agenda for the IS field', *Journal of Information Technology* 27: 87–93 <https://doi.org/10.1057/jit.2012.4>.

Zuboff, S. (2019) *The Age of Surveillance Capitalism: The Fight for a Human Future at the New Frontier of Power*, Profile Books, London.

CHAPTER 2

Enabling empowerment and platforms for learning: ICTs for strengthening maternal and child health in India

Arunima Mukherjee and Sundeep Sahay

India, which is aspiring to become an economic regional and global superpower, is often compared unfavourably with China. Despite its high aspirations, India lags behind many countries, even in the South, on foundational maternal and child health indicators, such as maternal mortality and child nutrition. In trying to improve this situation, the government has been engaged with deploying various digital-based interventions predicated on aggregate data, while shifting, over the past decade, towards more individualized data. The Mother and Child Tracking System (MCTS), one such pan-India initiative from 2008, had the initial policy intent of improving policymakers' trust in the data on pregnancies and child immunization being reported by the field nurses to the central level. To materialize this intent, the MCTS was initiated to collect individualized data on pregnant mothers and children due for immunization. This system, which was implemented with intensive and large-scale government backing, was unique in that it collected data for all mothers and children interacting with the public health system. While the system itself did not generate the desired result of improving health outcomes (and was replaced by another portal in 2014), this chapter argues that if one goes beyond the visible outcomes of a 'failed' system, some invisible learnings can be had (such as the empowerment of the health workers), which provide hope for the strengthening of digital health interventions in the future. Within our means-process-ends framework, digital intervention (MCTS in this case) is the means, while models of implementation provide the process that translates the means to desired ends. Although the ends achieved might be unintended, they provide hope for the future.

Context of maternal and child health in India

This chapter describes a case study on the implementation of health information systems (HIS) in the public sector in India. We start by providing the context of these ICT interventions, and then detail a particular intervention, the Mother and Child Tracking System (MCTS), which was designed to collect individual-level data such as on demographics, health status, and services to be provided, so as to improve mother and childcare services.

We analyse the case from the perspectives of the frontline field nurses responsible for the provision of care. We discuss the unintended consequences of this system, given that the state used the registered data primarily to strengthen its monitoring of the work of the field nurses. Although the system was replaced a few years later, there were 'invisible' lessons for the nurses that would help them engage with future digital initiatives of the state.

The MCTS was envisaged as the means for achieving the ends of improving maternal and child health in India, which continues to be poor in terms of health indicators. The process by which the state seeks to convert these means to better ends concerns the various strategies employed for implementation, including establishing the digital architecture and infrastructure, the approach to capacity-strengthening, and enrolling the field-level healthcare providers and building their compliance with central directives on system usage.

There was both explicit and implicit resistance from the health staff to the system, because they perceived it as enhancing the state's surveillance over them. However, the introduction of the health workers more broadly to digital systems served as a source of empowerment and learning that would stand them in good stead with the large-scale digital initiatives in the years to come – including the information systems response to the COVID-19 pandemic.

The case narrative has been developed based on the long-term engagement of the authors with both the research and practice of reform efforts in the national- and state-level Health Management Information Systems (HMIS). This engagement started in 2008, when the National Rural Health Mission undertook a large-scale reform effort of the public health systems, including the HMIS, through architectural corrections related to increased decentralization, the strengthening of the integration of systems, and making systems more action-oriented to promote evidence-based decision-making. As members of the national reform team, the authors were involved in the redesign of the data formats, including what data gets collected and with what frequency, and how these contribute to the generation of actionable health indicators. Mother and childcare services were the core focus of the reform effort. The implementation of the reformed systems, including the MCTS, started in states.

Since then, the authors have been studying the implementation of the systems, and of new initiatives such as the introduction of mobile phones, and the challenges and opportunities perceived, in particular, by field-level nurses known as Auxiliary Nurse Midwives (ANMs) in using the digital initiatives. Over a decade of this engagement with the HIS, including recent initiatives to support the COVID-19 vaccination rollout, informs the rich and longitudinal insights into the unfolding dynamics of these systems. Not least, we discerned how 'failures' in the short and medium run actually provided a base for cumulative learning and empowerment, which went a long way in building capabilities to support future digital initiatives in the health sector.

Health information systems for maternal and child health in India

While India, in general, does poorly on maternal and child health, there is great variation in performance across and within states. States such as Uttar Pradesh and Rajasthan have high rates of fertility and maternal mortality, but states such as Kerala and Tamil Nadu have rates comparable with other middle-income countries. India, with 16 per cent of the global population, has the highest number of under-5 deaths, with a total of 1.08 million such deaths in 2016. It is one of the six countries that contribute to 50 per cent of the world's under-5 mortality rate, and to 24 per cent of all neonatal deaths. India's infant mortality is 35 deaths per 1,000 live births, an alarmingly high rate. On nutrition, India is ranked 102 among 117 countries on the Global Hunger Index 2019, with more than 35 per cent of children under five years of age underweight, over 38 per cent stunted, and more than half of all children anaemic (Drèze, 2020). The government sees digital interventions as crucial in helping address these challenges. In 2008, after an intensive reform process, the HMIS was made web-based and states were instructed to report district-level statistics to the national portal (Sahay et al., 2017). In 2009, the Union Ministry of Health and Family Welfare (MoHFW) introduced the MCTS to address existing deficiencies in the HMIS to shift focus from aggregating statistics to tracking individuals. The stated aim of the MCTS was to help track all pregnant women, which would ensure that they received their complete antenatal and postnatal check-ups and that more mothers delivered in institutions rather than at home. The close follow-ups of individual pregnancies would help to detect high-risk cases early and ensure appropriate referrals for specialist cases. Similarly, the follow-ups of children would help minimize dropouts from the immunization schedule.

Between 1990 and 2016, under-5 mortality reduced from 114 per 1,000 live births to 39 per 1,000 live births, and the infant mortality rate from 81 per 1,000 live births to 34 per 1,000 live births. Between 2003 and 2017, the maternal mortality rate dropped from 301 per 100,000 live births to 122 per 100,000 live births (MoHFW, 2020). Despite these improvements, however, the current rates of both remain a cause for concern, especially for a country seeking to become an economic power both in the region and globally. Figure 2.1 shows as an example how India fares on under-5 mortality rates in relation to other LMICs in the South Asian Region. While India may soon meet the world average of 39 fatalities per 1,000 live births, three countries (Nepal, Bangladesh, and Sri Lanka) have already met this target. Interesting to note in this analysis is that Nepal and Bangladesh have lower per capita incomes than India, while Sri Lanka has higher per capita income.

Given the scale of the maternal and child health challenge, the MoHFW has put significant efforts into strengthening digital interventions in this sector. Aside from the HMIS and the MCTS, some of the other initiatives include the RCH (Reproductive and Child Health) portal and a mobile-based application called ANMOL (Auxiliary Nurse Midwife On Line, an acronym that also means

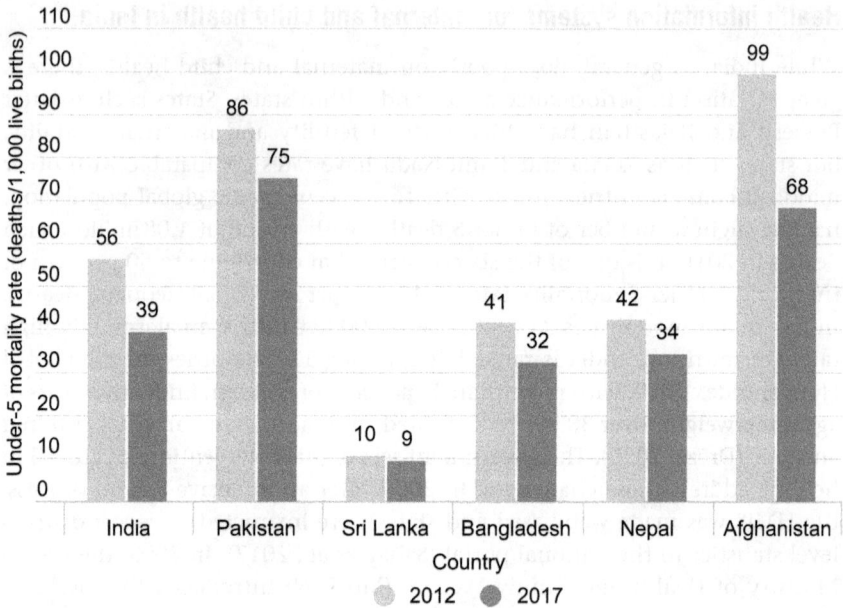

Figure 2.1 Comparison of mortality rates in LMICs

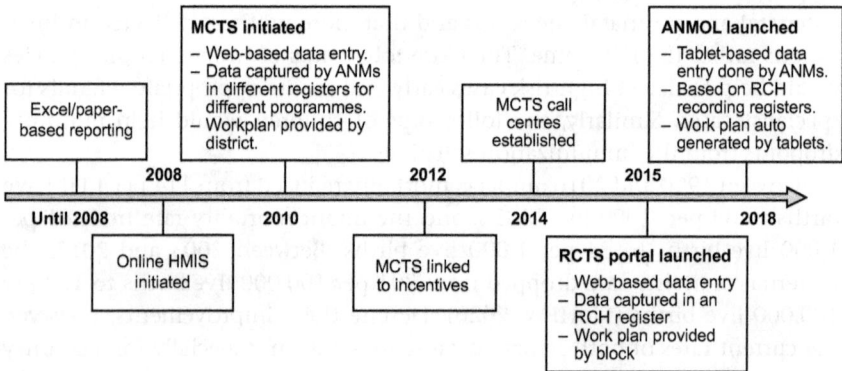

Figure 2.2 Comparison of decline in mortality rates

'priceless'), which were also rolled out in support and extension of these systems. An overview of the timeline of the rollout is depicted in Figure 2.2.

Prior to 2008, data was aggregated and primarily written on paper or, at most, Excel spreadsheets. In 2008, after a lengthy, centrally driven reform process, a web-based HMIS was introduced nationwide and catered primarily to aggregates such as number of babies born, or women given antenatal check-ups, within a particular time period and in a geographical area. In 2009, the MCTS began collecting individual case-based data – for example, the names and addresses of pregnant women and children requiring immunization.

Additionally, the name of the caregiver and her phone number were also noted. In parallel with the HMIS, the MCTS ran until 2015. It was then replaced by the RCH portal, which enhanced the scope of data collected, not only of pregnant women from conception to the postnatal period to the first five years of a child, but also of 'eligible couples', defined as married women in the reproductive age group of 15–49 years.

This led to a three-fold increase in the volume of data collected in the RCH, as compared to the MCTS portal. The RCH also introduced a significant change in how information was recorded. Conventionally, data was recorded in primary registers based on services provided by the ANMs to the catchment population. So, all data for antenatal care (ANC) services in one facility (consisting of about five villages) would be recorded in a single register. The RCH, however, mandated one register for each village, which resulted in the ANM needing five registers for the aggregated statistics of ANC services in her area.

The MCTS and its implementation dynamics

The origins of the MCTS can be traced to a public statement made by the health minister in a national daily where he doubted the veracity of aggregated figures reported by his field-workers:

> At present, the chief medical officer compiles the vaccine coverage data based on what states tell him, without going into the field. So, we are not sure if the data is true. As a pilot project, we are starting name-based vaccination with polio which is confined to just a few states. Once we have such data, we can simply call up a child's family and check whether he was administered the vaccine or not. We aim to eradicate polio in the next two to three years (Sinha, 2009).

Another health ministry official added:

> Once vaccination data becomes name-based rather than number-based, we will be able to account for the exact number of children vaccinated. The Auxiliary Nurse Midwife under the NRHM (National Rural Health Mission, MoH) will collect the data. At present, a lot of this data is fudged by states (Sinha, 2009).

Shortly after, a Government of India (GoI) notification announced (Ministry of Health & Family Welfare, 2011):

> It has been decided to have a name-based tracking system whereby pregnant women and children can be tracked for their ANCs (Antenatal Care) and immunization along with a feedback system to ensure that all pregnant women receive their ANC and post-natal care (PNCs) checkups; and further children receive their full immunization. An online module for the name-based tracking system is being developed and direction of use will be given soon.

In an annual review meeting, the health minister proudly announced that with the MCTS, even our partners in the US could ring up a pregnant woman in a rural Indian village and check if she had received adequate care services. As is typical of most government initiatives, the MCTS was designed by a government information technology agency in a top-down manner with limited effort to understand the work practices and the existing pain points of the ANMs, the primary users of the system. An ANM's work practices are complex. They involve a mix of care-giving, administration, data management, and community care, and nearly 60 per cent of her time is spent on data-related work. This work takes place both in outreach settings (in the villages where the beneficiaries reside) and in ANM clinics (called Sub-Centres), and involve much travel across the five or six villages (each with a population of about 1,000) that the ANM is responsible for.

While these are the government norms for population coverage, there are large variations across various states and districts. The ANM notes the care details (e.g. the first ANC check-up on a pregnant woman) in her field diary and, at the end of the day, transfers them to one of the 20-odd primary registers she manages. Each entry in the register is by the name of the beneficiary, his or her address, the service given, the next service due date, etc. At the end of the month, the ANM would have the figures verified by the facility's medical doctor, the name-based patient data then entered in the web-based MCTS, and the data made available to all levels nationally. Previously, the ANM only reported facility-level aggregate figures. Now, she was expected to send all person-based case records in a digital format, with the computer located not at her facility but at the Primary Health Care (PHC) facility responsible for the Sub-Centre. Primarily involving a lot of extra work for the ANM, this shift was radical. In addition, the HMIS application with the aggregate figures continued in parallel, with the ANM needing to enter data in both systems. The parallel running of these systems created redundancies and data duplications, with adverse implications on data quality and use (Khurana, 2021).

Prior to MCTS, the case-based details were recorded in primary registers maintained by the ANMs. This, while cumbersome, was available here and now. During our fieldwork, an ANM in a northern state said:

> My register is what I use to plan my everyday work to provide services. Everything else is only for reporting upwards. The information in these registers is available 'here and now'. I can read, mark things of importance, make notes to myself, [and] search for information at my pace without depending on anything or anyone.

The ANMs complained of always lagging behind with even a whole day of work. They had to line up at cybercafés close to their homes to update data entries in the evenings after work hours, and were often accompanied by family members for reasons of security. Some ANMs went to the extent of handing their passwords to cybercafés they contracted to enter data into the

MCTS – an action that could compromise data security. Another ANM said during an interview:

> I return from work by 5.30 p.m., rush into kitchen to get dinner ready and finish whatever I can to leave home by 6.45 p.m. to reach the cybercafé by 7 p.m. The shop closes at 8 p.m. Only if I put in one hour of data entry every day can I complete my registration workload. I am not quick at using computers, and my son does not understand the data. So, we both try to complete as much [as possible], as [I] cannot afford salary cuts.

The introduction in 2015 of the RCH portal and ANMOL created even more complexities, including those of integration and additional workload. An ANM said:

> All the pregnancies registered by me since 2011 in the MCTS and the RCH application are now being shown as 'pending tasks' in ANMOL, and I am being given periodic reminders to complete them. But the truth is that I have no pending tasks. In ANMOL, the first pregnancy in my follow-up schedule is from January 2011, and I must keep scrolling down to the present to find data relevant for today. Though we were told that we would be able to filter data by year, it is still not possible. This makes ANMOL very time-consuming and irrelevant for my everyday work.

The introduction of new systems required the ANMs to keep updating the baseline data in the new systems. Said an ANM:

> Another method we have been told about to get past this pending list is by completing the outcome information for each of the past pregnancies. But we do not have time to open all the previous registers, find the outcomes of each of the registered pregnancies, and enter these online. For me, this pending list does not matter, because this system is of no use to me. This is only for reporting upwards, and does not affect my providing of services, for which I use only my registers.

As data started to flow into the MCTS, administrators began monitoring system usage on parameters such as 'number of women and children registered yesterday and expected'. This message was communicated daily by SMS to the state health secretary first thing in the morning. Over time, comparative state rankings were added to these messages. So were reprimands for inadequate efforts. Gradually, approvals for state budgets became conditional on achievement of registration targets. The MoHFW started sending monthly letters to the states to enhance registration. A Government of India letter dated 10 February 2012 read: 'On close analysis of the data available in MCTS, it is noticed that only 77% of the mothers and 12.5% of the live births are registered in MCTS till date. Moreover, the services given to mother and child are not seen updated regularly.'

Two years later, the health minister proudly announced:

> Information is collected to track every mother and child by name, address and telephone for which a call centre has been set up in the ministry to verify the data and inform women of the check-ups and the immunization schedule, the health minister said. The Minister also made sample verification calls to registered women under the MCTS database to verify the database entries today (Ministry of Health and Family Welfare, 2011)

In November 2013, the MoHFW advertised a new Request for Proposal (RFP) for the setting up of a Mother and Child Tracking Helpdesk (MCTH) to strengthen data validation. It stated:

> MCTH shall validate records of health worker, pregnant women and children registered under MCTS by making outbound calls to the health beneficiaries and health workers. Errors/deviations that are generated in the validation exercise must be reported back to MCTS so that corrections can be made. Minimum 70-calls (outbound) and minimum 6-hours of actual calling in a day by individual helpdesk agent. The average time per call is expected to be 5 minutes (National Institute of Health and Family Welfare, 2013).

Feedback reports from the system to the ANM to improve care processes were limited. In the past, an ANM prepared lists of cases of pregnant women – including details of their demographics and health status (e.g. haemoglobin levels and the previous pregnancy) – whom she would visit during her outreach. Now, these lists were supposed to be generated by the central MCTS and returned to her, and she typically received them too late or even not at all. The reports were supposed to be colour-coded red-yellow-green, with red, for instance, depicting serious cases that needed immediate follow-up. However, in the printouts that the ANMs received, these colours were not visible, with everything showing up as black and white. Thus, the ANMs did not receive actionable information. Four years into the implementation, the MoHFW was still primarily focused on the processes of validating the quality of data being reported. The ANMs, fearing public reprimand, were struggling to complete data entry on time. Messages (typically reprimands) were being sent through daily SMSs, and there were press releases and reports on nonperforming facilities and ANMs, but discussions on output reports were limited. Locally situated processes of provision of care were transformed so as to exercise control, and reprimands were issued from a distance in real time. Letters of reprimand cascaded from centre to state to facility to the individual. Poorly performing ANMs were publicly shamed, with their names displayed on notice boards, and they were negatively flagged in their annual confidential appraisals.

An ANM in a northern state said:

> I am always lagging [behind] in my registration targets, and I am the lowest performer in my district. This has been told to everyone in every meeting. But what is not told is that I have seven big villages under my area with the highest load of mother-child registration in my block. It is always a race to complete data entries. My son and daughter help me complete, but they have college in the day, and internet shops are far from home, which does not leave me much time for them. Now, I have contracted the internet shop operator to complete my entries. I pay him from my pocket, which of course does not get reimbursed. We are a large joint family, and diverting the resources is not helping. But all this still does not help, as I have been now been labelled the worst performer, which is extremely demotivating.

While the centre made percentage of MCTS entries a condition for state budget approvals, some states went further and made the salaries of ANMs conditional upon registration percentages.

Said an ANM:

> The state has also started with salary cuts for not meeting targets. I have had three continuous salary cuts. I cannot afford this. The PHC has only one data entry person. The load is too much, so most of us have been asked to find our own ways to complete the entries. I am 58-years-old, and I do not know computers. I don't have computer shops near my house. I am struggling with my data entry. I need to take my registers to the computer shop, which is far away, and leave the registers there for three or four days. But, then, I also have a backlog of data entry in these registers. I had suggested using untied funds for completing data entry, but this was refused. All of us are now using our own money to complete data entry. This is not sustainable.

While discussing the matter of low registrations, one ANM pointed out that while the government had issued the MCTS format for reporting, the primary registers for recording, into which she transferred data from her field diaries, had not been revised.

An ANM told us:

> How do we report on data that we do not capture? I have been dealing with pregnant women and children since I joined the service 30 years ago. We always consulted our doctor in the monthly meeting at the PHC about cases we considered high-risk. But for three years now, our monthly meetings have only been about the percentage of names registered in the MCTS, show-cause letters issued to those not completing targets, and timelines to complete entries. We do not discuss cases or work-plans any longer.

At a sub-district monthly meeting, a data manager pointed out that none of the ANMs had completed data entry in ANMOL, while the ANMs insisted that they had completed them and showed the list of entries made. The bone of contention was whether or not the ANMOL data was synchronized with the database of the web-based RCH application, which was what the data managers accessed. To get round the impasse, an ANM worked on a tablet out of sight of her supervisors re-entering case data into the web application. After discussions, everyone divided the data entry work.

An ANM said:

> During the ANMOL training programme, we were told that once a record is entered, the system would manage the data by making work-plans or schedules based on service updates. For example, the system would ensure that those who had been permanently sterilized would disappear from the eligible couples list, or would filter the cases registered according to the year or area. None of these functionalities were actually functioning, although we were told that these would work in the subsequent versions of the application – which we are still waiting for in 2019. Until this happens, our work of reporting ANC and immunization data has tripled – RCH registers, ANMOL, and the RCH portal.

Another ANM remarked: 'All these portals and tablets are only there to monitor us. Data entered in these systems is not for us, it is for people at state or national levels [for monitoring purposes]. Most ANMs in the country will not see more than 10–12 pregnant women in a month to follow up. And we know these women, for which we do not need outside systems to plan visits.'

Although none of the ANMs denied the potential of ICTs, they found their experience 'complicated'. They viewed the systems as designed for top-down work surveillance instead of for supporting their care-giving. One clear inference is that the vast digital infrastructure deployed, particularly related to the collection and processing of personal data, has not yielded effective results. The MCTS was subsequently replaced by the RCH portal, into which data from nearly 225,000 public health facilities are flowing on a regular basis. While issues relating to the quality of data and its effective use in supporting health improvements continue, the process of data entry goes on unabated.

The MCTS was a foundational system, the precursor to not only various new digital initiatives for disease-specific programmes but also to the recently announced National Digital Health Mission (NDHM). The government has introduced various large-scale plans to convert many existing systems into name-based systems. Despite its short-term failure, the MCTS was a robust foundation for these planned and ongoing digital interventions.

Short-term 'failures' but long-term 'invisible' gains

On the face of it, the MCTS story can be seen as a typical implementation narrative from both the LMIC and the non-LMIC contexts. It had the usual constraints typical of top-down design insensitive to local work practices, high workloads of data providers, the existence of parallel, redundant systems, weak capacity, and inadequate time to stabilize new initiatives (Braa et al., 2004). The challenges of data quality and limited use continue. Seen through the lens of traditional implementation, we would infer that it is a suboptimal, failed system. But, in actuality, we would be inclined to go beyond this superficial finding to explicitly seek the positives and the 'invisible gains' from this experience, and the hope it creates for the future.

Other research has also highlighted the challenges in implementing the MCTS. Gera et al. (2015), for example, carried out an in-depth assessment of the MCTS, focusing on data quality and implementation challenges in the states of Rajasthan and Uttar Pradesh. In both states, the quality of data on both pregnant women and children was 18–34 per cent, indicating relatively poor performance. Data incompletion was attributed to the challenges of weak guidelines and processes, the heavy work burden of the frontline health workers, a lack of systematic monitoring and supervision, weak capacities, and, not least, shortage of consumables such as MCTS registers. These findings reinforce ours, although their understanding of factors was through a snapshot approach, which did not capture the processual dynamics of ANM work and systems implementation.

ICT4D projects are rife with conclusions of 'failures'. For example, through Heeks (2002) came the dramatic and much-quoted figure of 90 per cent full or partial failures. Sahay and Avgerou (2002) lamented the unrealized potential of ICT4D efforts in the health sector. There are two reasons why such inferences only present partial truths. First, they focus on defining success or failure in binary terms based on visible impacts such as systems not scaling up (Sahay et al., 2013), or sustaining themselves (Braa et al., 2004), or not being used for decision-making (Latifov, 2013). Second, the diagnoses of failures are based on the use or non-use of limited sets of system function-alities such as those related to data entry or data use. Such tight focus may, for instance, only study how an ANM uses the mobile phone to register and transmit data, ignoring how she uses the phone to talk to her peers and get technical or social support. To avoid this tunnel-vision trap, we have focused on two additional sets of issues: 1) empowerment, and the invisible elements of ICT4D projects; and 2) the creation of an enabling digital infrastructure to support future initiatives.

Empowerment: the invisible element of ICT4D projects

A snapshot view of IT projects leads to the implication that envisaged deliverables have not been met. While meeting deliverables is important, the label of 'failure' hides more than it reveals. This is illustrated through an exchange we had with a researcher who had come to review an IT project involving a hospital information system.

Four years after the system had been initiated in one hospital, the researcher tried to assess its success by analysing system-usage patterns. He created graphs that showed the number of patients registered as far higher than the number of outpatient department encounters. This led him to conclude that 1) the registration clerks were not optimally using the search function to identify revisiting patients, which was why most patients were registered as new – resulting in an inordinately high number of registrations showing in the system; and 2) since the outpatient department (OPD) doctors were resisting using the system, they were not registering OPD encounters in the system.

We challenged his perception on two grounds. First, the doctors had autonomously taken the decision to create system-generated OPD encounters only for chronic patients (such as those suffering from HIV, tuberculosis, and diabetes) who they felt required a longitudinal patient record. Since about 75–80 per cent of patients registering for hospital services were primarily non-chronic cases (such as fever and aches), they were registered in the system but not in the OPD record. Second, many of those registering in the system had come not for OPD services but for non-medical hospital services such as obtaining medical fitness certificates (required, for example, for employment or for a driver's licence) and did not need to meet the OPD doctor. As a result, the number of OPD encounters was significantly lower than those registered in the system.

This exchange serves to highlight the fact that the provision of healthcare is an extremely complex phenomenon, and cannot be adequately captured through simple quantitative measures and graphical analysis. There is much more than meets the eye. An 'invisible' impact was that the doctors were actually empowered by the system, and were now capable of directing the use of the system to where they felt it was needed most – for the care of chronic patients.

Understanding impacts through the lens of health worker empowerment helps to shift the focus from the supply side (the provision of technology) to the demand side (how the system adds value for the health worker). Empowerment, which boils down to expansion of choices, takes place within an institutional context, or an 'opportunity structure' within which choices are made (Alsop and Heinsohn, 2005). These choices are related to organizational hierarchies, laws, regulatory frameworks, and norms and conditions of legitimacy governing behaviour. It is important how these structures are built and mechanisms implemented. With regard to the MCTS, the mobile phone created a new opportunity structure in terms of enabling the ANMs to learn and use a novel means of reporting data, as compared to their existing, tedious manual system. However, the state authorities viewed the same opportunity differently: as enhancing surveillance over and control of health workers with new routines of daily reporting, SMS-based reminders. This had both positive and negative implications on agency (Kabeer, 2005). The difference lies in the phrases 'power to' and 'power over'. The former refers to the space people are given to define and exercise their choices. The latter represents how an individual or group (in our case, the state) overrides the agency of others. While there was a greater exercise of 'power over' health workers, there was also the percolation of 'power to' the ANMs.

Scott (1998) has emphasized that large-scale, state-initiated projects, such as those related to building identification schemes and cadastral mapping, tend to fail because they try to standardize and simplify social phenomena that are too complex to rationalize and order. Such projects represent a strong belief in a 'high modernist ideology', implemented through state power and passive acceptance by civil society. The MCTS case, one such large-scale pan-national initiative built with a high modernist ideology and state agenda, was by design inadequate for capturing the detailed and intricate work practices of ANMs. The state used the MCTS to exercise authoritarian power through constant reprimands, public shaming, and salary deductions. The fault in its plan was that the ANMs were not passive, and found innovative and improvisational means to deal with new situations (e.g. linking up with local internet kiosks and using the support of their children to do data entry). That the ANMs learnt how to manage their work when under an implacable remote gaze can be seen as their having been empowered.

In a different mobile health (mHealth) project in the same state, the ANM workers' union went on strike and stopped all reporting for nearly six months when rumours began circulating that the GPS feature in mobile phones was tracking their everyday movements (Mukherjee, 2017). Empowerment also means being able to organize collective action based on an understanding of the positive and negative implications of technology.

Empowerment helps people build cumulative capabilities over time through their varied experiences in ICT projects. Such learning resonates with Amartya Sen's (1999) distinction between 'capacity' and 'capability'. While 'capacity' refers to people's ability to use a technology, 'capability' refers to how this capacity enables people to achieve their individual wellbeing and pursue choices they value (Mukherjee, 2017). In the MCTS, while the state's focus was primarily on the former, the ANMs applied their cumulative learning from earlier experiences to the MCTS. With regard to the earlier mHealth project in the state, the ANMs, who had learnt to use the basic functionalities of the phone to carry out data reporting, themselves suggested mHealth technology a few years later when the state needed to conduct a household survey for cancer prevalence. By the time MCTS came around a few years later, the ANMs were already well-versed in the technology. We heard many anecdotes from them of how they were now using their mobile expertise to teach their children how to surf the internet and to use WhatsApp. This was unintended, 'invisible' empowerment.

Creating an enabling digital infrastructure to support future initiatives

Prior to the MCTS in 2008, what existed were chunks of aggregated data from districts or facilities collected and collated by manual systems, on Excel sheets, and then various genres of HMIS. The MCTS's pan-India coverage was an important positive factor. The challenge of mother and child health is a national issue complicated by state-level and interstate variations. Addressing this problem in a holistic sense requires data from the entire country, not just from isolated pilots. In that fundamental sense, the MCTS was essential for providing this large-scale, systematic data that could potentially be used to make a sea-change in improving mother and child health.

Since the advent of the MCTS, there has been a huge explosion of systems that seek to collect individual and case-based data such as those related to the Integrated Health Information Portal, Health and Wellness Centres, the Pradhan Mantri Jan Arogya Yojana (PM-JAY) insurance scheme, the National Health Protection Scheme, and the National Health Stack (Sahay and Mukherjee, 2020). Moreover, there are various disease elimination initiatives for malaria, leprosy, tuberculosis, etc., all of which demand individual data and have resulted in new information system initiatives. This burgeoning calls for novel capacities and infrastructure to manage and use the data.

Based on the National Health Policy of 2017, the GoI in 2019 announced the launch of the NDHM (now rebranded as Ayushman Bharath Digital Mission – ABDM). The National Health Authority is to implement this vision, including drawing up the blueprint of the technological infrastructure and implementing some pan-India digital initiatives. The idea is to create a national digital health ecosystem that supports universal coverage. Various building blocks have been thought of: a universal Health ID, a Digi Doctor registry of all practising doctors, a National Health Resources Repository, a Personal Health Record Management System titled MyHealthRecord, and others. These different apps are being launched in phases, with data from controlled pilot sites being continuously reviewed and scaled.

The MCTS project is no doubt a trailblazer. Many ANMs and medical doctors we spoke to acknowledged the positive potential of ICTs but urged a more decentralized model of implementation. We have not yet seen systematic efforts by the system designers to learn from previous experiences and understand the work practices of health staff. However, our recent experience of using the digital system to register citizens for COVID-19 vaccines administered by ANMs in health facilities was very pleasant. For the first time, the digital system enabled people control over their choices of when and where to get their vaccinations. This 'flipping the coin' from the state to citizens could arguably only have been made possible by more than 12 years of experience that the state and health workers have had with digital systems (Mukherjee, 2021). There are key learnings that the MCTS provides for framing future policy directions, key being to have clearly defined strategies for the systems to provide added value to health workers' everyday work, particularly related to care provision, and to reduce the work burden of (redundant) data collection.

For Sen (1999), development is about removing the barriers (or the 'unfreedom') that limit people from pursuing the choices that they individually value. If a family values good health, education, and play facilities for its child, the state should remove the constraints, and make provisions for a school, ensure bus transport, build proper roads, and provide a playground nearby. The various infrastructure-building efforts under the MCTS have led to opportunity structures being created, even if as unintended consequences. Internet in villages has expanded the choices of health workers on data-reporting and seeking medical help through messaging apps such as WhatsApp. ANMs, associated with a 'failed' MCTS system, arguably have built both skills and understanding of how not to approach implementation. Their opinions and suggestions, actively solicited through a participatory rather than a top-down, centralized approach, could be a valuable resource in the NDHM.

In fact, we would argue, the unintended outcomes have, through the large-scale empowerment and learning of the health staff, created a national-level digital infrastructure. This can only be better for future digital initiatives for the strengthening of healthcare services particularly for the marginalized population that is vastly impacted by unfit maternal and child health conditions.

However, digital systems by themselves will not guarantee positive outcomes. They need to be bolstered by changes in models of governance and of implementation that ensure increased decentralization. There must be active, free-flow mechanisms that allow designers and users to interact, for only through such symbiosis will designers be able to intimately understand the context of use. We have still not seen any systematic efforts to build a participatory approach.

Acknowledgements

The authors acknowledge insights on the Indian public health system developed through interactions and working together (2008–2012) with Dr T. Sundararaman, during his stint as the Executive Director, National Health Systems Resource Centre (NHSRC), Delhi, a think tank for the Ministry of Health. The long-term empirical engagement with reform efforts of national health information systems as members of HISP India, a not-for-profit NGO, is also deeply acknowledged.

References

Alsop, R. and Heinsohn, N. (2005) *Measuring Empowerment in Practice: Structuring Analysis and Framing Indicators*, Policy Research Working Paper No. 3510 [online], World Bank, Washington, DC <https://openknowledge.worldbank.org/handle/10986/8856> [accessed 20 January 2022].
Braa, J., Monteiro, E. and Sahay, S. (2004) 'Networks of action: sustainable health information systems across developing countries', *Management Information Systems Quarterly* 28(3): 337–62 <https://doi.org/10.2307/25148643>.
Drèze, J. (2020) 'New evidence on child nutrition calls for radical expansion of child development services', *The Indian Express*, 10 July [online] <https://indianexpress.com/article/opinion/columns/new-evidence-on-child-nutrition-calls-for-radical-expansion-of-child-development-services-7107810/> [accessed 20 January 2022].

Gera, R., Muthuswamy, N., Bahulekar, A., Sharma, A., Singh, P. and Singh, V. (2015) 'An in-depth assessment of India's Mother and Child Tracking System (MCTS) in Rajasthan and Uttar Pradesh, BMC', *Health Services Research* 15: 315 <https://doi.org/10.1186/s12913-015-0920-2>.

Heeks, R. (2002) 'Information systems and developing countries: Failure, success and local improvisations', *Information Society* 18(2): 101–12 <https://doi.org/10.1080/01972240290075039>.

Kabeer, N. (2005) 'Gender equality and women's empowerment: a critical analysis of the third Millennium Development Goal 1', *Gender and Development* 13(1): 13–24 <https://doi.org/10.1080/13552070512331332273>.

Khurana, N. (2021) 'Issue analysis: a use-driven approach to data governance can promote the quality of routine health in India – A Commentary', *Global Health: Science and Practice* 9(2): 238–45 <https://doi.org/10.9745/GHSP-D-20-00347>.

Latifov, M. (2013) 'Global standards and local applications: case of implementing ICD-10 standard in HMIS Tajikistan', *Journal of Health Informatics in Developing Countries* 7(1): 20–32.

Ministry of Health & Family Welfare (2011) 'Operational Plan for Mother and Child Tracking System' [online], Press Information Bureau <https://main.mohfw.gov.in/sites/default/files/6611655292draftopt.pdf> [accessed 20 January 2022].

Mukherjee, A. (2017) 'Empowerment: The invisible in ICT4D projects? The case of public health information systems in India and Kenya', unpublished doctoral dissertation, University of Oslo, Norway.

Mukherjee, A. (2021) *'Flipping the Coin' from State Controlled to Citizen Enabling Health Information Systems: A Decade of Reflections from Engagement with Public Health Systems in India*, Working paper, Information Systems Research Group, University of Oslo, Norway.

National Institute of Health and Family Welfare (2013) *Tender Document No: NIHFW/WS/20-18/2013*.

Sahay, S. and Avgerou, C. (2002) 'Introducing the special issue on information and communication technologies in developing countries', *The Information Society* 18(2): 73–6 <https://doi.org/10.1080/01972240290075002>.

Sahay, S. and Mukherjee, A. (2020) 'Where is all our health data going?' *Economic and Political Weekly* 55(1), 4 January.

Sahay, S., Sæbø, J. and Braa, J. (2013) 'Scaling of HIS in a global context: same, same, but different', *Information and Organization* 23(4): 294–323 <https://doi.org/10.1016/j.infoandorg.2013.08.002>.

Sahay, S., Sundararaman, T. and Braa, J. (2017) *Public Health Informatics: Designing for Change – A Developing Country Perspective*, Oxford University Press, New Delhi.

Scott, J.C. (1998) *Seeing Like a State: How Certain Schemes to Improve the Human Condition Have Failed*, Yale University Press, New Haven, CT.

Sen, A. (1999) *Development as Freedom*, Alfred A. Knopf, New York.

Sinha, K. (2009) 'Azad doubts data on child vaccination', *Times of India*, 15 September [online] <https://timesofindia.indiatimes.com/india/azad-doubts-data-on-child-vaccination/articleshow/5011257.cms> [accessed 10 March 2022].

CHAPTER 3

Empowerment of displaced persons through the smartphone

Thomas Hylland Eriksen

The smartphone revolution began in 2007, and the devices began to spread exponentially in the 2010s. By the time of the Syrian refugee crisis in 2015–16, a great number of services and affordances were available through smartphones. This chapter shows some of the main ways in which smartphones have become ubiquitous and indispensable for refugees. Through messaging services and social media, refugees are capable of instantaneous communication about practicalities, coordinating their movements, keeping in contact with family members, obtaining essential information about border crossings and control, and occupational opportunities, etc. Similarly, Global Positioning System (GPS) maps enable precise orientation in space. Moreover, dedicated apps facilitate orientation and procurement of services and assistance in new locations. Immigration authorities are aware of the empowering potential of smartphones, and have been known to confiscate or even destroy smartphones belonging to undocumented migrants. The vast majority of refugees on their way to, or having entered Europe, have mobile phones, most of them smartphones. The main argument is that the smartphone's potential to compress and stretch time and space has made it a necessary device for refugees, a means to an end.

The power of the smartphone

It was thanks to the smartphone camera that the world learnt about dramatic events unfolding in Tunis in the spring of 2011, eventually leading to the – ultimately ill-fated – Arab Spring. Ordinary townspeople filmed riots and unrest as they unfolded, immediately catapulting the grainy but compelling images across the planet, thanks to a technology and an infrastructure that did not exist a decade earlier. The Tunisian drama, which soon spread to other Arabic-speaking countries, was not created by smartphones and social media, but it was communicated and enhanced through them. The mass exodus of refugees, especially from Syria, in the subsequent years also involved smartphones from the outset.

The smartphone creates affordances hitherto unavailable, and its ubiquity, connected through an invisible global web of electronic networks, usually provided by private companies, has made it a very significant part of the global infrastructure. It is a means in the sense that is elaborated in the Introduction to this book (Chapter 1), but it is insufficient without the processes involving people making use of it, which, in turn, will be futile unless the ends are reached, improving the situation for marginal, excluded, and vulnerable people. This chapter presents some of the main ways in which the smartphone has empowered refugees, and will also note some caveats and unintended consequences of smartphone use.

In the expanding global middle-class, the smartphone is – among other things – an entertainment machine, a bottomless and endless source of encyclopaedic knowledge, a news service, a street map, and a weather forecaster. This aspect of the smartphone, which concerns information, can make it appear as a younger, shrunken, and deterritorialized relative of the newspaper, the magazine, cinema, and television. It miniaturizes, simplifies, and accelerates. It is, above all, superbly mobile, which is why refugees may be one of the groups that reaps the greatest benefits from it.

To refugees who find themselves in one of their liminal phases – ready to flee, on the move, in a refugee camp, waiting for their asylum application to be approved – the smartphone is perhaps mainly a descendant of the landline and the phone booth, the letter and the postcard, the physical meeting at the railway station or at one of the other sites where newly arrived migrants typically congregate. It has turned sockets and free Wi-Fi into desired, scarce resources precisely because it is a multifaceted lifeline. First and foremost, it is not a phone. It is a pocket-sized, incredibly powerful computer.

What these two otherwise very differently positioned groups have in common is that, in both cases, the smartphone contributes to the desta-bilization of time and space. It produces simultaneity and instantaneity, it compresses time and space, but it also has the potential to expand space and make time more flexible. It enables new forms of personal freedom and offers a bird's-eye view of the relevant social world, holding out the potential of a fluid, horizontal network society as an alternative to the hierarchical society of fixed, static relationships.

But it is also a tool for surveillance both at the macro level of the state and at the micro level of intimate social relationships. It becomes important as a means to the maintenance and expansion of personal networks for people who may have had a passive and indifferent relationship to the mobile before they were forced to flee. For example, a retired fisherman in Ireland told researchers that he had used his smartphone regularly while his daughter lived in Australia, but now that she had moved back, the mobile was scarcely used at all (Garvey and Miller, 2021: 122).

The difference between the way the temporalities of refugees and of securely settled people is affected by the smartphone should not be exaggerated. Much of the time, both groups simply use the phone to fill temporal gaps with games, music, social media, or websites helping them to fight boredom (Jacobsen et al., 2020).

In addition to its networking affordances and bottomless source of information (including rumours and fake news), the mobile functions as a storage room and an archive for refugees, since it makes it possible to freeze valuable moments in the past and store half-forgotten memories, a possibility which can be enormously valuable to people who have been forced to leave everything behind and flee not only from places, but also from people they are close to. As mentioned, the smartphone is rarely just a phone, and in this respect it is a miniaturized, powerful time-capsule that makes it possible to store, expand, and shrink time.

Through compression, the smartphone has brought time and space out of kilter. Networks, knowledge, and consumption have been appified. What you can't get into an app ceases to exist, for all intents and purposes. In this world, no borders are absolute, no delays in communication are necessary, and everything becomes comparable with everything else insofar as it can be squeezed into an app.

The same qualities of the smartphone that make it a flexible, compact networking tool create both opportunities and constraints for people who need to stay under the radar of the state and other institutions determined to limit their mobility. Refugees have become easier to monitor owing to digital networks. The increasing criminalization of refugees (and immigrants, generally) in Europe has been documented by Franko (2020), who shows how the European Union (EU) has turned the Mediterranean effectively into a border, and the ways in which the authorities use ICTs to intercept people on the move.

On the other hand, the smartphone has also provided refugees with new means to circumvent obstacles by accessing information about safe borders, legal rights, and so on. This, incidentally, also applies to criminals who, like refugees, are on the move much of the time. Text messages and mobile data are used as evidence in court, and investigators can, at least in theory, follow the movements of suspects. Yet, criminals may play the same game, leaving false traces behind and – not least – coordinating their movements with accomplices. Criminals have even developed their own, encrypted networks, making them difficult, if not impossible, to monitor. A widely used network of this kind was EncroChat, which had 60,000 users when it was infiltrated by the police and closed down in the spring of 2020. It is a matter of some concern that refugees and criminals (e.g. drug traffickers) are often treated in comparable ways, sometimes in violation of the UN Refugee Convention, a fact that has led criminologists to coin the word 'crimmigration' (Franko, 2020).

The tiny multimedia computer, spoken of as a polymedium by Madianou and Miller (2012), equipped with a swipable and thumbable touchscreen instead of a cumbersome, tiny keyboard, a slim, sleek rectangular object of metal, plastic, and silicon, which fits snugly in the inner pocket of a dinner jacket, the front pocket of a pair of jeans or a woman's handbag, was introduced only in 2007. The smartphone compresses, accelerates, and miniaturizes the user's relationship to the external world, and such is its penetration into the lives of millions that it may well be regarded as a bodily *extension* in McLuhan's (1964) sense. And as people joke, 'they say you can even make calls with it as well'.

I shall now look into the significance of the smartphone for refugees hoping to make a European country their new home, with a particular emphasis on the ways in which this minuscule, rectangular electronic device affects time and space. There is little doubt that the smartphone has transformed everyday life around the world; but it is no less obvious that these changes have taken place in different ways, for reasons of economy, social organization, network types, political regimes, scale, cultural values, and the situation in which actors find themselves. We should always be wary of simple generalizations. As pointed out by Vokes and Pype (2018), it cannot simply be assumed that the internet leads to time–space compression; time–space expansion is also a way of looking at it; the social space is expanded, and time becomes flexible in new ways. In fact, when social micro-coordination (Ling and Yttri, 2002; Ling and Lai, 2016) is mediated by smartphones, clock time becomes less important. The possibility of delayed response, as opposed to the required immediacy of the telephone call, is built into the social media platforms and text messaging, and the simultaneity and constant calibration of arrangements in the near future (e.g. social encounters) tend to replace categories such as '11:15 a.m.' with 'in five minutes' or 'just around the corner'. The coordination of a broad range of social activities can now take place as an ongoing flow of minute exchanges and adjustments, not as done deals finalized days or weeks earlier. It accelerates everything touched by it.

By integrating their lives into the temporalities mediated by mobile telecommunications, refugees planning to flee, being on the move, or having arrived at a detention centre are no different from everybody else. Yet, their lives have changed, and they have become reliant on smartphone apps for manoeuvring the social and cultural fabric of their surroundings. Thus, their precarious, liminal situation implies significant differences from settled populations with legal status, fixed abode, and stable daily routines. Strangers in a strange land, severed from filaments of belonging, linguistically impaired, and condemned to open-ended, debilitating, and humiliating periods of waiting, these people – whether huddled together in the hull of a barely seaworthy vessel, in a tent erected by volunteers or an NGO on a Greek island, or on the streets of Hanover – may offer a privileged site for an exploration of the ways in which the smartphone is transforming the social world and its temporal regimes, and how it can contribute to a less unequal world.

The transformation of space

The Europeans, who see the smartphone as a luxury item, associating it with leisure and convenience in the smoothly functioning neoliberal information society, misinterpret the ubiquity of smartphones among refugees as signifying that they belong to a leisured class. Refugees do not primarily flee from poverty; they may well have belonged to the global middle-class before having been forced to leave everything behind. Among Gillespie et al.'s (2018) informants are a well-travelled businessperson, an accountant, a shop-owner and technology student, a surgeon's assistant, an administrator with a law degree, and an international salesperson in clothing. They did not escape from poverty, but from violence and insecurity. They are you and me, and their access to smartphone affordances is urgent and crucial, even if they may sometimes, like other people, be caught unawares playing *Candy Crush* to fill gaps or kill time. Why shouldn't they, as long as the cushioned and smug majorities do?

Few of the Syrian refugees interviewed by Göransson (2018) and his collaborators owned a smartphone when they crossed the border to Lebanon in 2014 or 2015, but they were likely to purchase one soon after arrival, seeing it as essential for their new lives. Interestingly and by coincidence, the exponential growth in global smartphone ownership and use coincides with the period of war and displacement in Syria beginning in 2011. Although, as Gillespie (2016) found, 80 per cent of the refugees in their sample owned a smartphone, the gender disparity was considerable, with 94 per cent ownership among men and 67 per cent among women. There is, nevertheless, almost universal saturation, since a neighbour is exceedingly likely to have a smartphone if you don't.

In order to begin to understand the radical transformation in question, it may be useful to keep in mind that as late as 1960, just 9 per cent of the United Kingdom (UK) population, translating into roughly a quarter of British households, had a landline. The majority of the working-class and rural Britons accordingly relied on neighbours or the pub for urgent calls in or out. In other words, notwithstanding the development of a great number of platforms and services for the internet-enabled touchphone, simple phone coverage is also better in a Syrian refugee settlement in Lebanon than it was in the UK of a generation ago.

Together with people who are chronically ill or living with physical disability, refugees are among the groups for whom the smartphone has the most obvious benefits. Moreover, unlike the others mentioned, refugees often avail themselves of the location services enabled by GPS. In a highly original study, Frith (2015) argues that the most significant innovation represented by the smartphone consists in its character as a location medium. Much of the work it performs for the average user, he continues, consists in locating us, others, services, places of interest, and so on.

While this can be a fruitful perspective, my approach emphasizes the convergence between spatial and temporal identities. Where you are ceases to matter; this entails, says the social phenomenologist Alfred Schütz (1967) that mere 'consociates' may become contemporaries: they are aware of each other, however dimly, and can theoretically communicate with each other, regardless of physical location. In other words, the smartphone technology entails an inherent time–space compression (Harvey, 1989). This section and the next must therefore be seen as two sides of the same coin.

Location services are essential for refugees on the move. When they move from A to B, often in unfamiliar surroundings, sometimes in rough terrain, refugees rely on location services to find their way, and even simply to find out where they are. At the same time, they are often reluctant to keep the location services on continuously en route, since signals from the mobile phone may enable criminals and hostile authorities to discover their whereabouts. Those who cross the Mediterranean into Europe also risk their phones being confiscated by the authorities in order to check their contents, history, the logs, and so on, before – occasionally – destroying them, aware that mobiles are tools giving refugees greater freedom of movement and a degree of control of their destiny. The Police, Crime, Sentencing and Courts Bill ('Police Bill'), passed by the UK Parliament in 2021, actually provides for 'extraction of information from electronic devices' by immigration officers.

The precarity of the refugee situation, and the need to monitor one's own mobile use carefully, is evident not least as regards refugees from North Korea who have managed to cross the border to China, and who are on their way to South Korea via Vietnam (Kang et al., 2018). They use the mobile phone to stay in touch with one another, orient themselves geographically, and contact persons and organizations that might be able to help them. They are in an unusually vulnerable situation, even compared to other refugees. Whenever they turn on location services on the phone, they may in theory be traced by authorities. The migration is risky in other ways too, and some female refugees end up as sex slaves in China (ibid.). The Democratic Republic of North Korea allows nobody to leave, and China also does not accept North Korean refugees. They cannot send messages to family members or friends in their home country without jeopardizing their own situation and that of others, and they cannot post selfies on social media. Yet, they are totally dependent on the smartphone to navigate, communicate, and coordinate during the dangerous journey from one of the least connected countries in the world to its neighbour, which is one of the most connected, via China and Hanoi.

One of the most striking changes produced by the new technology of spatial location is its positioning of the subject. Unlike the paper map, the mobile map and related location services place the user at the centre of the universe. Formerly, one of the most demanding tasks when reading a map of an unfamiliar city consisted in locating oneself. That situation has now changed. With the smartphone, you always know where you are, but not necessarily what it looks like around you. The sociologist Marie Gillespie (2016) reports that more than a third of the refugees her team had interviewed in camps in the Middle East used Google Maps regularly. After arriving in a camp, they obviously knew where they were, but used location services actively to explore the territory and, not least, to search for opportunities to get into Europe, since Google Maps offers accurate information about distances and public transport options. In this way, distance becomes manageable and tangible in a different way than it would on a paper map. Information is easily accessible about the cost of an Uber, and how long it would take compared with a bus or train. The map even tells you how long the walk from the train station to the bus terminal takes, and the traffic situation on the road is updated continuously. Many have been surprised and perhaps impressed by the accuracy of Google's traffic information, but the explanation is simple. The file servers continuously receive mobile signals from everybody who is connected, and the density of these signals indicates with great precision the amount of traffic on a given road at a given time. The connected mobile phone is so ubiquitous that traffic information for São Paulo is just as reliable as it is for the greater Kuala Lumpur region or the main roads in and out of Stockholm.

A paradox is the fact that distance may come across as more tangible and concrete when filtered by an algorithm and represented on a small colour screen than when it was merely physical. By using the advanced functions available on the location apps for smartphones, everybody can become their own time-geographer; it becomes easy to calculate the relationship between time and distance. Time and space, thus, are not primarily compressed here, but translated into practically useful chronotopes, tangible and specific.

Location services can save lives. A news item some years back (Casciani, 2016) told the story about an Afghan boy who was travelling with other refugees in the back of a truck somewhere in England, when it slowly became difficult to breathe there. With some help from a translation app, he sent a message in English to a volunteer he had met in Calais, explaining that his group was about to run out of oxygen. The group survived because the French activist forwarded the message to a British colleague, who in turn contacted the police, which eventually found the vehicle. Thanks to the mobile phone, the group was rescued, unlike the 39 Vietnamese migrants who perished in a similar situation in 2019, the Essex lorry deaths (BBC, 2019).

Another story (Eide et al., 2017) concerns a boat en route from the Turkish coast to Samos, a Greek island in the eastern Aegean Sea known to Northern Europeans as 'the holiday island'. At sea, in the middle of the night in January 2016, the engines failed. The waves ran high, the boat was overloaded, and everybody was in great danger. Thanks to Google Maps, some of the passengers succeeded in locating the nearest islet, and the refugees managed to reach it by paddling with their hands.

Another group of refugees in the Aegean Sea had ended up in an uninhabited and remote part of an island. They were exhausted and uncertain of their whereabouts. From a hill, they were able to access a Turkish mobile network, and could use the GPS map to locate the nearest village, which was a couple of hours away on foot. Eide et al. (2017) also describe a Syrian refugee who had paid good money to get from Budapest to Germany, only to discover, the moment he connected to the online map, that they were on their way in the opposite direction – that is, towards the Romanian border.

To refugees on the move, as to many other people, the location services on the smartphone are not merely – or even mainly – means to orient themselves and navigate in physical space, but also a tool enabling them to locate other people, both old and new acquaintances. Notwithstanding the many useful services offered by Google Maps, this app has its limitations. Notably, it does not tell you how you can avoid being searched, arrested and/ or beaten up by police, or where you can go, having arrived in an unfamiliar city, to get a meal and a bed for the night offered by a friendly organization. For this purpose, other apps exist, identifying services such as soup kitchens, free legal assistance and interpretation, available accommodation, meeting places for undocumented refugees, and so on, always in several languages. These tailor-made apps, which may be seen as subversive by authorities, largely draw on technologies developed by Google, Foursquare or other major corporations. Indeed, SIM cards and even functioning mobile phones have in the past few years been offered by NGOs engaged in voluntary work among undocumented refugees.

Temporalities of the smartphone

As the foregoing has made clear, the smartphone has, just in the space of a few years, virtually become an extension of the body for hundreds of millions; it is now part of the air that we breathe, but to some, who find themselves between a rock and a hard place, that air sometimes has a foul smell.

As noted above, the smartphone also functions as a storage space and an archive. It is not just a tool for communication or a repository of information. It is also a miniaturized, powerful time capsule which makes it possible to store, expand, and shrink the passage of time. It is also a place substitute enabling the positioning in a virtual place when the concrete place is inaccessible.

There are good reasons why stories about refugees and smartphones are especially interesting. They tell of changes in the time–space coordinates in particularly dramatic ways, which are nevertheless relevant elsewhere, if in somewhat watered-down versions. Consider the aforementioned boy who saved his friends' lives and his own by texting a voluntary worker in Calais about the lack of oxygen; the refugee in a camp in Jordan who was able to trace his brother who had arrived in Germany; or people who reconnect with relatives and friends in their home country or another European country; or who use tailor-made apps to navigate through an urban jungle somewhere in Europe: all of these stories are unique, and they may give an exaggeratedly upbeat impression of the online life. However, they are no more or less unique than the story about the ski tourist who was found after an avalanche because his mobile transmitted GPS signals; the story about the man whose girlfriend broke up with him because he had run out of battery and was therefore unable to respond to her urgent texts; or the story about the woman who was criticized on social media after posting a cheerful little video on TikTok while she was stuck on a mountain shelf waiting for the rescue helicopter.

All of these stories, whether about refugees or not, tell about a new world where time and space are out of sync, where networks, knowledge, and consumption have become appified, where no borders are absolute, and where everything becomes comparable with everything else if it can be accessed through an app.

It may be the case that the late John Urry was right in arguing that sociology should no longer deal with assumed stable societies but about mobility (Urry, 2001). But it may be even more accurate to say, following Marx's analysis of financial capitalism in the mid-19th century, that all that is solid melts into air. The tangible is turned into an abstraction, and this is just as much the case regarding time as regarding space.

As pointed out before, in some respects, people who are planning to flee, who are on their way, or who have arrived at a reception centre or in a camp, are not very different from everybody else. After the introduction of the smartphone, their lives have changed, and they have become reliant on smartphone apps to manoeuvre in their social and cultural surroundings. A young Afghan man on the street in Marseille told the researcher that he found it difficult to imagine how people in the past, before the smartphone, were at all able to flee from Afghanistan to Europe. This casual comment speaks volumes about the extent to which these devices have transformed everyday lives.

Most refugees have smartphones, whether they are from Afghanistan, Mali, or Syria. They wait for paperwork to be completed in a camp, or the application for residency or asylum to be decided. They use the mobile to build and consolidate social networks, communicate with family members in the home country or elsewhere, and obtain information that makes it possible for them to make both short-term and long-term plans. The widespread reliance on mobile communication among refugees was graphically illustrated in a photograph taken in the main railway station of Budapest during the summer of 2015 and published in newspapers across the world. It depicted a row of men lying on makeshift mattresses along a brick wall, trying to rest while their mobiles were being charged, and their faces were illuminated by the flickering blue light from the small screens.

The temporality of refugees is not accelerated; in general, it is very slow. Most of the time, refugees are not on the move; their mobility takes place in spurts and, as noted, immobility – waiting – is far more typical. They develop new concepts of place and distance, but time is also changed by the gadget in their pocket. Refugees without a formal legal status are typically seen as liminal, in a limbo state, between a past they have been forced to leave behind and several possible futures. In their case, it is highly pertinent to ask about the specificities of 'the future': When is it? The possible futures imagined by refugees waiting for their applications to be processed are paused, open-ended and, indeed, actively sabotaged by bureaucratic sluggishness and institutions of Kafkaesque impenetrability and Byzantine complexity.

The significance of the smartphone for temporal coordination can barely be overestimated. In a not too distant past, when *le transport* ('people smugglers') did not arrive in time, you had no other choice than wait for them in the designated meeting place. You may now ask the driver or captain in real time why he is late, after having checked on social media about the going rate for the crossing and which pilots to trust. You can later use GPS to locate yourself accurately, send a message to your uncle in Munich about being on your way, ask your cousin in Düsseldorf whether he still has a job for you in the informal sector, update yourself on the kind of border control you might expect along European borders, and which parts of the Mediterranean are least militarized and where it may be safe to cross the border. This form of access to immediate contact with the outside world has enormous significance for people who cannot rely on formal channels for coordination and information-sharing.

Time and space are compressed in this way. Where you happen to be does not interfere with your online activity, and this is highly significant for people who are on the move and rarely sleep two consecutive nights in the same place. A landline would have been useless for them. Its archival function, alluded to above, can be illustrated through the electronic calendar and address book. Just consider what your electronic address book says about your life. Getting their hands on it would be a major scoop for your future biographer, but if you are an undocumented refugee, it is also highly interesting for the police in a country where the state has an expressed ambition to know as much as possible about those who find themselves within its boundaries (as indicated in the aforementioned 'Police Bill' in the UK).

The online person shrinks and compresses time, spreads it out (as when some may wait for a day or two before responding to electronic messages), watches an entire season of a TV series at a single sitting rather than one episode a week, at a time when linear TV has become a quaint subset of TV as such; and micro-coordinates with friends and family to preclude the need to shoehorn appointments in between existing plans. In sum, the smartphone makes consumption, communication, and production more efficient. It is a generous gift to global capitalism, relying as it does on increasing speed and efficiency.

It is therefore worth reminding oneself that the smartphone can also contribute to reducing the pace, as when you sit abandoned and cold in a refugee camp on a Greek island, killing time by watching music videos from your youth, or reading and re-reading messages from friends, NGOs, relatives, and others. You may play old games, or read about the poet Rumi on the Farsi version of Wikipedia. The nature of the mobile phone encourages the here and now at the expense of the there and then. It strengthens the tyranny of the moment (Eriksen, 2001), but it can also be used to draw long lines backwards, sideways, and forwards in time.

The mobility of refugees is now choreographed, handled, and managed in new ways through the medium of the smartphone. In order to expand the space and create new possibilities, refugees are obliged to develop relationships of trust with strangers, which was a less pressing matter before migrating.

The weak ties celebrated in Granovetter (1973) are kick-started through the migration process. The potential of the smartphone to build and nurture weak ties, thereby building social capital, is almost infinite. A former refugee told researchers about his route from a deadlocked situation in a resource-poor Libyan refugee camp to a permanent job in Beirut via networks that he partly exploited, partly built online through his mobile (Gillespie, 2016).

The far side of the *Mare Nostrum* – that is, the Mediterranean margins of the European Union – can often be seen with the naked eye from the Turkish mainland. Turkey lost nearly all its western islands to Greece after the Balkan war in 1913, and islands like Rhodes and Lesbos are much closer to Turkey than to the Greek mainland. In this region, human smugglers have engaged in lively marketing of their services via social media and messaging apps, where they offer first-class lifejackets, cold refreshments on board, and assistance to avoid immigration officers. Their activity would have been slower and more cumbersome without the smartphone.

Of course, transport of refugees and other migrants did take place, across the Mediterranean and along the West African Atlantic coast, long before the smartphone revolution. The business model and logistics were nevertheless more complicated at the time. The informal transport companies offered their services in person or through intermediaries, and information about cost and services was spread by way of the spoken word between acquaintances. Refugees had to wait longer in their villages and in the port city, but the boat would eventually set sail even then. The point is that this activity was, at the time, based on personal, physical contact. The role of the smartphone as a lubricant and accelerator in various kinds of transactions is confirmed in this kind of setting, as it is elsewhere.

All is not rosy. As pointed out by Awad and Tossell (2021), deterritorialized availability round the clock may add pressure to an already extreme situation for refugees. Some find the expectation of connecting with family members in the home country invasive and debilitating. One man explains how his wife, left in Afghanistan, cries and begs him to come home every time he calls. Another explains that social media and news media never bring positive news from home, and that he would have preferred an offline existence. They also argue that the widespread dependency on digital communication may be an obstacle to integration into society, since face-to-face encounters are more conducive to trusting relationships, and because many refugees lack the funds to be fully online. In brief, there is an ambiguity and duality resulting from smartphone dependence: it makes the user both freer and less free, more connected but also more disconnected, and so on. This duality is explored more fully in Eriksen (2021). The pressure to be connected in the host country, and to be constantly available for relatives and others in the home country, may add new problems to an already precarious situation, and this issue should be kept in mind in an overall assessment of the significance of the mobile phone for refugees. In spite of these misgivings, none of the people whom Awad and Tossell (2021) spoke to considered relinquishing the smartphone. It remained a lifeline, a networking tool, and an indispensable source of information, providing a sense of autonomy and offering hope.

Conclusion

The impact of the smartphone on refugee mobility from A to B forms part of a larger pattern and is consistent with other, less dramatic changes. Although sending an emoji to your partner is quite different from asking a remote acquaintance whether crossing the border is safe right now (process), the underlying principle of communication and the infrastructure (means) on which the activity relies, is the same. The effects are also comparable but far from identical (ends): the logistics run more smoothly, and efficiency increases.

Ling and Lai (2016: 834) conclude in an article about 'micro-coordination 2.0', that is, group chat and social media:

> Perhaps the most fundamental function of the mobile phone is to make us individually available to one another, thus facilitating coordination. Indeed, they afford us constant and ubiquitous connectivity. We can call one another to just chat, or to arrange (or rearrange) our plans. Until the rise of the smartphone and the mobile Internet, this was mostly limited to dyadic interactions. We could call and text to one other person at a time. Thus, we could micro-coordinate [or hyper-coordinate; Ling and Yttri, 2002] our interactions, but with only one person at a time. With the coming of smartphones and messaging apps, it became possible to expand this horizon. We are able to quickly construct groups of varying sizes to just chat or to coordinate specific tasks.

The world grows and shrinks simultaneously. In the 1960s, the cultural anthropologist Geertz (1963) wrote that no anthropologist travelling to Africa or Asia on fieldwork could now ignore the presence of nationalism, understood as the struggle for independence, and subsequent decolonialization. Anything else would be disingenuous, he argued, since the struggle for full independence was now so pervasive that it could not be bracketed. In the 2020s, one might make a similar statement regarding the smartphone. On the streets of Bogotá, hawkers offer chewing gum, cigarettes, and *minutos* (minutes) for SIM cards; in a provincial Chinese city, your host calls for a taxi through an app after you have eaten noodles from a street vendor, paying through the phone, while, in the next moment, he texts his friend to tell him that you are on your way; in the Seychelles, your colleague checks her Instagram feed covertly during a lengthy staff meeting; and in Kuala Lumpur, your student uses a translating app in order to communicate with an elderly ethnic Chinese Malaysian with whom she has no shared spoken language. Networks become denser, faster, more comprehensive than ever before in human history. Above all, time and distance are relativized. The world shrinks because everything is instant, and that which used to be remote becomes close; and it grows because the networks are independent of physical distance.

This chapter has shown some of the ways in which refugees in limbo, in unknown territory, on their way to an unknown destination, deprived of the routines of everyday life, and removed from their family, profit from this miniaturization and deterritorialization of communication. Its many affordances fuel hope among precarious people on the run.

Acknowledgements

Some of the examples in this chapter have previously been used in 'Filling the apps: the smartphone, time and the refugee', in Jacobsen et al. (2020: 57–72).

I am grateful to Christine M. Jacobsen for having invited me into the WAIT project and to the co-authors of this book, to Jenny Peebles and to Shirin Madon, for comments and inspiration.

References

Awad, I. and Tossell, J. (2021) 'Is the smartphone always a smart choice? Against the utilitarian view of the "connected immigrant"', *Information, Communication and Society* 24(4): 611–26 <https://doi.org/10.1080/136 9118X.2019.1668456>.

BBC (2019) 'Essex lorry deaths: 39 bodies found in refrigerated trailer', BBC News 23 October [online] <https://www.bbc.com/news/uk-england-50150070> [accessed 16 August 2021].

Casciani, D. (2016) 'Afghan boy in lorry texted: "No oxygen"', BBC News, 8 April [online] <https://www.bbc.com/news/uk-35998273> [accessed 15 July 2021].

Eide, E., Ismaeli, A. and Senatorzade, A. (2017) *På flukt med mobiltelefon: En dyrebar følgesvenn [On the run with a mobile phone: a precious companion]*, Pax, Oslo.

Eriksen, T.H. (2021) *Appenes planet: Hvordan smarttelefonen forandret verden (Planet of the Apps: How the Smartphone Changed the World)*, Aschehoug, Oslo.

Franko, K. (2020) *The Crimmigrant Other: Migration and Penal Power*, Routledge, London.

Frith, J. (2015) *Smartphones as Locative Media*, Polity Press, Cambridge.

Garvey, P. and Miller, D. (2021) *Ageing with Smartphones in Ireland: When Life Becomes a Craft*, UCL Press, London.

Geertz, C. (1963) 'The integrative revolution – primordial sentiments and civil politics in the new states', in C. Geertz (ed.), *Old Societies, New States: The Quest for Modernity in Asia and Africa*, pp. 105–57, The Free Press of Glencoe, New York.

Gillespie, M. (2016) 'Smart migration? The power and potential of mobile phones and social media to transform refugee experiences', *Humanitarian Aid on the Move* 18: 14–19.

Gillespie, M., Osserian, S. and Cheesman, M. (2018) *Mapping Refugee Media Journeys Smartphones and Social Media Networks*, Open University, Buckingham.

Göransson, M. (2018) *Apping and Resilience: How Smartphones Help Syrian Refugees in Lebanon Negotiate the Precarity of Displacement*, Clingendaal Institute, The Hague.

Granovetter, M. (1973) 'The strength of weak ties', *American Journal of Sociology* 78(6): 1360–80.

Harvey, D. (1989) *The Condition of Postmodernity*, Blackwell, Oxford.

Jacobsen, C.M., Karlsen, M-A. and Khosravi, S. (eds) (2020) *Waiting and the Temporalities of Irregular Migration*, Routledge, London.

Kang, J., Ling, R. and Chub, A. (2018) 'The flip from fraught to assumed use: mobile communication of North Korean migrant women during their journey to South Korea', *International Journal of Communication* 12: 3533–52.

Ling, R. and Lai, C-H. (2016) 'Microcoordination 2.0: social coordination in the age of smartphones and messaging apps', *Journal of Communication* 66: 834–56 <https://doi.org/10.1111/jcom.12251>.

Ling, R. and Yttri, B. (2002) 'Hyper-coordination via mobile phones in Norway', in J.E. Katz and M. Aakhus (eds), *Perpetual Contact: Mobile Communication, Private Talk, Public Performance*, pp. 139–69, Cambridge University Press, Cambridge.

Madianou, M. and Miller, D. (2012) 'Polymedia: towards a new theory of digital media in interpersonal communication', *International Journal of Cultural Studies* 16(2): 169–87 <https://doi.org/10.1177/1367877912452486>.

McLuhan, M. (1964) *Understanding Media: The Extensions of Man*, McGraw Hill, New York.

Schütz, A. (1967) *The Phenomenology of the Social World*, Northwestern University Press, Evanston, IL.

UK Parliament (2021) *Police, Crime, Sentencing and Courts Bill* [online] <https://bills.parliament.uk/bills/2839> [accessed 16 July 2021].

Urry, J. (2001) *Sociology Beyond Societies: Mobilities for the Twenty-First Century*, Routledge, London.

Vokes, R. and Pype, K. (2018) 'Chronotopes of media in sub-Saharan Africa', *Ethnos* 8(2): 207–17 <https://doi.org/10.1080/00141844.2016.1168467>.

CHAPTER 4

Building resilience to strengthen HIS response to pandemics: Case study from Sri Lanka

Sundeep Sahay[1]

This chapter provides a long-term (2010–ongoing) engagement in strengthening health information systems and health systems in Sri Lanka, through the collaborative efforts of the University of Oslo, the University of Colombo, the Ministry of Health of Sri Lanka, and various partners of the global Health Information Systems Programme (HISP) research and development (R&D) network coordinated by Oslo. The initial period (2010–19) of building capabilities for digital resilience involved the development of a master's in Biomedical and Health Informatics (BMI) programme for medical doctors, who after graduation went back to the ministry to take up positions as Health Information Officers. An interesting feature of the study programme was a thesis project in which the students built different health applications on the District Health Information Software–Version 2 (DHIS2), a free, open-source digital platform. The large-scale educational capacity coupled with the experience on the platform contributed to build capabilities for digital resilience.

This capability found application at the onset of the COVID-19 pandemic, when multiple systems needed to be built rapidly in response to the needs of information support. The DHIS2 platform, coupled with the existing capacity, extended by drawing upon global and national technical resources, helped build adaptability to the resilience of the digital capabilities and also raised the threshold complexity of the information systems. This was further extended with the second wave when systems needed to be designed to respond to the complex needs of the vaccination rollout. At the same time, systems built during the phase of adaptability gradually became part of the routine systems.

This process of incremental and ongoing developments, with integrated feedback loops, represents a form of 'multi-scalar' resilience, which we describe as the potential of digital transformability. The message of hope conveyed through this chapter is how a low-resource country like Sri Lanka could frugally build an effective and successful information systems response to the pandemic.

Resilience of health systems

LMICs comprise the majority of the world's population and strengthening their health systems is a key development priority. However, since most LMICs have weak health systems, they struggle to provide a decent quality of life to their populations. This contributes to adverse socioeconomic consequences. The fragility of LMICs is caused by poor economies, weak governance systems, inadequate infrastructure, donor dependencies, and conflict-related situations, all of which pose challenges in the provision of healthcare. The sudden advent of pandemics in these contexts, as exemplified by the COVID-19 crisis, puts huge additional pressure on LMIC governments, and threatens to collapse their health systems if not properly managed.

While the Sri Lankan health policy has historically emphasized preventive and promotive care services, in a pandemic these services get overwhelmed and exhausted, with critically ill patients requiring care in intensive care units (ICU). A similar trend has also been noted in better resourced countries such as the US and the UK, highlighting gaps in policy and investments designed to build preparedness for pandemics and similar emergencies. Health systems need to be resilient to be able to 'bounce back' from external stress caused by the pandemic, while also being able to 'bounce forward' to be better prepared to handle such external shocks in the future (Heeks and Ospina, 2019).

This chapter attempts to understand how the Sri Lankan health system strove to achieve digitally enabled resilience to deal with the external stress of the COVID-19 pandemic. COVID-19, like H1N1 and SARS earlier, is a relatively unknown disease, and calls for experiments and trial-and-error methods to learn and implement integrated responses (Somda et al., 2009). Pandemics have global implications that transcend international boundaries, affecting large numbers of people (Doshi, 2011) as well as food and animals. LMICs actively rely on digital technologies to detect and track cases before and after they enter the country, and to support the vaccination rollout. Various digital processes need to be in place, including agility in building and deploying the information systems, new forms of governance mechanisms that enable multisectoral coordination and decision-making, and the use of digital platforms that come without licensing encumbrances and can be rapidly deployed to handle evolving information.

This chapter is built on a long-term, empirical engagement of the author and his colleagues at the universities of Oslo and Colombo. This longitudinal engagement has enabled insights into the process of building capabilities over time, how they are applied with the external stress of the pandemic, the feedback and learning loops involved in the (ongoing) strengthening of systems, and the contributions of these processes towards enhancing both the capabilities of and the potential for digitally enabled transformations in health and information systems. An understanding of how Sri Lanka managed these provides hope to other LMICs that, despite their inherent constraints of resources and high disease burdens, they can be better prepared for managing external stresses.

Building digital resilience preparedness

Three aspects were central in building preparedness for digital resilience: 1) a strong and proactive public health system; 2) significant investments in creating health information capabilities; and 3) extensive exposure to a world-class free and open-source digital platform – the District Health Information Software–Version 2 (DHIS2).

The DHIS2 allows for the collection, processing, analysis, and dissemination of health data that is both case-based (such as details of individuals tested for COVID-19) and aggregated (such as details of total number of positive cases in a geographical area). The processing of case-based data allows for improving point-of-care practices (such as better tracking of positive cases), and aggregate data analysis helps in the computing of positivity and fatality rates. The DHIS2 has been designed as a generic and flexible platform that can be relatively easily configured to support different uses. Its versatility can be gauged from the fact that it is currently being used in more than 70 countries for a range of applications from routine health systems, disease registries, disease surveillance, and logistics management.

Strong and proactive public health system

Sri Lanka is an island nation in South Asia, surrounded by the Indian Ocean, and with an estimated population of 21.8 million. Sri Lanka has robust social indicators: a gross national income of US$3,800, placing it as a lower middle-income country; a human development index of 0.78, which is higher than most other LMICs; a literacy rate of 95.7 per cent (Ministry of Health and Indigenous Medical Services, 2020); and as one of the few countries in Asia that achieved its Millennium Development Goals targets (United Nations, Sri Lanka, 2015). The country provides many social services such as for health and education, including graduate and postgraduate medical education, free of charge to its citizens, making it a shining example of strong public systems. More than 90 per cent of its medical graduates join the government's medical service and contribute to the continuous strengthening of its public health system. According to its Ministry of Sustainable Development (Government of the Democratic Socialist Republic of Sri Lanka, 2018), Sri Lanka is already well on its way to meeting most of its Sustainable Development Goals targets on good health and wellbeing, including for maternal mortality, under-5 mortality, neonatal mortality, and control over malaria and tuberculosis.

Significant investments in creating health informatics capabilities

In 2009, a new postgraduate degree programme, the master's in Biomedical and Health Informatics (BMI), was established at the Postgraduate Institute of Medicine, University of Colombo, with financial and technical support from the University of Oslo, Norway. This programme envisaged a futuristic vision of producing 'hybrid' medical and informatics expertise among doctors in the public health system. This was a crucial step in building resilient capacity in the country, where the government plays a predominant role in decision-making, with minimal intervention from the private sector or development partners. The students go through two years of full-time academic studies while being fully paid by the Ministry of Health (MoH). They are exposed to various aspects of health informatics, including a one-year thesis project where they practically address real challenges faced by the ministry.

Extensive experience with DHIS2

The DHIS2, now considered a global standard, has been managed by the University of Oslo under the framework of the Health Information Systems Programme (HISP) for the past two decades (Braa and Sahay, 2013). Given that the BMI programme was built around collaboration with the University of Oslo, the DHIS2 became the core platform for learning in the BMI. The students typically use the DHIS2 to learn about systems design, development, implementation, capacity strengthening, and policy formulation. The postgraduates revert to the MoH where they assume duties as Medical Officers in Health Informatics. The BMI has so far produced more than 200 medical doctors trained in health informatics over the past decade who are now posted in all corners of the country.

Many of the prototype systems built by the students as a part of their thesis work were taken to full implementation in various departments of the MoH. Many new systems were also developed, such as for District Nutrition Monitoring System (DNMS), Electronic Reproductive Health Management Information System (eRHMIS), and tuberculosis and malaria information systems. The DNMS won the United Nations World Summit Award in 2016 for its impact on the health sector (World Summit Awards, 2016); the eRHMIS received Sri Lanka's eSwabhimani National Award for best innovative product in healthcare domain and the Commonwealth Digital Health Award in 2018.

Digital resilience has been prepared for by 1) creating an extensive core of health informatics experts now deeply institutionalized in the public health system; 2) deep and extensive experience on a world-leading free and open-source digital platform; 3) trust built between the MoH and the technical team behind DHIS2 (HISP Sri Lanka, a local NGO); and 4) building a networked national health informatics capacity, with the global Oslo HISP network providing a platform for continuous learning and innovations.

Applying digital resilience capabilities: building adaptability

The COVID-19 outbreak started off in China in late 2019. In the first month, it rapidly spread to many countries in Southeast Asia. Sri Lanka is heavily dependent on the tourism industry. Of the more than 1.9 million tourists who visited the country in 2017, a high number were from China (China Daily, 2017). Seeing this dependence as a major national threat, the MoH decided to take rapid precautionary measures to identify and contain the disease at points of entry. This involved multisectoral coordination between airport staff, immigration, quarantine, field health workers, doctors, and laboratory technicians, to name a few. Building this coordination was no small challenge, given the traditional culture of siloed departmental work, the novelty of the disease, and the absence of effective outbreak management systems. While there existed some manual or semi-computerized systems such as Flu Sys for the surveillance of influenza, they were primarily based on aggregate data and largely incapable of supporting the case-based information needs for COVID-19 required, for instance, for tracing contacts.

Enabling this coordination was the establishment of a high-level governance group with direct attention by the president, who assigned a task force that included the minister of health, the director general of health services, and various subcommittees including senior officials from other sectors such as defence and police. Surveillance and information management based on digital platforms was the responsibility of a specific committee under the Health Information Unit of the MoH, which enrolled BMI postgraduates and selected the DHIS2. They contacted HISP Sri Lanka, a regional node of Oslo's global HISP network, who collaborated with the Information and Communication Technology Agency of Sri Lanka, a government entity regulating ICT implementation and providing hosting infrastructure. The technical team, which identified some key limitations in the DHIS2 core platform, adopted means to address them such as enrolling freelance developers, organizing a hackathon, and reaching out to the Oslo core team. The hackathon was a two-day event to which software developers in the country were given an open invitation. New functionalities were developed, and collaborations between stakeholders were forged. Figure 4.1 summarizes the timelines for the development of the different modules.

Port of Entry module: 20–27 January 2020

Initial discussions between the MoH and HISP Sri Lanka were initiated around 20 January 2020. The design process involved creating the workflow of the initial registration of passengers at the ports of entry, and their subsequent itineraries. The system needed to capture information on their sociode-mographics, travels, and symptoms present on arrival, and make this data accessible to the community health staff for follow-ups, particularly the positive cases. The first version of the system was quickly developed using the platform capabilities of DHIS2. It was presented to and approved by the

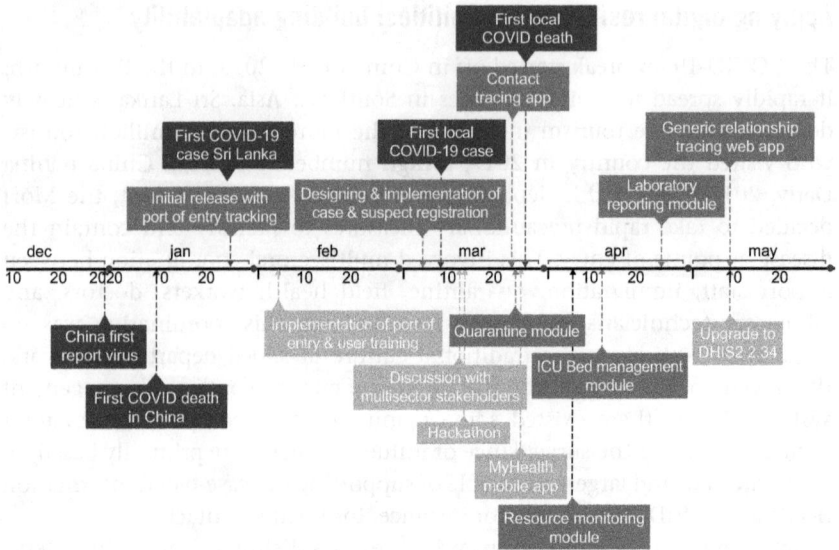

Figure 4.1 Timeline of events related to COVID-19 DHIS2 modules

director general of health services immediately before the country reported its first case of the coronavirus on 27 January 2020. Rapid training for users was conducted via Zoom, and then the system went live.

The first indigenous case, which was reported on 14 March 2020, catalysed the MoH into shifting its focus on the clinical management of confirmed cases, incorporating sociodemographic, clinical, and laboratory data, and on the treatment outcomes. The team rapidly built this functionality using the DHIS2 Tracker module, and subsequently extended it to track suspected cases. This process was not simple, as there were gaps in the DHIS2 core functionalities – such as restrictions in changing the initial health facility that a person was registered on and on which all future analytics were based; in automating the transmission of data; and in generating required visualizations such as those for contact mapping. Individual-level data was primarily available only to the health department, while aggregate data was shared with other departments.

To rapidly address the technical gaps, a meeting was held on or about 14 March 2020 between the ICT Agency, the MoH, academics from the University of Colombo, HISP Sri Lanka, and the Department of Immigration and Emigration. Following this, a hackathon was organized by the ICT Agency, attracting volunteer developers from public–private and national–global developers, putting into practice agile development methods. The hackathon generated specific modules for contact tracing application, ICU bed management, tracing location through mobile towers, and various integrations with other systems, enabled through the Open APIs (Application Programming Interface) of the DHIS2. While the institutional issues of permissions from regulatory authorities for using location data was enabled by the high-level governance structure, the technical issues were worked on by the Oslo core technical team. Subsequently, individual consent was obtained. The mobile tower data lacked precision, as it only provided a rough idea of the areas that a person had visited. These diverse resources working together helped create rapid innovations in weeks which would otherwise have taken months or even years.

Integrations and innovations through multisectoral collaborations: March 2020

A web application was built to analyse relationships and contact tracing, extending one of the outputs of the hackathon, to support epidemiological research based on the cohort of confirmed patients. The DHIS2 relationship model provided the functionality to link internally registered patients, but it lacked the visualization component to analyse the transmission process. This led to the development of a web application for contact visualization by a volunteer developer under the guidance of the DHIS2 core team at Oslo. Another functionality captured patient locations over the past two weeks, which might not have been divulged by a person (for various reasons). For this, with permission from the regulatory authorities, the mobile tower location data was shared with the MoH, which was used to develop a middleware component linking the contact tracing application with the tower location. The end users complained of data entry being very time-consuming, so an integration functionality was designed to enable data transfer directly from the immigration information system to the DHIS2 to avoid re-entry of data.

Tracking of imported cases: March 2020

From the second week of March 2020, many Sri Lankans living in high-burden countries like Italy and South Korea started returning home, leading to a sudden surge in cases towards the third week of March. This led to a change in approach from community follow-up of suspected passengers to compulsory quarantine at government-run facilities. The DHIS2 quickly supported this new demand simply by adding on a new tracker programme. This was subsequently extended to monitor the distribution of personal protective equipment resources across the country to identify impending shortages using analytical dashboards. Implementation was enabled through digital training approaches on Zoom.

The ICU care functionality: April 2020

With the increasing number of patients requiring ICU care, the MoH requested a critical care module which could be accessed by clinicians from all

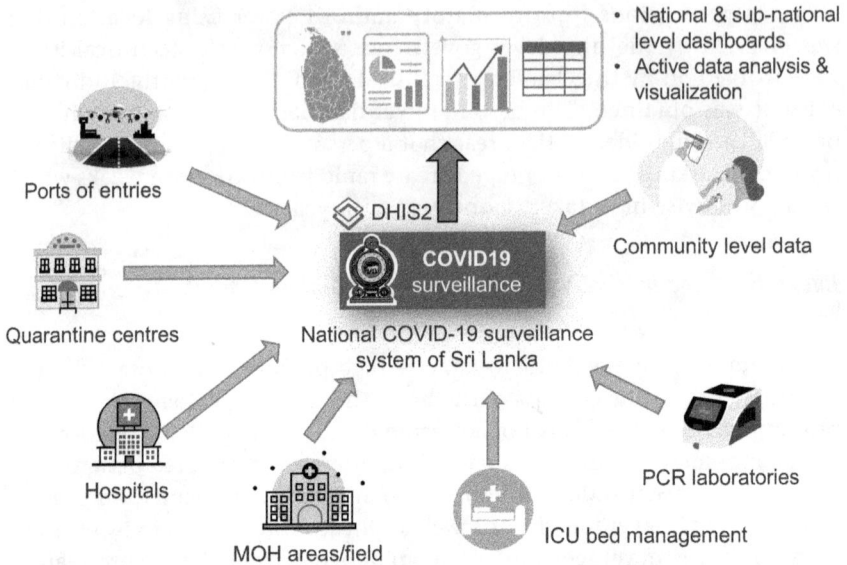

Figure 4.2 Components of the surveillance system

hospitals to help locate the nearest available ICU bed. The then ICU system of the ministry was non-functional. This was quickly developed including value-added functionalities of analytical dashboards with custom interfaces. The ministry requested an aggregate reporting component for COVID-testing laboratories to report daily summaries of the number of tests. This was designed in mid-April, and started to be used nationally. The different components of the surveillance system are depicted in Figure 4.2.

Globalization of local innovations: March–May 2020

The initial version of the contact mapping application developed by HISP Sri Lanka was shared in the global DHIS2 community, which started work on making this application more generic (Amarakoon, 2020). This led to a rapid eliciting of global requirements and the development of a generic contact tracing visualization app. Further developments in Sri Lanka were now guided by the global team. A dedicated post on the app was made available to the DHIS2 community encouraging regular feedback and improvements. Feedback received went into designing improvements, which, in turn, encouraged more countries to use the app. More developers from these countries joined in to adapt the app to the local context while also making contributions to the global development efforts.

Today, this package is being used in over 40 countries, and many success stories have been generated.[2] The package is continuously being enhanced based on feedback from a rapidly expanding user base. The biggest strength as well as the weakness of the implementation was to rapidly build the capacity of the end-users to engage with the system. The ongoing pandemic severely constrained the implementation team from conducting regular full-day physical training workshops for end-users. Instead, they had to devise teleconferencing platforms to conduct online training programmes that were supplemented by offline reference videos, single-page training manuals, a support hotline, and Viber chat groups.

Recent developments include the building of a third-party mobile app to enable citizens to self-report and monitor their health. The MoH is now promoting use of the DHIS2 dashboards by health administrators, focusing on real-time data as much as possible. To facilitate this, the platform was upgraded to the latest DHIS2 version (2.34), which had more advanced functionalities to support real-time analytics. Refresher training for users from hospitals, laboratories, and community centres was carried out. This whole process has contributed to strengthen the ministry's trust in the DHIS2 and HISP Sri Lanka. The potential for using the DHIS2 to create a centralized national data repository, which would integrate data from different systems, is now being explored.

Even as we write, the HISP Sri Lanka team is building systems to support the COVID-19 vaccination rollout. This is a task of tremendous complexity, as it involves making the database capable of holding the details of about 16 million citizens, a scale unaddressed earlier. Technical advice came from HISP Vietnam, which, while supporting countries such as Laos and Cambodia, had developed a solution on the DHIS2 for bulk import of person-based data. More complexities arose when the national system had to be integrated with another to support the generation of digital vaccination certificates, originally developed in India. Technical help for this came from the Oslo core team.

While these new systems were being developed, reflecting the bounce-forward adaptability of the digital capabilities, the health system also needed to ensure the bounce back, where the routine systems could stabilize and continue running. The digital COVID-19 response had positive effects on information systems, in general.

Figure 4.3 highlights the number of weight-monitoring events captured by the mobile-based nutrition information system, built prior to the pandemic, from a post-conflict district. The figure highlights a sudden drop of number of events captured from March to May 2020 that coincides with the reduction of service delivery due to a countrywide curfew. However, the reporting rates bounced back to pre-curfew levels, and achieved stability throughout the remaining months, highlighting the stability of routine systems even in resource-limited and fragile settings. This example illustrates how the robustness of the larger health system was relevant in creating a successful digital intervention even in a post-conflict district.

These different experiences in applying and building resilience contributed to building adaptability, a feature of resilience that is concerned with building the ability to deal with future challenges. This evolution has involved confronting challenges and finding innovative ways to work around them. A key strategy

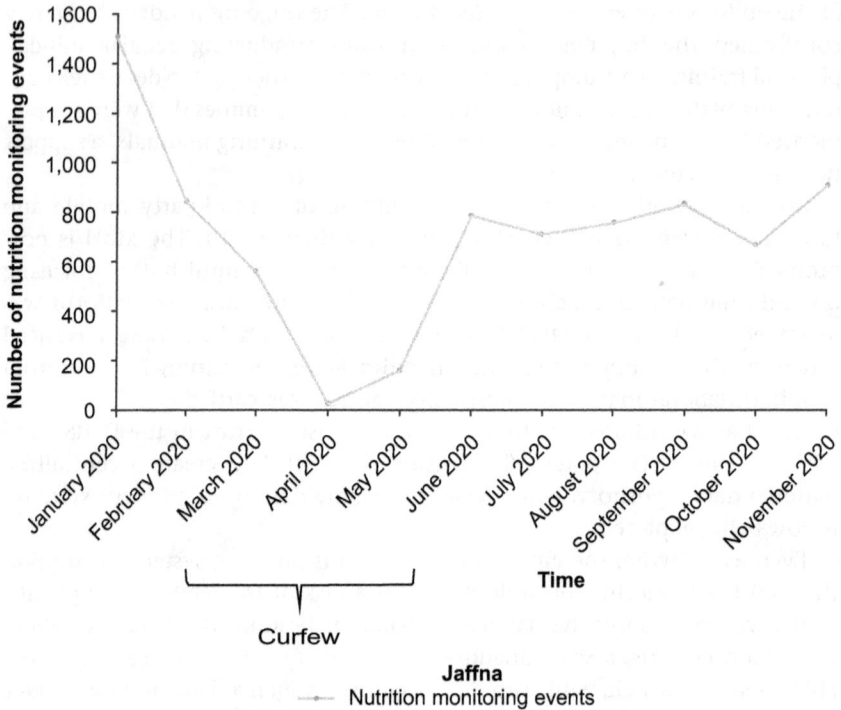

Figure 4.3 Reporting levels of nutrition information systems
Source: DNMS – Ministry of Health, Sri Lanka

in Sri Lanka has been to expand its national and global networks and draw upon their expertise in specific areas of support, often employing improvisations. For example, many health facilities were not ready to embrace the digital system due to resource limitations related to hardware, network connectivity, and people. The improvised solution was to capture data initially on paper, which required data entry in spreadsheets, which then needed to be synced with the central database. This was both a significant technical and logistical challenge, particularly given that the volume of data was rapidly increasing. Most rural health facilities did not have designated human resources for data entry; so, temporary staff were digitally enrolled, rapidly trained, and prepared. When patient loads reduced after the first wave of COVID-19, the temporary staff were transferred back to their original posts. In doing so, they added to the human resources capacity of the overall health system.

The process of building adaptability was enabled by a lean, multisectoral governance structure. While the structure facilitated the processes of early implementation, there were signs of renewed functional friction between different sectors, particularly when the virus was receding and there was limited transmission. Deeply embedded institutional behaviours are difficult to dislodge. The original crisis of the pandemic had helped to, at least temporarily, cut through some of these bureaucratic bottlenecks. The emergent friction will, of course, create challenges of sustainability for the governance and implementation models. It is a matter to be discussed and resolved among the policymakers.

Adapting a generic platform to local requirements in such a way that it can be again made generic was a non-trivial technical challenge, especially when there were many and an increasing number and types of custom require- ments spread across different modules. While the hackathon, for instance, was an effective platform for collaboration between local and global software developers, sustaining their contributions for updating and maintaining the applications for longer durations has been difficult. New means of support will have to be devised for the future.

Building and applying digital resilience: creating potential for digital transformation

We discuss first how the process of building and applying resilience is shaped by four sets of conditions depicted in Figure 4.4, which is then discussed particu- larly with respect to their potential to enable digital transformations.

Building resilience through capacity strengthening

A key means for building resilience capabilities has been long-standing investment by the government in fortifying public health systems, with significant input into strengthening research and education. Conventionally, in LMICs, the lack of capacity and adequacy of human resources have been major obstacles to effectively materializing digital initiatives. Contributing to this adverse situation are training approaches that tend to be short-term and

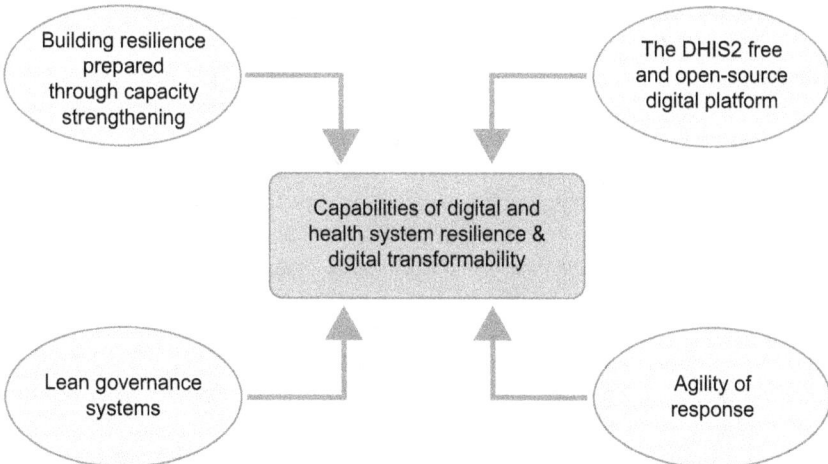

Figure 4.4 Socio-technical determinants of agility in times of uncertainty

skill-based, and that are discontinued after the system is deployed in the field. In contrast, Sri Lanka has wisely invested significantly on building human resources capacity through its policy of free education up to the postgraduate level. The training of medical doctors on informatics through the University of Colombo was a visionary decision taken over a decade ago that led to unique hybrid medical–informatics skills, the lack of which often hinders implementation initiatives.

The DHIS2 free and open-source digital platform

The DHIS2 digital platform was another critical means to build the surveillance system. The choice of platform was shaped by the knowledge and trust that the MoH had after extensive prior experience with it, largely through the BMI programme and the presence of its postgraduates in various departments. The ministry was convinced of the customization and adaptability of the platform, and the processual transparency and accountability it afforded. The decision to opt for the DHIS2 was a collaborative decision by the ministry, health informatics specialists, and administrators. There were no financials involved, and there were therefore none of the usual questions about procurement from a single source. Furthermore, the core team behind the DHIS2, the HISP Sri Lanka team and the medical postgraduates, were seen as 'insiders' committed to the national effort, unlike expensive external consultants who would be seen as in it for the short run and for monetary gains.

That the DHIS2 is free and open-source means that there are no licensing restrictions to its use. The ministry will own the source code and have the freedom to adapt it to different evolving needs. The open code base ensures transparency, inspiring confidence on how sensitive patient data is being used and by whom. Against concerns that open-source code compromises data privacy, the ministry saw it as enhancing security: there were no hidden back doors; and so many different groups working on the code heightened the potential for identifying and fixing code. The DHIS2 platform is designed for ease of use and flexibility. Most of the customization and adaptation work can be done by super-users, obviating the need for specialist computer science expertise. The required expertise was already available; for example, the first working prototype of the surveillance system was produced in four days using the pre-existing features of the platform. Moreover, no private sector entity was willing to try to build a new solution from scratch at the necessary speed.

The DHIS2 is the foundation on which outside parties can build complementary products or services (Tiwana, 2014). It is relatively easily able to accommodate custom developments as well as provide interoperability with existing information systems. Contact mapping visualization was not originally available in the DHIS2, but the developers designed a custom web application on top of the DHIS2 to facilitate it. Additionally, the DHIS2 fulfilled the stakeholder requirements of the non-health sector by being interoperable, for instance, with the immigration system and reducing the burden of data entry in the port-of-entry programme.

Agility of response

Agility in decision-making, and system development, and their implementation became an important element of the process by which the means (the capacity and the platform) was applied to manage the pandemic. For example, the system was quickly configured to capture data at the port of entry and transfer it to the health department for follow-up in the community. The COVID-19 pandemic created significant uncertainty in the world. Projections of the spread of the disease and the requirements of the health system, and the planning of the provisions of care, were difficult. The management of economies and key decisions such as the geographical extent of lockdowns were fraught with error. Agility became fundamental to decision-making, as did working incrementally and through trial and error. Agility played out on two levels: first, the level of institutional decision-making; and the second, the level of information systems design and development. Taken together, we describe it as a form of 'socio-technical' agility, which is reflected in application design, development, and implementation, and is situated in a dexterous governance framework within a rapidly changing disease and social context.

At the institutional level, the MoH along with its key partners anticipated the requirements of an efficient information system to manage the looming crisis arising from the entry of the virus in the country. With the gradual progression of the virus, the task force quickly anticipated and identified requirements and initiated system design, development, and deployment, and buttressed it with online training on a national scale.

Agility in the systems development process complemented the speed of the decision-making process, in which the development team efficiently and effectively responded to user requirement changes in a rapid and evolving manner (Lee and Xia, 2010). The first module of the surveillance system was the rapid development and rollout of the port-of-entry programme. By the second week of March, with increasing cases fuelled by returning Sri Lankans from Italy and South Korea, the case monitoring module was incorporated. With the introduction of compulsory quarantine in late March for all incoming passengers, a new module for quarantine management was incorporated. As the number of critically ill patients increased, an ICU bed-monitoring module was quickly developed and adopted. The local development team also mobilized other development resources by conducting hackathons, eliciting the support of volunteer developers, and bringing in additional expertise from the DHIS2 core team in Oslo. All this contributed to the development of a unique 'socio-technical' agility that goes beyond that typically described in software engineering literature.

Lean governance systems

Leanness was another key process element which enabled effective translation of the means to effective outcomes. Historically, Sri Lanka has had a formidable paper-based health information system, characterized by fragmentation and limited data sharing across vertical programmes. However, information requirements related to COVID-19 spanned various departments of the MoH as well as non-health sectors such as immigration and police. Coordination and rapid decision-making required strong processes of governance. The direct involvement of the president and the establishment of the multisectoral task force comprising senior decision-makers provided an effective governance structure.

For example, in late January 2020, the director general of health services approved the first prototype, which enabled the implementation process. Such high-level approvals would normally have entailed a time-consuming bureaucratic process. This quick governance permeated to the other non-health sectors. It led, for instance, to the ICT Agency giving approval for providing web-hosting services, which in turn enabled countrywide coverage by the surveillance platform. Also enabled was interagency data sharing, which led to the immigration department sharing data with the health department, enabling the monitoring of incoming travellers.

The governance structure derived its authority because, first, it was directly under the gaze of the president; and, second, the task force was multidisciplinary and was made up of the senior-most decision-makers from the various departments. National-level governance became effective at the local level. At a time when mobility of expert resources from the national level was greatly restricted, medical doctors trained in health informatics functioning as technical experts as well as administrators at the district level guided implementation all the way to the health facilities.

The means (capacity, platform) and process (agility and governance) have gone a long way in achieving the ends of a resilient health and digital system, with the potential of bringing out digital transformation at a fundamental level of the health system. The relatively stable running of the nutrition system is an example of a resilient information and health system. Resilience-building prior to the pandemic contributed to the development of many routine systems, some of which were nationally adapted. The onset of the pandemic raised two sets of challenges: one, the existing routine systems needed to be maintained to ensure no disruption in health services; two, new, adaptable systems needed to be developed. This happened from the first phase into eight or nine months of the pandemic.

However, as the next phase emerged in 2021, the new systems developed in the adaptability phase had to become part of the routine systems, while new systems, such as for vaccination rollout, needed to be developed. Each cycle of change has raised the threshold of complexity of the systems as well as the capacity of the health system to address the challenges. These incremental cycles of engagement create what Folke et al. (2014) term multi-scalar resilience that contributes to digital transformability. Achieving these elevated levels of resilience, however, requires extensive work – that of making systems born in the pandemic to be institutionalized and sustained as routine systems.

While it is possibly too early to comment on how this might play out, there are a few examples that give an idea of the possible direction it may take. There have been various integrations of the DHIS2 with other systems, such as for laboratory and immunization data, and immigration information. This interoperability can be contrasted with systems dedicated for particular purposes. The COVID-19 vaccination system has already triggered discussions on the adopting of the DHIS2 for general immunization information tracking. The dashboards have prompted discussions in the MoH about using the DHIS2 as a central repository for data analytics.

The story of hope: building digital resilience and transformation in a low-resource context

The three-decade-old civil war had significantly disrupted the accessibility of social services such as health, education, and the overall quality of life in the northern and eastern regions. Development was unequal. However, in the post-conflict era, there was high enthusiasm and commitment among the people to reconstruct the infrastructure of the region and enhance living standards. This enthusiasm and hope were crucial for the health sector, particularly at the district and community levels, to be accepting of new ICT-based initiatives as a path forward for reconstruction and rebuilding. ICTs were seen as adding value to their everyday work and an opportunity to learn new technologies, which they were deprived of during the conflicts. Particularly, free and open-source software was seen as a vehicle to build local capacity and sustainability, without undue dependence on the central level. One example of this was the nutrition monitoring system, which was implemented by HISP Sri Lanka and had better acceptance in the resource-limited, post-conflict district of Jaffna than in the three districts in central parts of the country where it had been introduced earlier. This sense of hope and aspirations arguably served as valuable resources to support these digital initiatives and social development more broadly.

To those who believe that digital resilience involves large-scale and expensive investments in digital technologies, the Sri Lankan experience provides an alternative and inspiring story of hope. By investing historically in strengthening public health and educational systems, including free and open-source digital systems, the two effective means of capacity and digital platforms were enabled. Lean governance, and agile systems development and institutional responses became important process elements that helped convert the means to the relevant outcome of a resilient health system, with inherent capabilities of digital transformability. This helps articulate a means–process–ends model highlighted in our analytical framework.

Acknowledgements

The author acknowledges the conceptual and empirical insights of Pamod Amarakoon, the primary person in building the information systems response in collaboration with HISP Sri Lanka. Discussions with my colleague Jørn Braa have been central in building the conceptual insights presented in this paper. The ongoing efforts of the HISP global R&D network are acknowledged.

Notes

1. This chapter draws upon content present in the following publications: Amarakoon et al., (2020), (2021); Kobayashi et al., (2021).
2. https://dhis2.org/category/covid-success-stories/

References

Amarakoon, P. (2020) 'DHIS2 Relationship Tracing App', DHIS2 Community [online] <https://community.dhis2.org/t/dhis2-relationship-tracing-app/39217> [accessed 5 September 2021].

Amarakoon, P., Braa, J., Sahay, S., Siribaddana, P. and Hewapathirana, R. (2020) 'Building agility in health information systems to respond to the COVID-19 pandemic: the Sri Lankan experience', in R.K. Bandi, C.R. Ranjini, S. Klein, S. Madon, and E. Monteiro (eds), *The Future of Digital Work: The Challenge of Inequality*, pp. 222–36, IFIP Advances in Information and Communication Technology Series vol 601, Springer, Cham <https://doi.org/10.1007/978-3-030-64697-4_17>.

Amarakoon, P., Braa, J. and Sahay, S. (2021) 'Building agility in COVID-19 information systems response in Sri Lanka: recommendations for practice', in Proceedings of the *IFIP WG 9.4 Virtual Conference on Implications of Information and Digital Technologies for Development* <https://doi.org/10.48550/arxiv.2108.09727>.

Braa, J. and Sahay, S. (2013) *Integrated Health Information Architecture – Power to the Users: Design, Development and Use* [online], Matrix Publishers, New Delhi <https://www.mn.uio.no/ifi/english/research/groups/is/research-library/integrated-health-information-architecture/prelims.pdf> [accessed 10 March 2022].

China Daily (2017) 'Chinese tourist arrivals to Sri Lanka record 3.5% growth in November', China Daily, 10 December [online] <http://www.chinadaily.com.cn/a/201712/10/WS5a2cf35da310eefe3e9a1424.html> [accessed 30 September 2020].

Doshi, P. (2011) 'The elusive definition of pandemic influenza', *Bulletin of the World Health Organization* 89(7): 532–8 <https://doi.org/10.2471/BLT.11.086173>.

Folke, C., Biggs, R., Norström, A.V., Reyers, B. and Rockström, J. (2014) 'Social-ecological resilience and biosphere-based sustainability science', *Ecology and Society* 21(3): 41 <http://dx.doi.org/10.5751/ES-08748-210341>.

Government of the Democratic Socialist Republic of Sri Lanka (2018) *Voluntary National Review on the Status of Implementing the Sustainable*

Development Goals [online] <https://sustainabledevelopment.un.org/content/documents/19677FINAL_SriLankaVNR_Report_30Jun2018.pdf> [accessed 21 January 2022].

Heeks, R. and Ospina, A.V. (2019) 'Conceptualising the link between information systems and resilience: a developing country field study', *Information Systems Journal* 29(1): 70–96 <https://doi.org/10.1111/isj.12177>.

Kobayashi, S., Falcón, L., Fraser, H., Braa, J., Amarakoon, P., Marcelo, A. and Paton, C. (2021) 'Using open source, open data, and civic technology to address the COVID-19 pandemic and infodemic', *Yearbook of Medical Informatics* 30(1): 38–43 <https://doi.org/10.1055/s-0041-1726488>.

Lee, G. and Xia, W. (2010) 'Toward agile: an integrated analysis of quantitative and qualitative field data on software development agility', *MIS Quarterly* 34(1): 87–114 <https://misq.umn.edu/toward-agile-an-integrated-analysis-of-quantitative-and-qualitative-field-data-on-software-development-agility.html>.

Ministry of Health and Indigenous Medical Services (2020) *Annual Health Statistics – 2018 Sri Lanka* [online] <http://www.health.gov.lk/moh_final/english/public/elfinder/files/publications/AHB/2020/Final AHS 2018.pdf> [accessed 21 January 2022].

Somda, Z.C., Meltzer, M.I., Perry, H.N., Messonnier, N.E., Abdulmumini, U., Mebrahtu, G., Sacko, M., Touré, K., Ki, S., Okorosobo, T., Alemu, W. and Sow, I. (2009) 'Cost analysis of an integrated disease surveillance and response system: case of Burkina Faso, Eritrea, and Mali', *Cost Effectiveness and Resource Allocation* 7: 1 <https://doi.org/10.1186/1478-7547-7-1>.

Tiwana, A. (2014) *Platform Ecosystems: Aligning Architecture, Governance, and Strategy*, Murgan Kaufman, Burlington, MA.

United Nations, Sri Lanka (2015) *Millennium Development Goals Country Report 2014: Sri Lanka* [online] <https://www.lk.undp.org/content/dam/srilanka/docs/mdg/MDG-Country-Report-2014.pdf> [accessed 10 March 2022].

World Summit Awards (2016) 'District Nutrition Monitoring System (DNMS)' [online] <https://wsa-global.org/winner/district-nutrition-monitoring-system-dnms/> [accessed 10 March 2022].

CHAPTER 5

Enabling sustainability qualifiers of health management information systems: Case study from Odisha, India

Sundeep Sahay and Arunima Mukherjee

The sustainability of digital interventions in LMICs remains a matter of enduring concern for both research and practice. Sustainability, which implies the capability of the digital system to endure over time and space, beyond the framework of external support, is also closely linked to the ability of the system to spread to different geographical and functional use cases. Health information systems (HIS) are particularly prone to 'sustainability failures', often because of the primary dependence on external donor support. Within this rather suboptimal landscape, it is important to understand how some digital interventions succeed in sustaining themselves, and what drives that to happen. This we conceptually understand through the notion of 'sustainability qualifiers'.

The case study presented in this chapter is set in Odisha, a state in eastern India, which is disadvantaged by low income levels and a high percentage of a tribal population. Their inclusion in the state systems for delivery of social services is weak. The state is periodically subjected to natural disasters such as cyclones. Despite these constraints, the state has managed to sustain and evolve the state HMIS since 2008. This remarkable achievement provides hope for other LMICs on how to harness their public systems.

The challenge of sustainability

Sustainability implies the capability of an intervention to endure over time and space, after external support has been withdrawn. It is a central concern in development interventions, both digital and non-digital. In HMISs in LMICs, the challenge of sustainability is acute. Heeks (2002) reported that nearly 90 per cent of such initiatives end up as partial or complete failures. The possibility of a slight exaggeration in this number, given the manner in which a system is classified as a failure or success (see also Chapter 2), does nothing to reduce the magnitude of the problem. The sustainability problem is described by Braa and Sahay (2012) taking the example from Uganda of 23 mHealth initiatives during the period 2008–09 in Uganda, but resulting in 'pilotitis' as all of them failed to be scaled and sustained. This led not only to a huge loss of resources but also to the undermining of governmental trust in digital technologies (Aid Leap, 2014).

Traditionally, ICT4D initiatives have adopted strategies of a 'supply-side push,' where sustainability tends to be equated with new and modern ICTs (Korpela et al., 1998). This approach ignores the 'demand-side pull' that arises from the aspirations of the users, and the socio-technical-cultural nature of the challenges in making systems work and provide value over time. Sustainability of systems often is compromised by the centralized nature of the initiatives, which marginalize the work practices of the end-users (Mukherjee, 2017). Health systems are typically characterized by multiple vertical systems, often organized around different disease-based systems, which promotes fragmentation and redundancies and constrains the use of unified information. Weak data use leads to poor demand for data, with increasingly less attention being paid to providing quality data. This contributes to a vicious cycle of data not being, leading to increasingly poor quality data and more non-use. The outcome of this vicious cycle is that the HMIS becomes unsustainable (Nhampossa, 2005).

The focus of this chapter is to understand how governments can achieve the ends of sustainable digital interventions for improving their citizens' access to quality health services. The World Health Organization (WHO) has identified the HIS as the building block for strong health systems, implying that the more robust they are, the stronger will be the state's capability to provide quality healthcare. The digital platform on which the HIS is built is a key means to achieving sustainability. It needs to be supported by appropriate implementation processes to ensure good quality data for the health staff that is then used for decisions on improving healthcare. This translating of means into desired outcomes presents complex, interconnected socio-technical-political challenges. It is not just about the embedding of modern digital technologies: it also calls for enabling governance, capacity strengthening, building ownership, and reinforcing data quality improvements.

The HMIS is the umbrella HIS in the government of the eastern Indian state of Odisha. This includes routine data on all health services being delivered to the population, from the lowest community level, to the district and the state, to the national level, and, finally, the global level. The HMIS provides data for strengthening local-level care processes and supporting state- and national-level programme management and policymaking. Given its comprehensive scope, the HMIS is the state's foundational informational tool for guiding healthcare delivery, especially to ruralites, who tend to be marginalized and cannot afford privately delivered, expensive care.

The concept we used to understand the digital HMIS is that of 'sustainability qualifiers'. We confront the paradox of the system being deeply institutionalized and owned by the state, and yet being flexible enough to evolve with the changing informational needs of the health system. Sustainability is critical for a digital initiative. Over time and as it gains experience, a state will build technical and institutional capabilities to better address evolving, local-level health challenges. Nor, with a sustainable system, does the state need to keep spending resources on new technologies.

That a resource-poor state like Odisha built these sustainability qualifiers over more than a decade of engagement with its HMIS provides hope that others in similar circumstances can do the same.

The context of the study

This is an especially interesting case to study for three main reasons: one, the HMIS implementation, based on the DHIS2 platform, has been evolving since 2008 – longevity that is rare in LMICs; two, the sustaining of the HMIS in Odisha, one of the most under-resourced states in India, makes it imperative to understand what has made it possible; three, given the socioeconomic challenges in the state, an understanding is crucial of precisely how the potential of the HMIS was harnessed and actualized to make things 'better' for its citizens.

The authors of this case study have been engaged with the design, development, implementation, and evaluation of Odisha's HMIS from the very beginning. This engagement has been in terms of both strengthening the systems and situated empirical research. The practical engagement was initiated in 2008 when the National Rural Health Mission, Ministry of Health, Government of India, began the process of reforming the health systems to strengthen public systems nationwide. This included making the HMIS more decentralized, standardized, and evidence-based. The first author of this chapter was seconded by the University of Oslo to the Indian health ministry and, as the National HMIS Advisor, was intimately involved in the reform process. He was also a founder member of HISP India, a local NGO that was a technical partner to the national agency to support the reform implementation. The second author of this chapter was also a member of HISP India, and part of the national HMIS reform team.

Odisha was a focus state for these reforms. In 2008–12, both the authors visited the state multiple times to support the design and implementation of the reformed systems. They conducted trainings, built local requirements on the DHIS2 platform, and balanced the information needs of the national and state levels. This implementation continued until 2012, after which Odisha made a bilateral arrangement with HISP India to technically support and evolve their systems, which process continues. The authors' ongoing engagement with strengthening the state HMIS complements the empirical research they conducted in March–July 2019, when a research team visited six districts, with three sub-district facilities (called blocks) in each, to understand how the system was being used, what challenges the users were facing, and how they were dealing with the challenges.

Odisha, located in eastern India, has a population of 41.97 million (Census 2011; https://censusindia.gov.in/2011-common/censusdata2011.html), with 22 per cent tribals, almost all of them with typically poor food security, low health indicators, and inadequate health access (Office of the Registrar General & Census Commissioner, India, 2011–2012; Routray and Schmidt, 2015).

Despite its resource limitations, the state has grown economically and socially. The *Odisha Economic Survey, 2017–18* (Government of Odisha, 2018) reported that the gross state domestic product increased by 7.14 per cent in 2017–18, which made it higher than the national average increase of 6.5 per cent. There has been a reduction in the infant mortality rate by 41 points (1998–99 to 2015–16); in the total fertility rate, or the average number of children per woman, from 2.6 to 2.0 (2004–06 to 2014–16); and an increase in the literacy rate to 72.9 per cent, an uptick of 9.8 per cent.

Infrastructure development has, however, been uneven. For instance, the spread of automated teller machines (ATMs) is lower than the all-India average; wireless teledensity was 79.58 compared to the national average of 91.09 (2018); and about 20 per cent of the villages do not currently have mobile connectivity. Even the physical connectivity of rails and roads is lower than the national figures. While the state has the highest rate in the country of poverty reduction, from 57 per cent to 24.6 per cent (2004–2012), significant regional disparities exist. The major development priority for the state is the improvement of health and social services to vulnerable groups in remote and poorly accessible areas where child malnutrition can run as high as 50 per cent. Since the state has a long coastline, floods repeatedly cause health problems. The July 2019 floods, for example, affected more than 8.5 million people making them vulnerable to health problems such as malaria.

The Government of India launched the Transformation of Aspirational Districts programme in January 2018 to strengthen development where it is needed most – in districts that show the lowest socioeconomic indicators. Of the 117 districts identified across 28 states, 8 were from Odisha.

The process of building HMIS sustainability

The history of HMIS implementation in the state is interpretively reconstructed over three phases.

1. Initiation of HMIS (2008–10)

Odisha was included in a situation analysis conducted as a part of the national reform process. In addition to the nationally mandated data standards, the state identified its local data needs, which were not to be reported to the national level. While defining the state's organizational unit-based hierarchy, we identified duplications and redundancies in nomenclature: for example, a Primary Health Centre (PHC) was referred to by different names, such as 'Mini PHC', 'New PHC', and 'Additional PHC'. Working with the state team, we built standardized nomenclature and incorporated then in the DHIS2-based HMIS. The database was gradually improved and standardized, and its deployment supported by a series of workshops, and orientation and training sessions. While the software and technical support were provided free by HISP India, the process was supported by a national budget, which continued until 2012. Following this, the state chose to work directly with HISP India for technical support.

2. Total transition to DHIS2 based systems (2010–12)

This phase involved a full transition from the paper-based HMIS to the DHIS2 digital platform. The configuration of the platform to simultaneously support state and national needs, capacity building, and troubleshooting support were major activities, and entailed working closely with both state- and district-level teams. Configuration primarily involved incorporating state- and district-specific requirements not addressed by the national process. Troubleshooting and bug-fixing issues were addressed on a continuous basis, and focused on strengthening work practices around data quality management and data use.

During this period, the central ministry tried to discourage the state from using a local system on the DHIS2, and to use the national portal instead. The state dealt with this pressure by arguing that, first, the DHIS2 dealt with state-specific needs; and, second, the state would ensure that it provided the central system required data on a monthly basis. Thus, Odisha became one of the few states that established its autonomy in selecting and using a software platform which it considered best suited to local needs. Most other states succumbed to central pressure and adopted the national system. Contributing to Odisha's stance of local autonomy could be their very visionary and stable structure of governance.

3. Consolidating the HMIS (2012–ongoing)

In 2012, when national-level support to the states was withdrawn, Odisha was advised to develop a bilateral relationship with HISP India if it wished to continue receiving technical support for the HMIS. By this time, the state HMIS team had gained an adequate understanding of the DHIS2, and had experienced its real-world ability to support local needs and improve data analysis with easy-to-use features such as dashboards. They found that the DHIS2 could rapidly support their evolving needs at a low cost, obviating the need to build new systems from scratch. The state's relationship with HISP India continues.

Three key outcomes of the implementation process were identified: 1) significant improvements in data coverage; 2) significant gains in data quality; and 3) a steady progression towards an 'integrated state data warehouse' based on the DHIS2.

Improved processes of data coverage

The transition from a paper-based to a web-based free and open-source digital platform helped address historical challenges related to redundant and inconsistent data formats, duplications across data recording and reporting practices, errors resulting from manual data processing, and time delays in reporting. While the earlier system had been geared primarily towards upward reporting to the central ministry, the DHIS2 allowed the district and sub-district local levels to see their own data and address long-existing problems of data quality and inflated reporting. With even the block (sub-district) users entering data into the DHIS2, the state gradually achieved 100 per cent data coverage.

Said a district user on the value of increased visibility of data:

> Increasing numbers of data elements means more data to be presented in monthly meetings. It becomes possible to focus on poor performers. Increasing data quality and reporting rate has also been seen in the district. Urban areas with many private facilities are currently the focus as they have lower reporting rates and poorer data quality.

The MCTS system was also used to identify poorly performing facilities and individuals. We believe that the health staff identified differently with the MCTS and the DHIS2. While the MCTS was seen as reprimanding the poor performers, in Odisha the DHIS2 was perceived as focused on understanding the reasons for the shortfall in data quality and how that could be addressed. In Odisha, these processes contributed significantly to enhancing data coverage supported by the participation of the health staff. The state created an environment in which the health staff felt the freedom and confidence to voice their opinions and give suggestions on, for example, what data elements to include and exclude.

A health worker had this to say:

> In our monthly meeting, a health worker asked to merge data elements from the Home Based Care for Young Child (HBYC) dataset into the HMIS dataset so that they would have one less dataset to report. We discussed with other health workers in the district for suggestions. And we had very good ideas on reducing data elements and merging data sets. I took this up at the state meeting with other districts, and everyone agreed to undertake the same process. This led to our state institutionalizing the rationalizing process every two years.

From the data reporting status of the PHC HMIS monthly dataset for the initial three years (2010–11, 2011–12, and 2012–13) and the last three years (2018–19, 2019–20, and 2020–21), we can see that in the initial three years, the reporting percentage increased from 0 per cent to 85 per cent in April and from 77 per cent to 87 per cent in March. In the last three years, the data reporting percentage is more than 95 per cent in both April and March. In terms of percentage of facilities reporting data, the figure has improved from about 80 per cent in 2011 (900 to 1,000 facilities of 1,200 existing facilities) to the current figure of about 95 per cent. The reporting rate increased from 28.8 per cent to 75.5 per cent over seven years.

Well-defined institutional protocols for data quality management were defined around data reporting and evolved through regular use. These protocols took into account pre-existing practices related to data collection reviews, processes of confirmation, and submission of data. The aim was not to eliminate the legacy practices but to build upon them and gradually make them more stringent and visible through digitization. To support digitization, explicit guidelines, responsibilities, and resources were agreed upon, such as establishing institutional responsibilities for the identification and correction of data validation errors generated by the system. Through data rationalization and removing duplications in data (such as different names for PHC facilities), the amount of data collected was significantly reduced, enabling improvements in data quality. The DHIS2 allowed for easy identification of facilities that did not report data, enabled correctness checks at the very point of data entry, allowed locking of the data once confirmed to prevent late changes, run data validation checks, and implement useful functionalities such as role-based user authorizations. In this way, digitization helped build new routines and practices that were not divorced from the past but sought to build upon and extend existing routines.

These technical improvements were only made possible through the establishment of supporting institutional processes. Validation committees at each level of the reporting hierarchy (state, district, and block) were set up to routinely review data quality and to provide support for making corrections. The validation committees did not seek to change the authority structure but to enhance the visibility and accountability of the information function using the digital affordances. Conversations around data between the validation committees and the data providers helped to increase awareness about the value of data and helped build a sense of pride around its upkeep. With increasing maturity in data quality, there was a shift from data use for performance evaluation and control to corrective action to strengthen service delivery. With this, increasingly more stakeholders got involved in conversations around data.

A block-level functionary noted:

> In 2006, there was a big booklet of around 25 plus pages that we had to fill. Each data element was disaggregated by Scheduled Caste, Scheduled Tribe and Others, and further broken down by male and female. Data was entered in Excel to be aggregated, which generated a lot of mistakes. The district level only had block level data and could not drill down. Now we are getting direct contact with the lowest level, we can look at their data, and call them if something is wrong. Even the state level is in contact with the lower levels as they can see their data. The state level is also contacting sub-centre facilities. In 2006, only one programme was included in HMIS. Now they have integrated multiple programmes to make reporting easier.

Building on the strong culture of bottom-up and participatory management, the local teams created structures for local review and correction of data. This process was not limited to the health staff but included functionaries from the village, who had a stake in the data: for example, to see how many children in the village had been immunized.

A health supervisor said:

> Now we ensure that only one number is reported for our village. So, every 4th of the month, we have a village meeting to discuss our monthly reports. The school principal, an *anganwadi* worker (village level health worker), the PHC medical officer, the village head, an accredited social health activist (ASHA) and I (health worker) are present. I bring my registers and the medical officer brings my data from system after validation check. For example, at any given point, there are not more than 5–6 pregnant women in the village, and not more than 8–10 children for immunization, so it is easy to discuss all the cases and identify referral cases. We validate our village data, which is signed by all, and a copy is kept in village office.

Often, data quality suffers because of the frequent turnover of health functionaries and the need to provide new incumbents with training on the HMIS, which is affected by resource and time limitations. However, the state organized matters internally to support new incumbents, and dispensed with engaging expensive external consultants.

A state-level functionary explained this process:

> We started the annual weeklong Data Manager Refresher Training for all block, district, and state teams. We use this for training on reporting forms, new features, and reports in DHIS2, annual data analysis, new processes, etc. We ensure that changes are done in the forms, and new data elements are added or deleted. A new appointee spends a week at the state level for training on the DHIS2. If the appointment is at the district level, then the neighbouring district supports the appointee's training for three months. If the appointee is at the block level, then the district supports the training for three months.

Gradual progress towards an integrated state data warehouse

Driven by the initial agenda of the HMIS, the early focus was on strengthening data coverage and quality, primarily for the national-level programmes. Over time, requirements emerged for national and state-specific programmes. As many as 10 programmes were integrated, and the DHIS2 incrementally evolved into a repository of all state health data. However, not all the integrations have been embedded well or adapted well for routine use. The uptake has been variable. Technical improvements need to be supported by appropriate institutional mechanisms such as assigning responsibilities for data use.

The focus now is on the use of data in the DHIS2, and on creating a more integrated usage and policymaking perspective.

The processes of integration was not driven only from the top, but also took place in the field. A health worker described how the community ANM and the ASHA shared and discussed data (e.g. to identify women suffering from anaemia).

> When, for two months, my block reports showed high severe anaemia cases, it had me worried. I checked for validations and typos. I matched the ANCs done with iron folic acid (IFA) distributed and haemoglobin checked for each facility. I found no error. I called a meeting with the ASHAs and the ANMs, and checked if the ASHAs were monitoring women taking IFA tablets. We found they weren't, and realized that after their initial reaction to the IFA, maybe the women were discontinuing taking them. We agreed to focus on the ASHAs personally administering the IFA (which is 3–4 per week per ASHA), and on anaemia and the IFA in our ANM meetings.

The health workers were not wedded to the digital systems, and always backed up information in their manual registers and forms.

A health worker told us:

> When I have to look up patients, I use my register – for which I don't need the internet, I don't need electricity, I don't need to login. And I can carry in it my bag, I can make small notes for myself without any predefined format. Sometime, it helps to draw and explain matters to the patient, and my register allows me to do so. I can also tear off a page to write a note to my patient. None of the technologies allows me to do so much!

What have been the sustainability qualifiers?

We identified three key sustainability qualifiers: 1) accruing of benefits and continued benefits; 2) routinization and institutionalization of processes; and 3) continued evolution of systems development. We discuss here how these qualifiers were achieved in the empirical case, from the perspectives of the data providers, and the monitoring and evaluation (M&E) and IT teams in the state. While the technical elements are critical for defining sustainability qualifiers, there are also visibly political and social qualifiers at play. For example, political sustainability is reflected in how the state created an environment for health workers, such as local level data validation committees, to exert their voice in relation to data handling. Social sustainability is visible in terms of the emergence of local structures including civil society actors such as the village leader who also was active in commenting on the data.

Accruing of benefits, continued benefits

For the data providers, data rationalization, which called for eliminating duplications and redundancies of data, reduced their workload. The digitization of these new data formats in the DHIS2 enabled a transition of reporting systems from manual and time-consuming work to an easier, more accessible, and more efficient process. The HMIS, which allowed the identification of and then support to weak performers, helped to gradually achieve 100 per cent data coverage. This also implied that data providers could avoid reprimands for nonattendance or late reporting. For the M&E team, all the data in one database enhanced the visibility of health status, and increased their ability to drill down to the lowest level of data to identify events and their causes in order to enable corrective action. This greatly strengthened their analytical abilities. The IT team had the opportunity to work with a state-of-the-art digital platform, the DHIS2, and also build individual technical capacities and strengthen local ownership. This was self-motivating.

Routinization and institutionalization of processes

The process of routinization and institutionalization of the DHIS2 and associated processes is well illustrated through the data management function. An explicitly defined protocol for data quality management based on the DHIS2 was established by the state, imparting it the necessary legitimacy to become routinely used across the state. Helping this process was that the protocols defined were not new. The process was based on legacy data management practices and expanded to incorporate digital aspects such as identifying data validation errors. The continuation of legacy practices also meant that the users did not perceive the protocols as a threat. Mechanisms such as the existing data review meetings and validation committees ensured compliance of practices and processes, leading to their gradual and deeper institutionalization. The participation of the health staff in the design and use of the systems contributed to the institutionalization of processes.

Continued evolution of systems development

Fundamental to the sustainability process was continuous technical and institutional development. For example, the guidelines for data quality management were continuously improved, and were disseminated at regular intervals after discussions with and clarifications from the relevant stakeholders. Technical improvements took the form of multilevel data quality checks, self-validation of data, supervisory approvals prior to report submission, and integrated reports at the sub-district level that were used during review meetings. Supporting these development processes was a stable and visionary governance structure based on realizing the need for a strong and low-cost technical partner such as HISP India. Whenever new features, modifications, or troubleshooting support were required, HISP India quickly responded, thus helping along systems evolution. These developments were enabled by the flexibility and customizability affordances offered by the DHIS2, and also that its use was not locked by proprietary licensing.

Table 5.1 Sustainability qualifiers shaping Odisha HMIS implementation trajectory

Sustainability qualifiers	Supporting practices	Institutional shaping of practices
Accruing benefits, continued benefits	*Data providers*: reduced data load; easier access to entry; improved quality.	Establishing *validation committees* to have monthly conversations around data.
	M&E team: Increased visibility of data; improved visualization and analytics.	*Monthly review meetings* based on HMIS data.
	IT team: Working on state-of-the-art technology with responsive HISP India support team.	Ongoing *support agreements* with HISP India continued over 10 years, being extended by the state on an annual basis based on the review of HISP India performance.
Routinization, institutionalization of processes	Routines of review meetings, data quality checks, data analysis, and use were clearly established, and imparted necessary legitimacy to be institutionalized, such as through budgets and human resources.	District and block level structures created for data quality review and use; at state level, dedicated IT team and data centre identified; state M&E team enhanced the demand for quality data, putting pressure on the supply side.
Continued evolution of systems development	Demand for new functionalities and modules rapidly incorporated; regular capacity building to build awareness and use.	State promoted the progressive policy of building an integrated data warehouse based on the DHIS2.

Some areas of development have, however, been tricky, such as the scaling of the malaria surveillance system, which had been successfully piloted in some districts. Since the malaria programme was directly controlled by the national rather than the state office, the state had ineffective say in what software was mandated at the national level.

In Table 5.1 we highlight the key sustainability qualifiers identified through the empirical analysis.

How striving for and achieving sustainability provides hope for low-resource contexts

Information systems research has developed different perspectives to understand the sustainability of (health) information systems (Greenhalgh et. al., 2004). The diffusionist perspective as proposed by Rogers (1983), synthesizing research from multiple diffusion studies, built a multidisciplinary perspective around a theory about the adoption of innovations among individuals and organizations. Rogers conceptualized the trajectory of an innovation and its adoption over time as an 'S' curve, which is primarily focused on the supply-side of an innovation, assuming that it takes birth at the 'centre', and is then gradually adopted at the 'peripheral' levels (Nhampossa, 2005). This is from a 'top-down' perspective that foregrounds issues such as donor funding, system usability, and technical fidelity as key sustainability concerns. Arguably, it is limited in how actively it considers the demand side of the user practices in social and institutional contexts. Research has highlighted that systems implementation needs to be based on local user needs and work practices (Walsham, et al., 1988), and the process is full of unexpected and non-linear events that often contribute to 'sustainability failures' (Best and Kumar, 2008). Nhampossa (2005) argued against the efficacy of the diffusionist perspective in the Mozambique context, critiquing the assumption that knowledge and innovation will only emanate from the centre, and that the periphery is incapable of building anything new. He advocates instead the adoption of a 'translation' approach, where the movement of technology is not seen as one giant leap from point A to B, but as a series of small steps (or translations) that enables the emergence at each step of new configurations of socio-technical networks that shape evolution as well as the contents of a technology.

Sustainability faces inherent challenges in low-resource contexts given the predominance of technocentric and top-down approaches that often depend on the short-term external support of donors, which their finite timespans render unsustainable. It becomes crucial for such contexts to develop locally driven and frugal approaches that minimize expensive and external dependencies. Braa et al. (2004) advocated a 'networks of action' approach to address the interconnected challenges of sustainability and scalability of HISs in LMICs. This approach is grounded in a research and action philosophy that is oriented towards enabling learning in collectives rather than in isolations. Such an approach avoids 'reinventing the wheel of mistakes' and undue wastage of resources (Yahya and Braa, 2011). Learning among peers fundamentally challenges top-down diffusionist thinking. The 'action' in this approach is that of enabling sharing of resources, ideas, and experiences across the various actors in an action network. This approach has been crucial in sustaining of the HISP network in more than 80 countries over two decades (Sahay et al., 2019). Enduring the test of time and scale is active proof of sustainability.

Our research approach is based on a practice-based methodology (Orlikowski, 2000), which operates at the micro and pragmatic levels and is based on the assumption that systems become sustainable only when they are routinely used and institutionalized, and add value to everyday work practices. Networks of action include the various stakeholders with an interest in the HMIS. They engage them in joint activities, particularly those oriented towards addressing recurring problems. While a prime requisite of sustainability is the institutionalization of processes and systems, a challenge exists about how to translate these systems into practice. Fleiszer et al. (2015)

describe these as 'qualifiers of sustainability'. Our empirical analysis identified three such qualifiers: 1) accruing of benefits, continued benefits; 2) routinization and institutionalization of processes; and 3) continued evolution of systems development.

Reflecting as they do enhanced capabilities of the state in owning a well-functioning HMIS that delivers crucial health services, these sustainability qualifiers serve as indicators of hope. Our case represents a rare example of a HMIS in a LMIC that has endured and continues to thrive even after 12 years. Despite frequent changes in the state government's administration, the Odisha governance structure has been consistent in supporting the DHIS2 and the HISP India technical team.

However, these are necessary but not sufficient conditions for promoting the effective use of data, which requires similar progress on data use. This would require additional qualifiers such as institutional incentives, dissemination of successful case studies and stories, and the foregrounding of exemplary data users. This could also benefit by expanding the network of stakeholders beyond the health sector, such as the local politicians and district administrators who are involved in implementing development programmes. Such an expansion would make for a self-reinforcing mechanism strengthening the demand side, and, by its sheer spread, creating top-of-the-line data users who would attract other users and innovations.

We believe that this story from Odisha gives rise to general principles relevant to other contexts and systems. A guiding principle is the need to focus on sustainability from the perspective of the state. An important lesson is that sustainability must be incrementally developed through a process that might take years. While we have identified three sustainability qualifiers, other contexts would need to identify relevant qualifiers to specific contexts and institutions. However, what is common to all these qualifiers is the need to focus on adding value and not extra work to the everyday users.

Acknowledgements

The long-term (since 2008) engagement of HISP India in supporting and strengthening Odisha state's Health Management Information System to make them self-reliant and sustainable is duly acknowledged. Empirical work carried out in Odisha by Jyotsna Sahay and Anna Basiston is deeply acknowledged.

References

Aid Leap (2014) 'Is there too much "innovation" in development?' [online] <https://aidleap.org/2014/11/20/is–there–too–much–innovation–in–development/> [accessed 20 August 2021].
Best, M.L. and Kumar, R. (2008) 'Sustainability failures of rural telecenters: challenges from the sustainable access in rural India (SARI) project',

Information Technologies and International Development 4(4): 31–45 <https://doi.org/10.1162/itid.2008.00025>.

Braa, J. and Sahay, S. (2012) *Integrated Health Information Architecture: Power for the Users: Design Development and Use*, Matrix Publishing, New Delhi.

Braa, J., Monteiro, E. and Sahay, S. (2004) 'Networks of action: sustainable health information systems across developing countries', *MIS Quarterly* 28(3): 337–62 <https://doi.org/10.2307/25148643>.

Fleiszer, A.R., Semenic, S.E., Ritchie, J.A., Richer, M.C. and Denis, J.L. (2015) 'The sustainability of healthcare innovations: a concept analysis', *Journal of Advanced Nursing* 71(7): 1484–98 <https://doi.org/101111/jan.12633>.

Government of Odisha (2018) *Odisha Economic Survey, 2017–2018*, Planning and Convergence Department, Government of Odisha [online] <http://www.desorissa.nic.in/pdf/Economic%20Survey_2017-18.pdf> [accessed 23 August 2021].

Greenhalgh, T., Robert, G., Bate, P., Kyriakidou, O., Macfarlane, F. and Peacock, R. (2004) 'How to spread good ideas: A systematic review of the literature on diffusion, dissemination and sustainability of innovations in health', Technical report, National Co-ordinating Centre for NHS Service Delivery and Organisation R&D (NCCSDO), UK.

Heeks, R. (2002) 'Information systems and developing countries: failure, success, and local improvisation', *The Information Society* 18(2): 101–12 <https://doi.org/10.1080/01972240290075039>.

Korpela, M., Soriyan, H.A., Olufokunbi, K.C. and Mursu, A. (1998) 'Blueprint for an African systems development methodology: an action research project in the health sector', in C. Avgerou (ed.), *Implementation and Evaluation of Information Systems in Developing Countries. Proceedings of the Fifth International Working Conference of IFIP WG 9.4*, pp. 273–85, London School of Economics and Political Science, and Asian Institute of Technology, Bangkok.

Mukherjee, A.S. (2017) *Empowerment: The Invisible Element in ICT4D Projects? The Case of Public Health Information Systems in India and Kenya*, Unpublished dissertation, University of Oslo, Norway.

Nhampossa, J.L. (2005) *Re-thinking Technology Transfer as Technology Translation: A Case Study of Health Information Systems in Mozambique*, Unpublished dissertation, Department of Informatics, University of Oslo, Norway.

Office of the Registrar General & Census Commissioner, India (2011–2012) *Annual Health Survey Report: A Report on Core and Vital Health Indicators. Part I* [online], Institute of Economic Growth <https://www.censusindia.gov.in/vital_statistics/AHS/AHS_report_part1.pdf> [accessed 10 March 2022].

Orlikowski, W.J. (2000) 'Using technology and constituting structures: a practice lens for studying technology in organisations', *Organisation Science* 11(4): 404–428 <https://doi.org/10.1287/orsc.11.4.404.14600>.

Rogers, E.M. (1983) *Diffusion of Innovations*, 3rd edition, Free Press of Glencoe, New York.

Routray, P. and Schmidt, W.P. (2015) 'Socio-cultural and behavioural factors constraining latrine adoption in rural coastal Odisha: an exploratory qualitative study', *BMC Public Health* 2015(15): 880 <https://doi.org/10.1186/s12889-015-2206-3>.

Sahay, S., Sundararaman, T. and Braa, J. (2019) *Public Health Informatics: Designing for Change: A Developing Country Perspective*, Oxford University Press, New Delhi.

Walsham, G., Symons, V. and Waema, T. (1988) 'Information systems as social systems: implications for developing countries', *Information Technology for Development* 3(3): 189–204 <https://doi.org/10.1080/02681102.1988.962 7126>.

Yahya, H.S. and Braa, K. (2011) 'Mobilising local networks of implementers to address health information systems sustainability', *EJISDC* 48(6): 1–21 <https://doi.org/10.1002/j.1681-4835.2011.tb00342.x>.

Building citizen trust in public health systems: Hospital information systems in India

Sundeep Sahay and Arunima Mukherjee

This chapter describes the process of designing, developing, implementing, and evolving a hospital information system (HospIS) in a network of secondary and tertiary care hospitals within the public healthcare system of the state of Himachal Pradesh in northern India. This state is pioneering in India in its efforts to strengthen its public systems of health and education, and enhancing the digital capabilities seen as important. HospIS was an integrated hospital information system built on a free and open-source digital platform called the Open Medical Record System (OpenMRS) and supported over the past 10 years and more by HISP India. While the HospIS is important in achieving a stronger public healthcare system, the building of citizens' trust is equally significant. We identified the various benefits of the HospIS, such as improving patient experience in hospitals, giving them a platform to voice their concerns and suggestions, and empowering them with the necessary information. We analysed these to understand how they contribute to the building of institutional and interpersonal trust and strengthen interactions.

Hospital information systems in LMICs

Healthcare in LMICs has focused largely on primary and community healthcare services that concentrate on preventive and promotive care services, with a primary focus on maternal and child health. Specialist services such as surgeries and advanced diagnostics are provided through the tertiary hospitals at the district and state levels. Efforts to strengthen health information systems in LMICs have primarily focused on the primary healthcare domain, while hospitals have been largely neglected (Braa and Sahay, 2012). This neglect is problematic from the perspective of strengthening the broader health systems as the hospital sector provides a significant proportion of health services to the population. With large-scale urbanization, rise in non-communicable diseases such as cancer, there is the increasing need for specialized hospital-based services and patient-centric care, emphasizing the need for an effective hospital information system (HospIS). This need has been acknowledged by the GoI's efforts in launching the National Digital Health Mission (NDHM) (National Health Portal, 2020).

District hospitals in India are complex sites for various reasons. First, they experience high patient loads of 500–800 outpatients daily, with each of the 60–70 patients in a doctor's daily shift getting only four or five minutes. Second, these hospitals provide a wide variety of preventive, promotive, and curative services, which require a great deal of coordination across medical and administrative departments. Third, due to historically low budgets, these hospitals tend to be insufficiently provisioned for resources and infrastructure, and are largely dependent on manual information systems. Fourth, citizens mistrust public health systems, their perception being that the system at large does not really care for their health (Rao, 2017). Generally speaking, a visit to a public hospital in India is an unpleasant experience, because of its location, which may involve a long trek by a villager, long queues in overcrowded spaces, and no guarantees that a doctor or medicines will be available at the end of the odyssey (Kumar, 2017). Consequently, many Indians have come to rely on the private sector, which is both expensive and inaccessible, especially to the rural poor.

Context of study

The state setting

Himachal Pradesh, in northern India, is situated in the foothills of the Himalayas. Along with Kerala and Tamil Nadu, it has been identified as having excellent public services, including health – a direct consequence of constructive state policies (Drèze and Sen, 2013). Pioneering healthcare reforms through innovative and ICT-based solutions, the state has been ranked among the top in the country on the Human Development Index. Much of the population accesses public health facilities through district hospitals. The results of these improvements in digitization, the medical infrastructure, and social inclusion are now evident in the state's high levels of health and educational attainment. For example, the public sector in the state caters to nearly 80 per cent of the population, which is more than double the India country average.

The state decided as far back as 2009 to computerize its more than 20 district hospitals, when most states had not. The state believed that electronic medical records would help the patient get better care, that there would be greater continuity in treatment, and that administrators would get a more granular view of the workings of various hospital departments. The state health department entered into an agreement with HISP India to design, develop, and implement a scalable HospIS based on the Open Medical Record System (OpenMRS). HISP India had already been working with the state on strengthening its routine HMIS, and had earned the trust of the state.

Technical details of HospIS

HISP India built the HospIS (figure 6.1) on the OpenMRS digital platform from scratch, starting with a pilot hospital located in the state capital Shimla, and through intensively engaging with the hospital's many departments. This approach provided the foundation for the standardization of data and information flows, a model that could be taken to other hospitals. Starting with one hospital in the first year, the system was rolled out to all 20 district hospitals by the end of the fifth year. HISP India is still supporting all these hospitals. The system has also been implemented in other health facilities such as teaching hospitals and primary healthcare centres. The initial agreement with HISP India was for three years, but it was extended for one year at a time, and, 10 years later, the project continues and is evolving. The project began by focusing on the development and stabilization of systems in hospitals, while the current efforts are focused on improving information flows and strengthening sustainability.

The initial design process involved detailed discussions with doctors, radiologists, lab technicians, pharmacists, and administrators, among others. The system was designed to be modular. It had a minimal 'core' that was limited to patient registration and outpatient clinical consultation, and the modules addressed the needs of the laboratory, the pharmacy, radiology, inventory, inpatients, and billing. Individual modules were loosely coupled with other modules, and could be turned off when not required. A facility could initially use only the core patient registration and billing, and gradually add on other modules as required. The HospIS was designed with enough elasticity to ease scaling up and down.

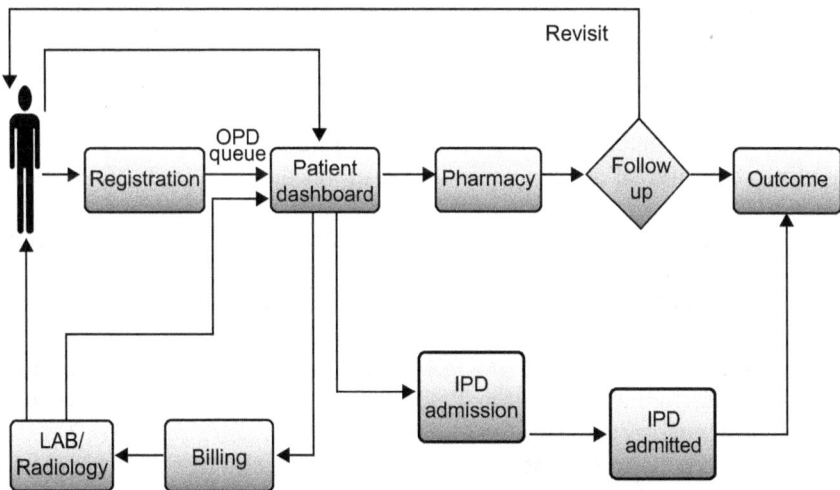

Figure 6.1 Architecture of the HospIS
Note: IPD, inpatient department.

The HospIS had 10 modules, including a 'Hospital Core' that coordinated communication between all modules. Its development involved analysing user requirements, building prototypes, obtaining feedback from users, trouble-shooting, and reporting on project progress, among other allied tasks (Aanestad et al., 2014). The development of the first version of the HospIS for the pilot hospital took approximately 12 months. Patient registration and billing were implemented first because these were relatively independent of the others, were easy to execute, and their outcome visible to patients immediately after deployment. The HospIS was designed to be deeply embedded in the hospital workflow, with added value features provided at pain points such as registration of high numbers of patients.

The registration desk consists of two data entry operators each for two separate queues for male and female patients. Some hospitals have added another queue for senior citizens. The patient was mandatorily registered, and a unique 16-digit Computer Registration Number (CRN) was printed on the registration slip. Since this slip mentioned the room number for their consultation, it did away with patients urgently searching for the radiology or the pathology labs, for example. Patients were added to relevant queues for the OPD at the registration desk itself, and they were told their position in the queue. Jumping queues, a regular practice prior to the HospIS, became a thing of the past. While all this invariably meant additional work for the registration clerks, it improved the information process flow significantly for the hospital.

The billing module was operated by clerks who would charge patients for diagnostics based on standardized rate lists. The billing module did not permit charging a patient for an unavailable test, which saved the patient the hassle of getting refunds. The system enabled the tracking of inventory, and sent out alerts when replenishment levels were reached. The centralized billing system improved cash flows, compared to the past, when various departments collected their own fees from the patients. Audit trails were embedded in the system to curb pilferage, and the staff were trained to handle all cash-related reports to ensure multilevel transparency. Printed prescriptions and laboratory reports (with more contextualized information, such as mentioning normal ranges) allowed patients to themselves make inferences. With reports in hand, patients could now choose to get a second opinion, which was previously not possible (Sahay and Walsham, 2017).

The HISP India team visits the deployment sites frequently for interaction and feedback from system users and other actors, besides capacity building and system-specific training. This gives them a sense of the users' comfort levels and strengthens operational efficiencies, improves overall delivery of service, and enables the assessing of needs for additional features. The system designers keep their suggestions and specific requests in logs for effective implementation (Aanestad et al., 2014).

As researchers, we were concerned with understanding the value of these systems from the perspective of patients. Specifically, we wanted to know how and if the perceptions of the patients had changed towards the public health system following the introduction of the HospIS, and whether or not the system had helped improve their trust in public health facilities.

Understanding the building of citizens' trust

A research team was formed that consisted primarily of researchers from the University of Oslo and HISP India in collaboration with the hospital staff wherever possible. Two rounds of fieldwork were carried out (in 2015 and 2019) to study the changing degree of trust over time. This learning was crucial for administrators and policymakers to assess the value of their investments, and to figure out what more they could do to enhance trust.

By 2015, the HospIS had been deployed in all 20 district hospitals in the state. Seven hospitals where the HospIS had been in operation for at least six months were chosen for the study. Patients were asked about their experiences in the various departments, focusing on whether the additional system-generated information that was provided to them presented them with additional choices about how they received care. A total of 63 patients were interviewed. The research team also observed patient–doctor interactions after prior consent. Key themes were identified from the data, which was then theoretically interpreted (Sahay and Walsham, 2017).

In 2019, the second round of fieldwork was conducted, with patients and their attendants assessing the impact of the HospIS on their overall experience in the hospital. This time round, all district hospitals that had the HospIS operational for more than a year were chosen as research sites. One of the hospitals, located in the state capital Shimla, catered to approximately 600 patients every day. The other four hospitals each had a patient load of about 300 daily patients. A total of 66 patients and attendants were interviewed (Kaur et al., 2020). OPD patients were contacted at various locations in the hospital, for example, near the registration desk, the waiting areas, outside doctor's chambers, the imaging labs, and the pharmacy. Since there were concerns about medical conditions and hygiene, the researchers deliberately avoided interacting with patients in the inpatient department (IPD). However, patients' attendants were generally consulted on relevant issues, as were doctors and nurses on how they used computer-generated outputs in their interactions with the patients. We also had discussions with state and hospital administrators to get their perspectives. We asked the respondents to give suggestions on what improvements in the system could advance the patient experience.

Enabling the patient's self-awareness of the care situation

Patients expressed limited awareness of the workings of the HospIS. They had little knowledge of what data of theirs was stored in the system, or even that they were entitled to printouts of their transactions. The research team encouraged them to demand prescriptions, OPD slips, and lab reports. The system had, after all, been built with their tax money. These documents would allow for a second opinion. Nor would they be locked into one hospital. In the erstwhile paper system, the doctor would rarely write down the diagnosis. In the computerized system, however, a 'provisional diagnosis' was a mandatory field, and it potentially enhanced the doctor's accountability.

Improving the patient's experience in hospitals

We had had the opportunity to witness the unruly crowds at the registration desk prior to computerization. It was impressive, therefore, to see the registration desk fully computerized and a long, orderly line of patients receiving their printed slips, complete with the CRN, for consultation. Ease of registration is important in facilitating access to healthcare services. Even the billing counters were entirely functional.

That there were separate queues for women and men, and that registration was done on the basis of numbers that marked position in a queue, made a distinct difference. According to a female patient, 'Earlier the stronger men would push the weaker lot and get to the queue and doctors first but that cannot happen now'.

Once a prescription for a laboratory test (imaging or pathology) was made, the patient would be directed to the billing counter to pay for the specific test, receive the necessary equipment (such as tubes and syringes), and then go to the lab for the X-ray or the sample to be collected. Patients said they wanted to receive their test results via SMS, and, if possible, in Hindi. They also welcomed not having to pay for unavailable tests in advance. The clinical modules of the OPD and the IPD were mostly unused across hospitals. The doctors justified this by saying that it was more important for them to give direct care to the patients than to enter details into the system.

Improved patient-specific documentation

Many patients noted the absence of calculation errors in the printed bills generated by the system. Although the prescriptions issued to patients were still largely handwritten by doctors (since they tended not to directly use the system), the test reports included the desired test ranges. The patients appreciated this comparative information. They could also request an annual medical summary of their treatment that detailed the diagnosis, the laboratory test reports, and the drugs prescribed.

Enabling local innovation

The implementation of the HospIS created employment for the local youth. The capacity building workshops that HISP India conducted over the years helped train the local youth in data entry, hardware support, and server maintenance. It was a frugal business model in which HISP India provided low-cost services and built capacity for local staff in the hospitals. For the state, a local support team helped reduce dependencies on high-cost donors and business entities.

Information enabling patient empowerment

In 2019, we witnessed the reinforcement of existing themes and the development of new ones. In the second round of fieldwork, patients were found to have acquainted themselves considerably with the use of the HospIS, as compared to 2015. Many knew that their unique CRN could help them retrieve their past medical record. Some suggested that, in case of a referral or transfer to a bigger facility, medical files could be transmitted to other hospitals through the system itself. The earlier practice entailed the manual handing over of bulky dossiers full of medical paperwork. Some patients suggested enabling registration through a mobile phone, which would both save time spent physically in the queue and reduce the work of the registration clerks.

We had found insufficient data entry resources within the OPD a matter of concern during the first round of fieldwork. However, during the second round, in one of the hospitals, a data entry operator was seen assisting each OPD in the entering of patient-specific details so that printed prescriptions were generated. In addition to being relevant to the internal hospital process, this data could also be of great importance to medical researchers studying clinical outcomes over a period of time. A number of patients reported retrieving their lost medical documents from the system using their unique CRN. In the first round, we had encouraged patients to demand printed slips from their doctors based on the CRN. Now, we found the patients relatively more demanding of information from the hospital staff, and also suggesting system-specific features for further improvements.

However, not all hospitals offered printed prescriptions and test reports for all patients. A significant proportion of the prescription slips were handwritten, but many were electronically generated. When they were system generated, not only did the printed documents give the patients confidence in the treatment but also reduced the medical errors. For instance, several patients mentioned that they crosschecked what the pharmacist gave them against the printed prescriptions, which were far more legible than handwritten prescriptions. Printouts also gave patients the option to consult local physicians, and thus avoid travelling great distances for routine health issues.

Enabling integration across public health schemes

Integration of public health was unique to the second round, because popular public health schemes such as PM-JAY and the Himachal Health Care Scheme (HIMCARE) had been implemented. Patients acknowledged being aware of other public health schemes such as the National Health Insurance Scheme and free treatment for pregnant woman and children under the age of five. Some respondents were already using smart cards issued under these schemes, while others were curious to know how they could enrol in and benefit from the HospIS. A pregnant woman suggested that awareness about various zero-bill schemes linked with the individual identification number Aadhaar card of the users should be promoted.

The research team recommended to the state to expand the dissemination of information through pamphlets or radio. Such schemes, when linked with the HospIS, could help remove the bottlenecks in fair distribution of benefits. While some of these integrations had not yet materialized, there was a growing awareness of the need to do so.

Improved coordination among hospital staff and patients

The hospital staff was well-acquainted with the system, and could independently undertake small tasks such as dealing with printer and server issues. A negligible number of participants reported misbehaviour by lab staff or doctors. In general, despite their heavy loads, doctors listened to patients calmly and conducted thorough diagnoses. In any case, a registered patient's past record would show up on the doctor's screen, which did away with the need to decipher subjective narratives. But the growth of this interpersonal trust was restricted by the fact that many doctors did not use the OPD and IPD modules. The turnover of patients could be the reason: doctors saw 80–100 patients in three or four hours. They believed that the three to four minutes they got with each patient would be spent more fruitfully providing care rather than entering details in computers. Doctors at some of the bigger facilities, however, had data entry operators to process patient information into the system.

Patients were asked if they had recently recovered from illness following the doctor's advice, and if they had taken a second or a third opinion. Surprisingly, patients expressed enormous trust in the doctors of the surveyed hospitals, particularly in the gynaecology, surgery, and orthopaedics departments.

A patient during an interview said, 'I know there was huge queue waiting outside for this doctor, but he never avoided answering repeated questions about his prescription. Had I been at his place, I would definitely have given an irritated response. I really appreciate his service intent.'

An attendant at the gynaecology department said:

> Earlier, patients would jostle against each other to know about their turn. Even repeated requests to them to take their seat in the OPD waiting room would fall on deaf ears. However, with the queuing system facilitated by the HospIS, they sit patiently for their turn as they already know their order in the queue for a particular OPD. This is such a relief for us. Patients used to accuse us of favouring

some of them over others, and sometimes spoke to us harshly or abusively. Now, there are no grudges because it is on a first come, first served basis.

Foregrounding issues of equity and justice

Another change witnessed by patients was related to treatment by the hospital staff. We received mixed feedback from the surveyed patients regarding this aspect. Prior to the HospIS, a patient known to a member of the hospital staff often would bypass the queues and directly approach the doctor. This jumping of the queue would infuriate the other patients. It would also negatively influence their institutional trust. Vulnerable and disadvantaged patients were the most affected. The HospIS contributed to rendering this behaviour largely a thing of the past since the queues were now automated by the CRN. It also disciplined those who were used to being favoured. We noticed a senior government official furious at the registration clerk for not allowing him to meet the doctor directly. We were told, however, that the trend of favouritism continued in the smaller hospitals.

'The hospital staff don't bother following the registration order with villagers like me. I always have to spend the whole day waiting for treatment, while staff members bring their relatives and get them treated immediately', said a patient at a hospital distant from the capital city.

This could be attributed to the lack of administrative control and monitoring of district hospitals. Strict controls on hospital staff are required to implement a policy of 'absolutely no undue favours to any relative or friend' (Ozawa and Sripad, 2013), which is a key determinant of institutional trust. Most patients surveyed said that they received free treatment at the hospital irrespective of whether or not they knew a staff member.

Potential of temporal analysis of clinical data

Since some of the modules are not yet functional in all the district hospitals, there remains the unrealized potential of temporal analysis of time-series data that might show trends and patterns in diseases with respect to territories (lower, middle, or upper Himalayas), the effects of prescribed medicines, and other correlations between demographics and certain diseases. The HospIS data may also be relevant in analysing the effectiveness of various systems linked to public health schemes, for example the number of citizens enrolling under these schemes and obtaining the benefits.

Faster and improved registration

Patients today spend 2–20 minutes in the registration queue, in stark contrast to the hours they would have spent earlier. More orderly queues have made life easier for senior citizens, women, and critically ill patients. The room numbers mentioned in the printed registration slips are complemented by signboards around the hospital. At their own discretion, doctors sometimes summon older patients whose age they can check on their computer screens. 'We are no longer pushed back by stronger and younger fellows for the registration slip', said an elderly patient whom we interviewed.

Retrieval of medical records from the HospIS

An old man waiting at the surgery OPD was extremely worried that he had forgotten his lab report at home, and that he had no one accompanying him who could fetch the report. We informed him that he need not worry: if he had an old prescription with his CRN number, he could retrieve his record at any time, including a discharge slip.

Strengthening pharmacy and laboratory systems

The pharmacy is an important unit in the hospital system. At the least, it informs the doctor about the unavailability of a particular medicine and enables an alternative prescription. Unfortunately, the pharmacy module had not been utilized to full potential in all the hospitals surveyed. Many patients complained about long waits in pharmacy queues only to be told that medicines were not available. Eventually, they would be forced to buy medicines from private pharmacies, at a greater cost. The public pharmacies mostly catered to below poverty-line citizens or to other low-income groups. It was hardly desirable that they should spend their meagre incomes on privately buying medicines to which they were entitled from the public health system. However, to get these benefits, the utilization of the pharmacy module needs to be strengthened, which is currently not the case across all hospitals. Nonetheless, despite these drawbacks, we saw a steady growth in OPD registrations.

Analysing the growth of citizen trust over time

Trust is a core enabler of a positive relationship with the state and their interventions including related to ICTs, and it evolves over time. It reflects how a citizen will instinctively go to a state facility for care even if there may be other alternatives available. At the outset, the citizens of Himachal Pradesh had a strong trust in the state, because of the progressive policies of the state more broadly in strengthening public systems and the strong reliance of citizens in state systems, where about 90 per cent of the population rely on the public health sector for accessing care services. Positive uses of the state in using ICTs, such as for strengthening their health management information systems, also contributed to the building of this inherent trust. This can be seen as a form of institutional trust and citizens also develop interpersonal trust because they see the same healthcare personnel over time in the public healthcare facilities.

Many of the staff would tend to know the patients and their families with a degree of intimacy. As the hospital information system was implemented and citizens started to get benefits from it, such as improved patient experience in the hospital, there was automation enhancing trust. Over time, we can see an intricate intermingling of institutional, interpersonal, and automation enabling trust, which has contributed to a more robust and evolving sense of trust of citizens in the state health systems.

How do we understand trust? Trust represents 'an instantiated informal norm that promotes co-operation between two or more individuals' (Fukuyama, 2001) and contributes towards societal development (Gunnar and Gert, 2015). In the context of health, with trust, patients can become more receptive to counselling, and to encourage relevant medical disclosures, which can contribute to better health outcomes. While in rich countries, trust is often understood in terms of willingness to share health data (Platt and Kardia, 2015), in LMICs the priorities may be different. In a resource-constrained setting, the access of the patient to printed information on her or his medical condition may be more relevant. While this access can be taken for granted in the West, in an LMIC it signifies enhanced choice for a patient in terms of being able to consult another doctor and to build a better under-standing of health status.

Institutional trust and technical reliability are intimately intertwined, and improvements in technological outcomes can help enhance trust (Adjekum et al., 2018). Trust in technology can be shaped by the reduced time a patient needs to spend at the hospital or having improved access to information, both at the institutional and individual levels. Flipping the logic, trust can break down when patients experience frequent system breakdowns and failures, which create delays and frustration in not knowing what to do next. Trust is more than an attribute, but represents a process that is built gradually over time based on interactions between the trustee and the trustor and shaped within an institutional context. Both institutional and interpersonal conditions and their intertwining become important in shaping processes of trust, both positively and negatively (Luhmann, 1988). Institutional trust represents a form of public trust indicating the structural aspects of the healthcare system, while interpersonal trust is built upon institutional trust, taking place at interaction sites or 'access points' where the individual and institution interact with both facework and faceless commitments (Giddens, 1990). Facework commitment is reflected by personality-related facets such as professionalism, communication, general mannerisms, and caring attitude exhibited by a system representative, while faceless commitment is created by legitimacy and technical expertise, leading to higher quality services. In a health setting, a patient is situated in a web of interactions with the hospital staff, including doctors, lab technicians, pharmacists, and registration clerks that span both institu-tional and interpersonal forms of trust relationships. How did this trust build in the case of the HospIS?

Automation enhancing trust

The HospIS helped enhance capabilities of patients by offering improved opportunities to vulnerable groups such as pregnant women, the elderly, and patients living with disability. Prior to the HospIS, the physically stronger, socially better connected would push these disadvantaged groups aside and jump the queues to access treatment first. The automated system of queuing numbers through registration helped to a large degree in mitigating this. All patients now democratically wait their turn. This automation of the queuing system enhanced institutional trust and removed interpersonal mistrust.

These systemic enhancements helped public facilities provide services on a par with the far more expensive private hospitals. In the hilly terrain of Himachal Pradesh, which is limited in private care facilities and where access to healthcare is challenging, these innovations have reinforced trust that the institution is acting in an equitable manner.

Enhancing citizens' voices

Over time, patients became confident enough to voice their opinions and give suggestions. These processes largely grew organically over time, rather than through the state's focused information dissemination campaigns. While being appreciative of the attempts at strengthening governance and transparency, patients suggested a stricter implementation of guidelines without bias. The implementation of their suggestions will further serve to provide superior care to the patients, increasing their institutional and inter-personal trust.

In conclusion, there is no doubt that the HospIS has brought about positive changes in access to care in the public hospitals in Himachal Pradesh. However, even after a decade of the system's use, all we can venture is that its full potential has not been realized, and that there remain many areas of improvement. For instance, the wealth of data collected over the years has not been subjected to systematic epidemiological analysis.

Acknowledgements

The authors deeply acknowledge the support of HISP India, the builders, implementers, and long-term (since 2009 and ongoing) supporters of the HospIS in Himachal Pradesh, and the State Health Department of Himachal Pradesh which trusted HISP India to support them. We deeply acknowledge the contribution of Dr Harleen Kaur, who conducted the primary research to understand citizen trust in the HospIS. This chapter has drawn upon prior collaborative research between Dr H. Kaur and the authors of this chapter.

References

Aanestad, M., Jolliffe, B., Mukherjee, A. and Sahay, S. (2014) 'Infrastructuring work: building a state-wide hospital information infrastructure in India', *Information Systems Research* 25: 834–45 <https://doi.org/10.1287/ isre.2014.0557>.

Adjekum, A., Blasimme, A. and Vayena, E. (2018) 'Elements of trust in digital health systems: scoping review', *Journal of Medical Internet Research* 20(12) <https://doi.org/10.2196/11254>.

Braa, J. and Sahay, S. (2012) *Integrated Health Information Architecture: Power for the Users: Design, Development, and Use*, 1st edn, Matrix Publishing, New Delhi.

Drèze, J. and Sen, A. (2013) *An Uncertain Glory: India and its Contradictions*, Allen Lane, London.

Fukuyama, F. (2001) 'Social capital, civil society and development', *Third World Quarterly* 22(1): 7–20 <https://doi.org/10.1080/713701144>.

Giddens, A. (1990) *The Consequences of Modernity*, Polity Press, Cambridge, UK.

Gunnar, S. and Gert, S. (2015) 'The puzzle of the Scandinavian welfare state and social trust', *Issues in Social Science* 3(2): 90 <https://doi.org/10.5296/ iss.v3i2.8597>.

Kaur, H., Sahay, S. and Mukherjee, A.S. (2020) 'Patients' trust in public health system mediated by hospital information system in context of LMIC', in K. Bandi, C.R. Ranjini, S. Klein, S. Madon, and E. Monteiro (eds), *The Future of Digital Work: The Challenge of Inequality*, pp. 207–21, IFIP WG 8.2, 9.1, 9.4 Joint Working Conference Proceedings, Springer, Cham.

Kumar, P. (2017) 'Do we care? India's health system', *Indian Journal of Community Medicine* (Official Publication of Indian Association of Preventive & Social Medicine) 42(3): 186 <https://doi.org/10.4103/0970-0218.212072>.

Luhmann, N. (1988) 'Familiarity, confidence, trust: problems and alternatives', in D. Gambetts (ed.), *Trust: Making and Breaking of Cooperative Relations*, pp. 94–107, Basil Blackwell, Oxford.

National Health Portal (2020) *National Digital Health Mission* [online] <https:// www.nhp.gov.in/national-digital-health-mission-(ndhm)_pg> [accessed 23 March 2022].

Ozawa, P.S. and Sripad, P. (2013) 'How do you measure trust in the health system? A systematic review of the literature', *Social Science & Medicine* 91: 10–14 <https://doi.org/10.1016/j.socscimed.2013.05.005>.

Platt, J. and Kardia, S. (2015) 'Public trust in health information sharing: implications for biobanking and electronic health record systems', *Journal of Personalized Medicine* 5(1): 3–21 <https://doi.org/10.3390/jpm5010003>.

Rao, K.S. (2017) *Do We Care? India's Health System*, 1st edn, Oxford University Press, New Delhi.

Sahay, S. and Walsham, G. (2017) 'Information technology, innovation and human development: hospital information systems in an Indian state', *Journal of Human Development and Capabilities* 18: 1–18 <https://doi.org/10. 1080/19452829.2016.1270913>.

CHAPTER 7

Mobile payments as a means to an end

Thomas Hylland Eriksen

Only elites in the Global South have bank accounts, but the need to make transactions is almost universal. This chapter describes the growth and spread of mobile payment services, with the successful Kenyan M-Pesa venture as a starting point, showing how mobile money is used and some of its wider implications. Any mobile phone can be used for mobile money. Over the past two decades, networks and devices have become widespread in most of Africa, even in many rural areas. Millions of families rely on remittances from family members working abroad, and mobile payment makes transfers inexpensive and frictionless. Moreover, the majority of Africans and Indians work in the informal sector, where mobile money has enabled faster and more efficient turnover. Although mobile money is unlikely to lead to economic growth at the societal level, it increases the efficiency in small-scale economic relationships.

The means for development are obvious in this case (the phone and a mobile money app), as are the ends (an improved quality of life), whereas the processes leading to the ends vary between countries. In some large countries like Nigeria, transactions are mainly cash-based; and, in spite of sustained efforts, mobile money has made a less major impact on the microeconomics of Haitians than expected. In a concluding discussion, the significance of trust in abstract systems is discussed as a possible key factor in determining the success or failure of mobile money.

Mobile money

Since making its entry with the Kenyan M-Pesa in 2007, mobile money has spread very quickly in some countries in the Global South. This mobile phone affordance offers a range of banking services to people for whom a regular bank account is difficult to get, or is simply unavailable. Mobile payment presupposes that the user has a mobile phone – not necessarily a smartphone – which most adults in cities by now do, even in poor neighbourhoods. The infrastructure comprising the cellular networks, the service providers, the mobile banking apps, and the actual devices are the means. The people using mobile payments in different ways, not always along the lines envisioned by the providers, create the processes that connect the infrastructure to ongoing social life. Finally, the potentials of mobile money to improve the quality of life for its users comprise the ends.

Yet, the translation from map to territory is never simple, and the road from departure to destination can be rocky. This chapter shows how mobile money has accelerated, streamlined, and simplified monetary transactions in parts of the world where the formal sector of the economy is inaccessible to the majority. There are, nevertheless, caveats and unintended consequences as well, which policymakers and NGOs need to keep in mind before whole-heartedly embracing the affordances of mobile banking.

All other things being equal, the extent of the informal sector in a country is, in this day and age, proportional to the percentage of the population to whom the smartphone is economically important. Mobile money is trans-forming practices of remittances, trading, work, and social networking in the informal sector, which is defined as that part of the economy that is not officially recorded or recognized. People working in the informal sector, which amount to the majority of the working population in most of the Global South, from Peru to India, are either self-employed or work for someone who is; they pay no taxes, have no written labour contract, and have no formal rights (ILO, 2018). It should nevertheless be noted that the boundary between the informal and the formal sector tends to be blurred. There are continuous interactions between actors in the two sectors. Informal work supports the formal economy, and many individuals shift between the two sectors, sometimes on a daily basis. For example, small-scale corruption, known as 'tea-money' in Kenya, helps people working on meagre salaries in the formal sector to make ends meet. Similarly, employees in registered companies may supplement their income by taking on informal work outside regular working hours.

At the time of writing in 2021, the urban African population's access to the internet was between 28.5 per cent (International Telecommunication Union, 2021) and 39.3 per cent (Internet World Stats, 2021), which is a massive increase from the 2 per cent coverage reported in 2006, yet well below the global average of 64 per cent. Besides, internet access is unevenly distributed along class and urban/rural dimensions. In the Democratic Republic of the Congo (DRC), the coverage is officially around 15 per cent for the total population; it is much lower in the rural areas and considerably higher in the capital Kinshasa. In South Africa, about 57 per cent of the population officially has internet access, while the figure for Mauritius is more than 72 per cent; the global average is nearly 59 per cent (Internet World Stats, 2021).

While the methods of measurement are uncertain, and the results vary accordingly, there is consensus about the phenomenal growth in smartphone ownership and internet use in the continent since the turn of the millennium. In Zambia, the number of mobile subscriptions was less than 1 per cent of the population in 2000, while the figure for 2019 was more than 95 per cent. (This does not mean that nearly all Zambians have a functioning SIM card; some have several, some have none, and some share a phone.)

Comparable figures can be found with respect to other African countries as well. There may today be as many as 40 countries, most of them in Africa, where more people have access to the mobile network than to the electric grid (IEA, 2020) or toilets. Investments in fibre-optic cables and mobile transmitters enable the new connectivity, but they would never have been undertaken had there not been a market for the services. This market does not appear *sui generis* the moment mobile providers offer affordable SIM cards and set up antennas. First and foremost, people must own gadgets. These have, to a great extent, been brought to Africa along one of the new Silk Roads. According to the anthropologist Gordon Mathews (Mathews and Yang, 2012), who studied the relationship between China and Africa in the early days of the smartphone, about 20 per cent of all African smartphones were likely to have passed through a single building in Hong Kong, namely the bustling trading emporium Chungking Mansions. Among the regulars were African buyers, Indian resellers, and Chinese exporters. Smartphones in a price range beginning at €10 were sold there in great quantities; most of them were produced in China, with many pirated copies of established brands. (There is an irony in the fact that these very phones contain rare minerals, often mined artisanally by adults and children in the Democratic Republic of the Congo.)

In this way, many Africans acquired smartphones, and they would soon also acquire network coverage even in the smaller towns and villages. This change took place in just a few years, from around 2010 to around 2015. The world would never be quite the same again in the markets of Lagos or on the savannah in Kenya. The figures are, nevertheless, of limited value in themselves, since they say little about what the mobile phone means to people and how they use it. Having 'access to the internet' is not straightforward in societies where connectivity is uneven and money is scarce. In a village in Botswana, studied by the social anthropologist Jo Helle-Valle (2020), nearly all adults now have a mobile phone, but mobile money is still unknown, and most only use the internet rarely owing to a lack of funds, or of need, or both. On the other hand, actual coverage may be greater than the statistics indicate, since several members of a household may share a phone. So even if, say, just a third of a population has a mobile subscription, the proportion with access to the internet may be more than half. Conversely, many belonging to one or several elites may have two or three phones with different SIM cards and numbers. In order to unpack the actual situation in a locality, it is, therefore, necessary to carry out research, preferably with qualitative methods.

An expensive smartphone from a famous brand is a status symbol on par with expensive sunglasses or a prestige vehicle. Only a few people at the top of the hierarchy have an iPhone, but there is a broad price range. In a working-class quarter in Kampala, Uganda, researchers found that just 8 per cent of the people interviewed did not have a mobile phone. However, 36 per cent had a smartphone. This is still an impressive percentage in a neighbourhood where people struggle to get by (Miller et al., 2021: 109). Most smartphone owners used it as much as they could afford to, mainly using WhatsApp and similar platforms. The 57 per cent who just had a 'dumb phone' tended to send messages instead of making calls. It was cheaper and often more convenient.

Urban poverty is not alleviated merely through the introduction of a new technology. Yet, as I will argue, the smartphone technology has obvious empowering potentials. In Chapter 3, I indicated how refugees use smartphone apps to improve their situation in a variety of ways; the urban poor face different challenges, which may nevertheless also sometimes be addressed through this formidable network machine.

In some African countries, such as the Seychelles, Mauritius, and Kenya, access to the internet is very high (keeping in mind the caveats mentioned), while the percentage in countries like Madagascar, Niger, and both Congos hovers between 10 and 15 per cent. The least connected African countries at the time of writing in 2021 are Western Sahara[1] (4.6 per cent), Eritrea (6.9 per cent), and South Sudan (7.9 per cent) (Internet World Stats, 2021). These numbers change almost monthly. In most countries in the Global South, the mobile is transforming everyday life, and mobile money is a driving factor. The shift from banknotes to digital money, and from formal banking to mobile banking, is ongoing and highly consequential, enabling development from below (Mathews and Yang, 2012) through a network rather than a fixed hierarchy (Castells, 1996). It must, nevertheless, be kept in mind that the means are not sufficient: they depend on processes leading to an end.

Remittances

One of the uses of mobile money consists in remittances, which are still to a great extent transmitted via other means such as Western Union, but where mobile money makes the transfer faster, more flexible, and less expensive. The total number of households that depend on remittances from family members working elsewhere, usually abroad, is unknown, and it is also a matter of definition what to 'depend' on something means. In some countries, cities, or neighbourhoods, the proportion of families that need regular remittances to get by is, nevertheless, very significant. Moreover, as pointed out by Peggy Levitt (1998), who coined the term 'social remittances', migrants send home more than money: they transfer social capital and connectivity to another country along with the money. The amount of remittances sent has grown rapidly. Although a precise estimate is difficult to make owing to the informality and interpersonal character of remittances, according to the International Organization for Migration, 'available data reflect an overall increase in remittances in recent decades, from USD 126 billion in 2000, to USD 689 billion in 2018' (IOM, 2020: 35). According to the World Bank Group Factbook (2016), between 2006 and 2014, remittance flows to developing countries increased by 77.7 per cent (Darmon et al., 2016). Figures are uncertain, and data are incomplete, but there are strong reasons to assume that remittance flows have increased very significantly in the first two decades of this century. In some countries, remittances from abroad are significant as proportions of GDP. This would definitely be the case in Tonga, where remittances account for 35 per cent of GDP, Kyrgyzstan (34 per cent), Tajikistan (31 per cent), Haiti (30 per cent), and Nepal (28 per cent). As confirmed by the International Monetary Fund, remittances represent an average of 4 per cent of GDP in low-income countries (Ratha, 2017).

In the 19th century, the institution of the remittance functioned in an opposite way to the present. Just as migration often took place from the colonial power to the colonies through permanent or temporary settler colonialism, remittances typically went from the natives of the metropolitan country to relatives settled in a colony. A 'remittance man' in 19th-century Britain was usually a 'black sheep', a person of good family who had fallen from grace, often due to excessive drinking, and had been sent to a tropical colony, there leading a modest life as the recipient of remittances from home. Today, remittances are generally sent by those who have left to those who stay at home, from richer to poorer regions. In the Norwegian version of the transnationally popular (but always locally adapted) board game Monopoly, which was first produced in the 1930s, one may be so lucky as to draw a card that reads, 'You have received a thousand kroner from an uncle in America'. The proverbial American uncle, who was rarely or never actually seen, was a staple character in local Scandinavian folklore at least until the late 1960s, with poor relatives in the mother country receiving, out of the blue, a generous inheritance or a lavish Christmas box.

The remittance is not tantamount to a flow of people (although it is a result of it) nor of deterritorialized services (as in India-based American call centres), but of money tinged with guilt and bad conscience, love and affection, duty and kinship obligations – money through which the life of the exile reverberates. But if we replace the microscope of the ethnographer with the geographer's macroscope, it becomes apparent that remittances reflect some of the complexities of the global system as well.

As suggested, remittances are not new; they were not invented in the post-1991 world. In the early post-war phase of migration from the Caribbean to the UK and North America, money orders and barrels of food and clothes were familiar and much appreciated arrivals at Christmas in many Caribbean ports.

It is an indication of increased global interconnectedness that the value of remittances has grown quickly and continues to do so in an era of electronic transactions. By the early 21st century, the remittances from the US were several times larger than the total value of official American development aid. The total global amount of remittances sent overseas by migrants far exceeds the amount transferred in development assistance from rich countries to poor ones. As noted above, in some countries, formal remittances account for a substantial part of the national economy, and millions of households depend on these transfers.

The extent of informal remittances, money, and other valuables transmitted outside the formal financial system is not known, but is believed to be considerable. According to some estimates, the official numbers on remittances may underreport the actual amounts by as much as 50 per cent. A limitation of official remittances statistics is that not 'all small transactions by migrants conducted via money transfer operators (such as Western Union), post offices, mobile transfer companies (like M-Pesa in Kenya) are included in all the countries, neither are informal transfers (such as via friends, relatives or transport companies returning to the origin community)' (IOM, 2020).

Whichever way one measures it, there is no doubt that a massive transfer of wealth is going on from the rich countries to the poor ones, following the transfer of wealth from the poor to the rich through the profits extracted from migrant labour. The remittances are transferred at an individual, low-key, small-scale level and are, therefore, relatively unknown outside the narrow circles of research and policy. They indicate the extent of interconnectedness between migrants and the people they have left, which has intensified enormously since the coming of mobile telephony and, subsequently, the possibilities for easy money transfers via the phone. A precondition for remittances to function efficiently is trust and moral obligation, which continue to be operative years and decades after a migrant's departure. At this time, the moral bond between migrant and family members can be confirmed, strengthened, and communicated continuously, as opposed to the time, not very long ago, when the letter and the occasional phone call were the only available means of communication.

Like all smartphone innovations, the shift has been fast in this domain as well. In 2009, the *hawala* (money transfer) system of remittances practised by Somali migrants in Europe led to controversy. The money was relayed physically, in kind, through a network of trusted couriers monitored through *hawala* offices, and police investigators suspected that the money went to fund Islamist insurgents in Somalia. As a consequence, one of the leading Somali *hawala* organizations, al-Barakaat, was closed, and its funds were frozen in November 2001 by the United States authorities (Tharmalingam et al., 2009).

Today, money travels easily and digitally, without needing to be turned into physical notes and coins until it arrives at its destination. Electronic transfer of money through mobile phone apps can also liberate the people performing transactions from the kinship networks on which they formerly depended, and which carried with them further obligations which could be difficult to fulfil. The growth in remittances since the beginning of this century can be linked to the emergence of mobile payment services. Darmon et al. (2016) show that households with access to mobile payment services are more likely to receive remittances than households that lack it. Mobile payments go under the radar of the World Bank and ministries of finance. Nobody knows their extent in the realm of remittances, but it is believed to make a major difference. Migrants are now connected with their families not only via FaceTime and WhatsApp, but also through the medium of easy, instantaneous, deterritorialized, abstract transactions: mobile money.

Mobile money: M-Pesa

Mobile payment is a recent development from gold and silver, coins, banknotes, and cheques, but it has developed rapidly since the beginning of this century. Reporting from Jamaica in the early 2000s, Heather Horst (2006) shows that remittances and phone calls are two ways of staying in touch, and that they sometimes merge. She tells a story about an elderly lady somewhere in Jamaica who urgently needed some money, who phoned a family member overseas, and who then received the amount in one hour. Until very recently, these kinds of transnational network were rarely given much attention in the literature on either migration or globalization, but which in important ways create and maintain powerful webs of transnational commitments worldwide. Most significantly, these networks are entirely based on interpersonal relationships, unlike a lot of the other transnational or global networks often considered in research on globalization, especially concerning financial services and transactions, which have until recently been centralized, top-down arrangements.

In the years after Horst's pioneering work in Jamaica, genuine mobile payment systems – where the mobile networks are not just auxiliaries for other services – have spread rapidly. They are easy and inexpensive to access, flexible, and user-friendly, offer a range of services which are understood to be necessary, and have all but eclipsed other means of transaction. The change is of a magnitude that can be compared with the introduction of general-purpose money in societies where market exchange had formerly been restricted to a few commodities, characterized by 'economic spheres' (Bohannan and Bohannan, 1959). The advent of mobile payment has changed the nature of money in societies where formal banking services are unavailable to most people and other means of transaction are cumbersome and expensive. The change is far more radical and fundamental than most are aware, comparable to the replacement of cowrie shells with pound notes.

The first and most famous genuinely mobile payment system was M-Pesa, introduced in Kenya in 2007 by the leading mobile telephony provider, Safaricom. In a country where the vast majority of everyday transactions had until then been cash-based, electronic payments through the phone represented a major change. Since most adult Kenyans have a mobile phone and are familiar with its use, the additional services were easily learned and did not require new hardware or, for that matter, an evaluation of the person's creditworthiness. It enables person-to-person (P2P) transactions, payment of bills, tickets or airtime, as well as banking services such as saving and withdrawals. Cash, or general-purpose money, is disembedded and decontextualized. It loses none of its value by being moved from one locality to another, or even internationally. With mobile money, the disembeddedness of cash is taken one step further, since the physical object (coins and banknotes) does not have to accompany the transaction.

The impact of M-Pesa is easily visible in rural Kenya. As a schoolboy in Nairobi in the mid-1970s, I remember villages as being devoid of much commercial life. There would typically be a snack shop, sometimes with a diesel generator for cooling the soft drinks, and a few market stalls selling food and clothing, but not much more. On a revisit in 2002, I noticed the presence of Western Union offices, and kiosks where one could buy phone credit. Another decade later, most of the Western Union branches were gone, and in their stead were M-Pesa outlets doing brisk business every day with the old and the young, men and women.

In a much-cited paper, Suri and Jack (2016) estimate that access to M-Pesa increased per capita consumption levels and lifted 194,000 households, or 2 per cent of Kenyan households, out of poverty in less than a decade after its launch. While such assessments are difficult to evaluate, it is clear that mobile payments serve as a lubricant and accelerator in small-scale economic systems. The M-Pesa payment system combines several features of the new technology: it is seamlessly integrated with apps for messaging, social networks, and voice calls, and is thus an extension of the pocket-sized polymedium which is the smartphone.

The informal Zambian marketplace

It is important to keep in mind that the smartphone does not create an entirely new social space but is incorporated into, and modifies, what was there already. For this reason, ethnography is often an indispensable method for studying digitalization. The ultimate explanation of the difference between the Kenyan and the Haitian situation may be found here. In Wendy Willems' (2019b) research on media and digitalization in Zambia, we are reminded that trust in strangers does not develop merely through Facebook encounters and personal messages. The lack of trust in strangers, characteristic of societies with strong kinship organization and a weak formal sector, prevents the scaling-up of transactions and business networks that, in principle, is enabled by digital technology. Thus, the disembedded anonymity online effectively prevents expansion of economic activities into new domains in societies where trust is mainly interpersonal and not between persons and institutions.

Smartphones have, nevertheless, enhanced productivity and efficiency in small-scale markets by lubricating existing networks, but also through the gradual introduction of mobile money. Willems' research in the markets of Lusaka, Zambia indicates a rapid change since the technology became widely available during the 2010s. In 2011, a young male market vendor told her that he 'was unable to afford a smartphone but had a keen interest in technology (manning a second-hand computer stall)' (Willems, 2019b: 8). However, in the intervening decade, the smartphone spread epidemically in Zambia, and, in all likelihood, this particular man has one by now. Consider a woman running a vegetable stall in Soweto Market in Lusaka. If she ran out of tomatoes by midday back in 2015, she had no option but to wait for the wholesaler or their assistant to pass by the next day with a fresh supply. She can now send them a text, offering to pay a bonus if they deliver the tomatoes within an hour. The wholesaler will go out of their way to do so, and both parties benefit (as, indeed, does the farmer).

In a later study from Lusaka, Willems (2019a) concludes that the phone has entered into small-scale business in a serious way post 2010:

> Mobile phones are considered to be vital in the business practices of farmers, small-scale traders and market vendors. For some, they have enabled small business to communicate more effectively with customers or suppliers or made it possible for farmers to access market price information on livestock or agricultural commodities (Willems, 2019a).

Like other countries in the Global South, Zambia is changing quickly owing to the rapid spread of the apps and their devices. Between 2015 and 2019, the extent of mobile payment grew by a factor of 25 in the country, from Kwacha 2.07 bn (€72.6 m) to K49.45 bn (€1.8 bn; Malakata, 2020). The woman stallholder and her supplier may well have shifted to mobile money by now.

The ambiguous case of Haiti

Considering its obvious advantages, it is worth considering why mobile money has not been similarly successful in other countries. Let us first consider the Haitian case, which can be considered neither a dismal failure nor a resounding success in this domain.

Haiti is the poorest country in the western hemisphere. It was the first to liberate itself from colonialism, in 1804, in the aftermath of the French Revolution a decade and a half earlier. Deeply indebted, boycotted by major powers, and manipulated into economic subservience – initially by France, subsequently by the USA (Farmer, 2004) – Haiti has an undeveloped formal sector, and a large proportion of the population relies on subsistence agriculture.

Mobile money was introduced in Haiti in the aftermath of the devastating 2010 earthquake, through an initiative from the Bill & Melinda Gates Foundation known as the Haiti Mobile Money Initiative. After two years, 800,000 Haitians out of a total population of 11 million were active users of mobile money (Choute et al., 2015).

Immediately after the introduction of mobile money, a group of researchers began to study its impact (Taylor et al., 2011). One of the persons they spoke with was Jean Yves, whom they encountered in a cybercafé in Port-au-Prince about to deposit 100 gourdes (about one euro) into his TchoTcho Mobile account. His brother Michel, who owns the café, has advised him to use this service for reasons of security, since he will then not have to walk through town carrying cash. Jean Yves deposits the money and withdraws it when he reaches his destination. An hour's drive away, in the busy port city Saint Marc, Carmen receives a text message informing her that an aid organization has deposited $40 into her T-Cash account. She picks up her shopping bag and goes off to the nearest food stall to buy rice and beans with her mobile. Just 15 per cent of the Haitian population have a bank account. About 18 per cent have access to the internet, but more than 60 per cent have a mobile phone and are, therefore, in theory, able to avail themselves of the services offered by the mobile payment systems. There are currently two alternative services with slightly different profiles, T-Cash and Mon Cash (formerly TchoTcho Mobile).

The introduction of mobile money in Haiti has not led to an economic revolution or a runway leading to economic 'takeoff', but could potentially make everyday life easier for millions of Haitians. They can at any time send and receive small sums, pay for goods and services instantly and, if they own a business, increase their turnover owing to the simplified and deterritorialized logistics. The flow of money accelerates, although the sums are mainly small.

Typical usages of the mobile payment services in Haiti were:

- I want to repay a friend the HTG20 that she paid for my transport across town. If we are both T- Cash customers it will cost me nothing to repay her. If we are not both T-Cash customers, then I will not be able to repay her using mobile money since the cost of transfer will be the same or more than the amount owed.
- A friend bought me lunch and a drink, costing HTG125. If we are both T-Cash customers, it will cost me HTG2 to transfer him the money; if we are both Digicel customers it will cost me HTG6. If my friend is not registered for either service, it makes no difference which I choose to use; in either case, it will cost me HTG20.
- I want to send HTG1,000 to my brother who lives in Aux Cayes. T-Cash and TchoTcho Mobile charge the same amount to send more than HTG600, so which service I choose will probably be decided by which mobile phone carrier I am with, and which mobile money agents are within reach of our homes (Taylor et al., 2011: 5).

Like in Kenya, mobile payments are simpler and faster than other types of transaction, and the money is located in cyberspace, which makes it independent of physical location. In both countries, the major telecommunications providers offer mobile money solutions, which means that the customer base was already substantial before the introduction of mobile payments. Yet, the growth in Haiti has been far slower than in Kenya, despite sustained marketing.

A more recent Haitian initiative, FINCA (Foundation for International Community Assistance), which is aimed towards both individuals and small businesses, has been moderately successful in recruiting clients to use its range of financial services, with loans as a main product. Yet, mobile money, which has been an instant success in Kenya, has not taken off in Haiti. Its popularity is also highly variable in other countries with a large 'unbanked' population and widespread access to mobile telephony. This variation requires an explanation based on empirical research (Choute et al., 2015).

Three possible explanations are connected with trust, cost, and relevance. Mobile money is abstract and invisible, and its value hinges on the credibility and perceived legitimacy of the mobile companies, which is not self-evidently high in countries where cronyism, corruption, and informal networks are rampant in politics and the economy alike. Second, if a hefty commission is charged for transactions, it may also easily put people off. As the examples above show, transactions can be dear if sender and recipient do not subscribe to the same service. In Kenya, this is not an issue since M-Pesa has, in practice, a monopoly. Finally, in many communities, the perceived need is limited, since scale, frequency, and size of transactions are limited.

This last argument is the most interesting one. Mobile money may itself generate activities that were formerly non-existent by facilitating and accelerating transactions. Loans may be negotiated more easily than with conventional banks, trading at a small or even tiny scale can proceed more smoothly than before, and small remittances which may make a difference beyond mere consumption can be transferred in a frictionless and immediate way. With mobile banking, Europeans have, in just a few years, become accustomed to paying their bills while lying on the couch, getting their movie tickets on their phone and not on paper, and paying their children pocket money through a mobile payment service and not in kind. There are young people who have no idea what banknotes look like, because they never handle them. During the COVID-19 pandemic, many businesses in Norway refused to take cash payments, referring to the risk of contagion.

Although mobile money is less widespread in Haiti than in Kenya, it is well known and had more than a million users by 2021. During the pandemic, the government distributed relief money to more than 20,000 families using the mobile service Mon Cash. If this kind of service becomes more common, trust in the system is also likely to increase.

The situation in parts of the Global South is, by now, comparable to that of the drift towards a cashless society in the Global North, notwith-standing the difference in wealth and degrees of formality in the economy. Economic transactions at any scale and reach have become immensely easier. Mobile telephony was boosted in Africa both from above (fibre-optic cables, telecom corporations) and from below (trading along the new Silk Road and in African markets). Mobile payment displays a similar pattern in that it is enabled by telecom giants functioning increasingly as banks, and it is difficult for small start-ups to enter the mobile money market of, say, Haiti (Bellini, 2021). In spite of the dominance by corporate power, the affordances offered by mobile payments create opportunities for sideways scaling, network-style, across boundaries, both physical and social, that could formerly have been seen as insurmountable. Marketing and distributing goods, searching for work, and developing new ways of working via apps (owing to the possibility of deterritorialized communication) follows as an option in the wake of the introduction of smartphones, and mobile money apps are ideal for small P2P transactions, be they domestic or related to work or consumption.

The paucity of mobile money in Kinshasa

The smartphone has been a blessing for many, not least in the Global South. It has given displaced people the ability to maintain their networks and build social capital; it makes it possible for traders or employers to increase the turnover rate; and it makes it easier to keep in continuous contact with family and friends in settings where few have a landline and sending letters is unusual and impractical. This is not least the case for single women in Kinshasa, the capital of the DRC, the metropolis just across the mighty Congo river from Brazzaville, the capital of the Republic of the Congo. Whenever the wind blows away the mist and smoke, it is perfectly possible to see the neighbouring city on the other side. Congo-Brazzaville (*La République du Congo*, the Republic of the Congo) is a former French colony, while the much larger *République démocratique du Congo* (Democratic Republic of the Congo), for a period the personal property of the Belgian King Leopold II, may have been the territory containing the greatest concentration of human suffering during colonialism.

Kinshasa, like many of the world's great cities, is a place of scarcity and abundance, and as always in Africa, the contrast between the two is striking: there are glittering façades and ostentatious villas with armed security guards; there are ramshackle, dilapidated blocks of flats, informal settlements built of cardboard and plywood; there are frequent power cuts and street vendors roasting corncobs on charcoal, lively nightclubs, and noisy traffic; it smells of kerosene, perfume, sweat, soot, diesel, and decomposition; and it is a city renowned for its music and visual arts. Nearly 18 million people live in Kinshasa (in 1950, the population was 200,000, meaning that it has grown by nearly 10,000 per cent in 70 years), and it is located so far from the eastern parts of the country that hardly any *Kinois* (French for Kinshasans) are aware of the atrocities taking place in the war-torn Kivu region, near the Rwandan and Burundian borders.

Nobody knows the proportion of Kinshasa's population that possesses a smartphone, but those who do not have one often know someone who does. Young, unmarried women in Kinshasa are often searching for men who can support them, preferably comfortably if not luxuriously. If they have the opportunity, they use the phone to a considerable extent, to find eligible men and to organize meetings with men they have found or met. It is commonly known that infidelity has become far easier after the introduction of the mobile phone. For those who are not in a relationship, the mobile and its apps make it easier to make relevant connections, maintain them, and set up meetings. Monetary transactions can also be conducted via mobile payments – just 4 per cent of the population in the DRC has a bank account – although cash payments are still far more widespread than mobile banking, unlike in many other African countries.

A survey indicates that just 11 per cent of mobile users in the country have ever used mobile money (Élan RDC, n.d.). It concludes that 'awareness, trust and understanding of mobile money remain low'. The contrast with Kenya, where mobile payments are ubiquitous, or Zambia, where they have grown by 2,500 per cent between 2015 and 2019 (Malakata, 2020), is striking. Even in India, where mobile money is still incipient, the number of people using mobile money grew by nearly 1,000 per cent between 2014 and 2019 (Saxena, 2020). The period of the pandemic, beginning in earnest in March 2020, is believed to have increased the prevalence of mobile money considerably in India, as in many other countries. For millions, while mobile money is the future at the time of writing, it will be, in all likelihood, the present by the time this book reaches its readers.

So why is mobile money so slow to enter the domain of small-scale transactions in the DRC? A closer look at a part of the informal sector in Kinshasa may give some answers.

The anthropologist Katrien Pype, who has carried out research in Kinshasa for many years, has looked at the phenomenon called *bolingo ya face* (love via Facebook) in Lingala, the lingua franca of the city (Pype, 2020). *Libala ya face* (marriage via Facebook) is also not unknown. After the onset of the pandemic, weddings on Zoom have also become fairly widespread among the affluent. Parents-in-law are relieved. They save a considerable sum with this kind of solution.

A young woman in Kinshasa whom Pype calls Flavie has several active relationships with Congolese men, but her dream is to marry a Congolese who is doing well in Belgium or France. She uses Messenger, WhatsApp, and other mobile platforms to coordinate her relationships and make certain that the men do not learn about each other. Flavie has three mobile phones. She has uploaded flattering profile photos, taken by a professional photographer, and uses platforms such as Badoo, WEConnect, and Meetic in order to meet men. Tinder, the preferred platform in other parts of the world, is less widespread in Kinshasa.

Like nearly everybody else, Flavie also uses the mobile to stay in touch with family and friends, but she does not relate to YouTube or news channels. She typically communicates at night, since bytes are cheapest between midnight and 5 a.m. To her, the smartphone is smart because it is a social network amplifier and a means of production. It also has an element of security, since she can easily contact friends nearby, and ask for help if a visitor does not behave himself. At the same time, she is perfectly aware that there is an element of make-believe and acting on the tiny screen, and that this applies just as much to her as to those she encounters online. In the interstices between the online and the offline worlds, a certain playfulness enters into the existential involvement and earnest search for connections.

The two spheres – online and offline – overlap regarding both personnel and content, but they follow different logics. In the online world, it is usually possible to take precautions to prevent two lovers from learning about each other's existence. This is not always possible in the analogue world. One evening, Flavie entered a restaurant in order to meet a man, but immediately discovered that four of her male friends were already there, seated at different tables. She, naturally, fled and may have missed a date, unless she texted her beau about the change of plans.

Hers is a world of limited trust and accountability. The government is distant and considered untrustworthy, and the gleaming façades of the financial institutions belong to a different world. Like in Nigeria, where mobile money has similarly not become very widespread, the DRC is a country of huge scale, patchy government, and a low level of trust in formal institutions. Cash is tangible, unlike money in cyberspace, and to precarious and vulnerable people like Flavie, the necessary trust is simply not there. However, it should be added that this situation might have been alleviated through a different marketing strategy. In so far as mobile money is associated with high finance and/or the government, it is unlikely to catch on. Had it been marketed as an easily accessible and eminently useful affordance available to ordinary people, purchased as easily as one buys a soft drink and from the same little shop, attitudes might have changed. M-Pesa kiosks in Kenyan villages are low-key, unglamorous, often mere shacks redecorated in the bright colours of Safaricom, with a low entrance threshold.

Accelerating networks and consumption

A universal dimension of the mobile phone is its enhancement of efficiency through the acceleration and facilitation of communication. Examples show how interpersonal relations can be expanded and deepened without being mediated by the state or the formal market, and are, thus, relevant for potential economic activities. Whereas a major debate in the North Atlantic region concerns potential surveillance by the tech companies and the state, the everyday discourse about new technologies in African societies is different and has a focus, instead, on local empowerment and lateral networks rather than hierarchical control.

One of the fastest growing smartphone markets is the Indian one. In Indian villages, the smartphone contributes to social change in many ways, not least by making it possible for people to spread their networks outwards, both to other castes and other villages. The Bagdi caste in one of these villages was among the last to get electricity; unlike the higher castes they did not have television or radio for years (Tenhunen, 2018). They got onto the grid around the same time as inexpensive smartphones appeared on the market. They were, thus, able to leapfrog technological stages that others had been through, such as linear television, cameras, and music players, since the smartphone makes these devices superfluous. Like others, the Bagdi use Facebook and other apps to stay in touch with people they already know, and also to expand their network. Mobile use can be economically profitable and liberating, not least for women trying to escape unacceptable family conditions. In rural India, the use of text is limited, since many are functionally illiterate. They listen to radio and music instead of accessing news sites, and many need the assistance of a literate relative to communicate on text-based platforms. To them, YouTube may be a bottomless well of knowledge and insight.

Much of the small-scale economic and networking activity taking place today in the Global South as well as the Global North presupposes that people have access to a mobile phone. The range of uses continuously expands. Until around 2019, doctors in Norwegian hospitals still carried a small flashlight in their pockets. They now use their smartphones to look down patients' throats. For wilderness enthusiasts, the smartphone has replaced the compass; for pupils, it has replaced the ruler; for builders, the spirit level; for musicians, the tuning fork. In rural Fiji, salespeople fidgeting with their mobiles has long been a common sight, but it is only recently that they have upgraded from simple models to smartphones full of free apps, advanced messaging services, and internet connectivity.

There is no doubt that the proliferation of smartphone areas of use, as shown by the examples in this chapter, has increased productivity and turnover for producers and resellers in markets where the formal sector is underdeveloped. Waiting time is shortened, and uncertainty can now be curtailed, owing to the improved logistics enabled by this technology. It has become easier to sanction nonperformers, and to pester latecomers and debtors. It has become more difficult to cheat customers, since one's reputation is publicly viewable online. The mobile payment systems, of which the Kenyan M-Pesa was the first, enable transactions between people who do not have a bank account ('the unbanked', seen from the perspective of the formal sector).

A question that needs to be raised is, thus, why has mobile money taken off in some societies with limited access to formal banking, but not in others? The short, immediate answer is that the differences are due to a lack of trust. This difference, in turn, needs to be explained.

Conclusion

Mobile money is an important innovation that takes a long trend in the history of human civilization a step further. In the ancient world, be it in India, China, or the Mediterranean, monetary instruments derived their value from their rare and precious qualities, and were mainly made of gold, silver, or gemstones. This was still the case in medieval times, but paper money was known in China, and made its entry in Europe in the

18th century. It represented – symbolized – gold or silver, and could be exchanged for them in a state bank. Since the global departure from the gold standard in 1973, led by Richard M. Nixon's US government, the value of money has been based purely on market psychology and subjective estimates, because notes and coins no longer have a gold equivalent. At the same time, the financialization of the world economy, typically characterized through 'future trading', divorced financial value from equivalents in the physical world, thereby confirming Marx's famous dictum about abstraction and financialization, namely, that 'all that is solid melts into air' (Marx, 1848). Mobile money, typically operating on a smaller scale than the financial economy, represents a comparable shift at the grassroots level, from cowrie shells to pounds and shillings, via the chequebook and bank account (for some) to money that exists only as a postulate and as digits on a small screen, but which continues to work in so far as there is trust in it. The key difference between Haiti and the DRC, on the one hand, and Zambia and Kenya, on the other, seems in this regard to consist precisely in trust versus mistrust in the actual functioning of abstract, digital, invisible money as opposed to old-fashioned coins and banknotes. Without basic trust in the reliability of abstract money, the practical advantages of mobile money become irrelevant, since it is uncertain, to potential users, that it works at all. There may be a parallel with Bitcoin and other cryptocurrencies in the Global North, as there remains uncertainty as to whether it actually works as a currency. Therefore, attempts to introduce mobile money, or to strengthen its position in societies where it already exists, need to take the following into account:

- How do people use their mobile phones at the outset? Do they mainly use them for social networking, or also for purchases, communication with local government, school, or the health system, etc.?
- What kinds of credit and transaction systems are people accustomed to? Are credit unions, microfinance institutions, or regular banks trusted and widely used?
- Are the benefits of mobile money sufficient, and sufficiently well known?
- To what extent do people trust a 'what' as opposed to trusting a 'who'? Is there trust in institutions as well as individuals, and if yes, how can this abstract trust be transferred to mobile money? And if no; how can people be convinced that mobile money is real, even if it cannot be seen and touched?

Policy needs to look at experience. Where has this innovation worked? Where has it failed? And why? What are the lessons from societies, or social milieux, or networks, where mobile money has empowered people and contributed to an improvement in their lives? Notwithstanding structural differences between societies, this is where one has to start: What works, and why. The means (mobile money) and the ends (a better life) are easy to pin down, while the processes are diverse and not always capable of connecting the two. While trust in abstract, invisible webs of connections is essential for mobile money to work in practice, it is necessary to ask specifically about the ways in which people are capable of using this affordance to generate hope for a better future. Means do not automatically lead to the intended ends, since the intervening processes may point in different directions, depending on structural opportunities and constraints.

Note

1. The territory of Western Sahara is disputed. Eighty per cent of the area is occupied by Morocco, while 20 per cent is controlled by the self-proclaimed Sahrawi Arab Democratic Republic under the leadership of the Polisario independence movement.

References

Bellini, P. (2021) 'HaitiPay did everything right. It still got crushed', *Rest of World*, 1 March [online] <https://restofworld.org/2021/haitipay-did-everything-right-but-that-didnt-matter/> [accessed 19 July 2021].

Bohannan, L. and Bohannan, P. (1959) 'The impact of money on an African subsistence economy', *Journal of Economic History* 19: 491–503 <https://doi.org/10.1017/S0022050700085946>.

Castells, M. (1996) *The Rise of the Network Society*, Blackwell Publishers, Malden, MA.

Choute, D., Jacques, C.C. and Hicks, B. (2015) *Haiti Mobile Money Business and Merchant Survey Results* [online], Dagmar and Imagines LLC <https://www.woccu.org/documents/Haiti-Mobile-Money-Business-and-Merchant-Survey-Results> [accessed 25 August 2021].

Darmon, E., Chaix, L. and Torre, D. (2016) 'M-payment use and remittances in developing countries: a theoretical analysis', *Révue d'économie industrielle* 156: 159–83 <https://doi.org/10.4000/rei.6469>.

Élan RDC (n.d.) 'Branchless banking' [online] <https://www.elanrdc.com/branchless-banking> [accessed 25 May 2021].

Farmer, P. (2004) 'An anthropology of structural violence', *Current Anthropology* 45(3): 305–25 <https://doi.org/10.1086/382250>.

Helle-Valle, J. (2020) 'From no media to all media: domesticating new media in a Kalahari village', in J. Helle-Valle and A. Storm-Mathisen (eds), *Media Practices and Changing African Socialities: Non-Media-centric Perspectives*, pp. 184–217, Berghahn, Oxford <http://dx.doi.org/10.2307/j.ctv1k3nqqs.11>.

Horst, H.A. (2006) 'The blessings and burdens of communication: cell phones in Jamaican transnational social fields', *Global Networks* 6: 143–59 <https://doi.org/10.1111/j.1471-0374.2006.00138.x>.

International Energy Agency (IEA) (2020) 'Mobile phone ownership and electricity access in selected sub-Saharan African countries, 2015–2016', February 2020 [online] <https://www.iea.org/data-and-statistics/charts/mobile-phone-ownership-and-electricity-access-in-selected-sub-saharan-african-countries-2015-2016> [accessed 25 May 2021].

International Labour Organization (ILO) (2018) *Women and Men in the Informal Economy: A Statistical Picture*, 3rd edn [online], ILO, Geneva <https://www.ilo.org/wcmsp5/groups/public/---dgreports/---dcomm/documents/publication/wcms_626831.pdf> [accessed 25 August 2021].

International Organization for Migration (IOM) (2020) *World Migration Report 2020* [online], IOM, Geneva <https://publications.iom.int/system/files/pdf/wmr_2020.pdf> [accessed 25 August 2021].

International Telecommunication Union (ITU) (2021) 'Digital trends in Africa 2021: Information and communication technology trends and developments in the Africa region, 2017–2020', ITU [online] <https://www.itu.int/pub/D-IND-DIG_TRENDS_AFR.01-2021> [accessed 24 January 2021].

Internet World Stats (2021) 'Internet penetration in Africa' [online] <https://www.internetworldstats.com/stats1.htm> [accessed 25 August 2021].

Levitt, P. (1998) 'Social remittances: migration driven local-level forms of cultural diffusion', *International Migration Review* 32(4): 926–48 <https://doi.org/10.1177/019791839803200404> [accessed 25 August 2021].

Malakata, M. (2020) 'Zambia records 126% growth of mobile money payments', IT Web Africa, 26 June [online] <https://itweb.africa/content/G98YdMLYRnwqX2PD> [accessed 25 May 2021].

Marx, K. (1848) 'Bourgeois and proletarians', in *Manifesto of the Communist Party* [online] <https://www.marxists.org/archive/marx/works/1848/communist-manifesto/ch01.htm> [accessed 25 August 2021].

Mathews, G. and Yang, Y. (2012) 'How Africans pursue low-end globalization in Hong Kong and mainland China', *Journal of Current Chinese Affairs* 41(2): 95–120 <https://doi.org/10.1177/186810261204100205>.

Miller, D., Rabho, L.A., Awondo, P., de Vries, M., Duque, M., Garvey, P., Haapio-Kirk, L., Hawkins, C., Otaegui, A., Walton, S. and Wang, X. (2021) *The Global Smartphone: Beyond a Youth Technology*, UCL Press, London [online] <https://discovery.ucl.ac.uk/id/eprint/10126930/1/The-Global-Smartphone.pdf> [accessed 25 August 2021].

Pype, K. (2020) '*Bolingo ya face*: digital marriages, playfulness and the search for change in Kinshasa', in J. Helle-Valle and A. Storm-Mathisen (eds), *Media Practices and Changing African Socialities: Non-Media-centric Perspectives*, pp. 93–124, Berghahn, Oxford [online] <https://www.academia.edu/41979938/Bolingo_ya_face_Digital_Marriages_Playfulness_and_the_Search_for_Change_in_Kinshasa> [accessed 25 August 2021].

Ratha, D. (2017) 'What are remittances?', International Monetary Fund [online] <https://www.imf.org/external/pubs/ft/fandd/basics/pdf/ratha-remittances.pdf> [accessed 25 August 2021].

Saxena, R. (2020) 'India's mobile money accounts rise 95-fold in five years: IMF', BloombergQuint, 10 November <https://www.bloombergquint.com/business/indias-mobile-money-accounts-rise-95-fold-in-five-years-imf> [accessed 25 May 2021].

Suri, T. and Jack, W. (2016) 'The long-run poverty and gender impacts of mobile money', *Science* 354(6317): 1288–92 <https://doi.org/10.1126/science.aah5309>.

Taylor, E.B., Baptiste, E. and Horst, H.A. (2011) *Mobile Money in Haiti: Potentials and Challenges* [online], Institute for Money, Technology and Financial

Inclusion <https://www.imtfi.uci.edu/files/images/2011/haiti/taylor_baptiste_horst_haiti_mobile_money_042011.pdf> [accessed 25 August 2021].

Tenhunen, S. (2018) *A Village Goes Mobile: Telephony, Mediation, and Social Change in Rural India*, Oxford University Press, Oxford and New York.

Tharmalingam, S., Gaas, M. and Eriksen, T.H. (2011) 'Post September 11 legal regulations of the hawala system: the predicament of Somalis in Norway', in A. Hellum, S.S. Ali, and A. Griffiths (eds), *From Transnational Relations to Transnational Laws: Northern European Laws at the Crossroads*, pp. 251–77, Routledge, London [online] <https://www.researchgate.net/publication/274248636_Post_September_11_Legal_Regulations_of_the_Hawala_System_The_Predicament_of_Somalis_in_Norway> [accessed 25 August 2021].

Willems, W. (2019a) '"The politics of things": digital media, urban space and the materiality of publics', *Media, Culture & Society* 41(8): 1192–209 <https://doi.org/10.1177/0163443719831594>.

Willems, W. (2019b) 'Digital development imaginaries, informal business practices and the platformisation of digital technology in Zambia', in J. Helle-Valle and A. Storm-Mathisen (eds), *Media Practices and Changing African Socialities: Non-Media-centric Perspectives*, Berghahn, Oxford [online] <https://www.researchgate.net/publication/338176274_Digital_development_imaginaries_informal_business_practices_and_the_platformisation_of_digital_technology_in_Zambia> [accessed 25 August 2021].

World Bank (2016) *Migration and Remittances Factbook 2016*, 3rd edn [online], Open Knowledge Repository, World Bank Group, Washington, DC <https://openknowledge.worldbank.org/bitstream/handle/10986/23743/9781464803192.pdf> [accessed 25 August 2021].

CHAPTER 8

ICT-enabled counter networks for peace: Mitigating violence in Kenya

Arunima Mukherjee and Sundeep Sahay

This case narrative concerns how communities and other state and non-state actors came together to form a 'peace network' to jointly engage in achieving the ends of conflict mitigation and peacebuilding. The case is set in the eastern counties of Kenya, which have been experiencing large-scale acts of violence, such as cattle theft, robbery, and killings, for more than 50 years. Providing the means to address this conflict was, first, the creation of the peace network, comprising people who had a stake in ending the violence; and, second, the use of ICTs in the form of an Early Warning and Emergency Response System (EWERS).

This relatively simple, locally developed SMS-based system was relevant to the context as it helped anonymize the complainants who had received messages of violence and removed their fear of intimidation. Furthermore, SMS allowed messages to be relayed to responders quickly, prompting rapid action to diffuse acts of violence. Supporting this action were systems of accountability: for example, messages would simultaneously be sent to the superiors of the responders, who would act out of fear of reprimand. Prompt messaging and action contributed to a virtuous cycle: the message-senders would see their messages being acted upon, and gain trust and confidence, which enabled them to continue to act without fear.

We identify two sets of interconnected processes to be crucial to converting means to ends: one, the process of building the peace network, which we refer to as a 'counter network' because it challenged the dominant networks; and, two, the process of social capital being leveraged by the peace network to help it grow. ICTs helped break down some of the bonding social capital based on intra-ethnic relationships, and promoted the linking of social capital relationships across ethnic divides. We can now discern a significant drop in acts of violence in the region. While the case study is based on research starting in 2017, we also draw upon prior experience of work in the region.

ICTs and violence mitigation

Ethnic conflicts are a widespread problem in the African continent, with devastating effects on human security through loss of life and livelihood, and increased hatred between communities contributing to large-scale displacement (Torbjörnsson, 2016). Ethnic violence is often invisible, where the parties involved feel solidarity with their 'own', and victims are chosen based upon ethnic membership (Horowitz, 2000). In Africa, some of the worst-hit countries from such violence include Nigeria, Ethiopia, Somalia, Sudan, Kenya, and Uganda (Elfversson and Brosché, 2012), each reflecting different modes and intensities of violence, and which change over time (Rohwerder, 2015). Kenya experiences much higher levels of ethnic violence than elsewhere in Africa (Dowd and Raleigh, 2013), contributed to by poor governance, cattle rustling, land-related conflicts, political boundaries, the politicization of ethnic relations, the proliferation of small arms and light weapons, and the effects of climate change (Mbugua, 2013).

As ethnic violence continues to flare across many LMICs, researchers and practitioners are exploring ways to integrate ICTs in violence mitigation and peacebuilding efforts (Kelly, 2019). For example, mobile phones have been used for a variety of measures, such as mapping and countering hate speech and rumours, mapping risks to livelihood, collating and analysing citizens' perceptions of risk and conflict, mapping violent incidents, tracking armed groups, and enabling early warning and response, often on a real-time basis (Convergne and Snyder, 2015; Perera, 2017). Pro-government civilians have used ICTs to effectively collaborate with security forces to suppress rebels, thereby decreasing violence. For civilians without access to communication networks, it is far more difficult and dangerous to inform on rebel groups as they cannot benefit from the anonymization such networks provide, and thus have greater difficulty living among a civilian population for fear of repercussions (Berman et al., 2018). Table 8.1 summarizes some important ICT-based applications being used for peacebuilding efforts in LMICs.

The Free Pentecostal Fellowship in Kenya (FPFK) initiated its own system because all the existing systems were more at a macro level, and could not

Table 8.1 ICT platforms for violence mitigation

Name of application	Location	Type of application	Comments
Ushahidi Platform	Kenya	Early warning platform	It is an app and requires internet for effective operation
Uwiano Platform for Peace	Kenya	Early warning platform	It is used for awareness-raising reporting
Umati	Kenya	Monitoring hate speech application	Customized for monitoring hate speech
Sisi Ni Amani	Kenya	Civic education and violence prevention platform	It is a crowdsourcing software relevant for use in crisis situations and when violence is about to occur
Infocrim Online system	Sao Paolo, Brazil	Violence tracking platform	It has been credited for reducing homicide cases from 12,800 to 7,200 within 5 years

Source: Mukoya, 2020

handle the local dynamics of information generation and transmission within the peace network. Most of those already existing systems were connected to international or regional early warning systems, making the response to local conflict challenges difficult. For example, the Uwiano platform had the number 108, run by a government agency, where the public could send information, but it had no local response mechanism. Other systems like Ushahidi were connected to the early warning system based in Ethiopia with no local monitoring and response mechanism. With the aim of providing appropriate solutions to local problems faced by the communities, the FPFK, therefore, created a system in-house.

ICTs come with the potentials and risks of mitigating as well as enhancing violence. While the rapid spread and access of low-cost ICTs has led to their increasing use in violence prevention and peacebuilding, they have also contributed to groups using them to facilitate organized violence by coordinating across militant groups (Pierskalla and Hollenbach, 2013). Stories of the use of ICTs in supporting violence are easily disseminated through the internet and social media, and they often serve as inspiration for other groups to emulate (Weidmann, 2015). These often contradictory effects make it important to develop a more nuanced understanding of the role that ICTs play in peacebuilding efforts, and how these play out in particular social contexts with implications for violence mitigation or enhancement. This chapter seeks to understand the interplay between ICTs and the social context in the mitigation, or otherwise, of ethnic violence. We examine this interplay through the lenses of social capital and peace networks.

The ends of violence mitigation are noble, and critically required to foster development processes, particularly in the LMICs. Since incidents of violence typically take place in communities, how they are socially organized (which is understood through the idea of peace networks) to experience, perpetrate, or engage with mitigation efforts (studied through the lens of social capital) defines the means of achieving the ends of a more peaceful life. The efforts of ICTs, increasingly embedded within these peace networks, become an important means in peacebuilding. How ICTs are socially embedded within these peace networks, and are scaled and sustained over time, represents the processes through which social collectives can engage with the violence.

The context of the case study

The case is a study of the long-standing engagement of the FPFK, a faith-based organization that has been working since 2009 on various development projects, with violence mitigation and peacebuilding. Their sites of engagement are in the north-east of the country, spanning the counties of Kisumu, Nandi, and Kericho which form the Muhoroni region conflict cluster, and comprising the dominant warring communities of the Kipsigis in Kericho, the Nandis in Nandi, and the Luo in Kisumu. The second conflict cluster is of Mount Elgon, which includes the Bungoma and Trans-Nzoia counties, where the Luhya,

Iteso, and Sabaot communities live. Both these clusters have been embroiled in violence since 1963; the violence is deeply embedded, socially and historically, and, thus, difficult to dislodge. ICTs provide an avenue of hope to try to mitigate this violence.

Some key determinants of ethnic violence in these clusters include:

1. Cattle theft between the Luo and the Kalenjin communities, where the latter are primarily pastoralists. The most affected areas are Jimo East, Gem Rai, Kaplelartet, and Kapsoit, where cattle theft is rife, magnified by poverty, unemployment, and adverse weather conditions such as drought, which create food shortages. The police collaborate with livestock traders who benefit from the stolen livestock. The business people give the police some money to dispense with the cases and ignore livestock thieves. Corruption in the police force, which is promoted by livestock business people, escalates cattle theft of up to 1,000 animals per month.

2. Politically driven ethnic discrimination creates conflict between majority and minority ethnic groups. For instance, in Kiguta, the Kalenjin are the majority, and the Luo, the minority, are discriminated against in accessing elective posts and resources. The majority control the instruments of security, and deliberately refuse to provide adequate security in areas dominated by the minority. This results in the widespread prevalence of firearms among civilians, gender-based violence, and drug and substance abuse.

3. Land and boundary disputes are the bone of contention along the borders of the Kericho, Kisumu, and Nandi counties, with each community seeking to protect its ancestral land/territory. With the increasing population, land and water have become limited resources, and lead to land invasion and illegal grazing. Administrative boundary disputes also contribute to denial of administrative services: for example, in Muhoroni, Sondu, and Maraboi, where different communities claim ownership.

4. The emergence of militia groups in Mount Elgon is a major cause of tension among the residents. Militia groups such as the Sabaot Land Defence Force, the Moorland Defence Force, and the Brokers have terrorized the region for quite a while, and their use by politicians to instigate violence has led to the growth of new militia groups. Politicians mobilize their ethnic-based political formations at both intracommunity and intercommunity levels to their personal advantage, seeding divisions within and between communities (Mukherjee and Mukoya, 2019).

ICT-enabled mitigation efforts

The FPFK started its peacebuilding efforts in 2009. In 2013, it developed an SMS-based Early Warning and Emergency Response System (EWERS), which was introduced in the Mount Elgon region to facilitate the prevention of intra- and inter-ethnic violence. During the 2007–08 election violence, FPFK staff visited camps with internally displaced persons to offer psycho-social counselling and provide food and non-food items. During the counselling sessions, the victims were grouped based on age and sex, and were asked to narrate their ordeals during the violence using word games, drawings, and storytelling. Many children played burning games where they demonstrated lighting bonfires and shouting the way the militia did. Others drew men carrying guns, houses burning, people running, and images of soldiers. The women, especially the widows, narrated stories about the disappearance of their husbands, who were probably abducted by the militias long before the violence broke out and never seen again. This was confirmed by Human Rights Watch (2008). Some youths who escaped from the militia camps also narrated stories of being abducted and forced to mutilate and kill people.

These experiences motivated the FPFK to initiate its peace and human rights project in Mount Elgon in 2009. It was aimed at restoring trust, human dignity, and a peaceful coexistence among the affected communities. Its primary work focused on promoting peace through dialogue and mediations, the rehabilitation and empowerment of militia groups and women, and the promotion of indigenous peoples' rights. The FPFK also engaged with social support and peace groups to both buttress the rehabilitation and reintegration of militia members with their spouses and contribute to the restoration of mental health and economic status of widows. These groups were trained in lobbying and advocacy for peace and conflict management, with strong components of indicator mapping and monitoring, and good governance involving security agencies. Registered with the government as legal entities, they were provided with badges that identified them as community advocates and champions for peace.

The FPFK approached other NGOs and community-based organizations such as Kenya Red Cross, Handicap International, Mercy Corps, Human Rights Watch, the Catholic Peace and Justice Commission (JPC), and various others working in the region to join this largely informal peace network. Their acceptance helped expand it. There was also the involvement of various state actors such as the departments of health, and child and women welfare; internal security agencies including the police and the military; and government leaders at the county levels. A combination of these state, non-state, and citizen groups, and mechanisms for coordination and engagement, contributed towards the establishment of the peace network, of which the FPFK was the de facto coordinating agency. The components of 'response' and 'action' were, thus, better integrated. The actions taken motivated the network's members to participate in it even more. Propelled by this success, in 2012 the FPFK initiated processes to expand the network to Trans-Nzoia, Bungoma North, parts of West Pokot, and Turkana South, which contributed to the 2013 general elections being largely violence-free (TAABCO Research and Development, 2013).

In one of the meetings of the peace network, members raised concerns about the victimization of community members who reported potential perpetrators. These members emphasized the challenges in communication among themselves, and with the community at large, the security agencies, and the government. They asked how they could be motivated to share information with the network and the authorities without being victimized. How might the relationship between the security agencies and the community members be improved? What was the role of the network and other non-state actors in preventing the violence? How might ICTs be used to prevent violence?

It was in response to these questions that the FPFK proposed the idea of the ICT-based EWERS. Local ICT specialists would be involved in its design, with the anonymous sharing of information from community members to responders being a key consideration. A technical working group was formed comprising conflict management practitioners and ICT specialists from across partners. They were responsible for analysing dialogue reports and extracting all the indicators. Community members had pointed out that they were always aware of upcoming acts of violence, but when they warned the authorities, they became victims of retribution by the reported groups. These members were, in fact, reported to the militias by the authorities themselves.

To deal with this issue, the technical group defined indicators that reflected proxies for violence, which were then coded for levels 0, 1, 2, and 3. Levels 0 and 1 indicated peace and calmness, level 2 showed seriousness that needed action, and level 3 was treated as an indicator of violence. Response procedures were designed, and responders identified.

The peace network has indicator monitors: teams of 75 well-trained field agents each, all selected from the community, and well-acquainted with the hotspots. They are equipped with normal phones with a reliable network provider for easy communication via both SMS and voice. They work on a 24-hour basis, are anonymous, and have their data safeguarded even at the FPFK itself. Their primary role is to collect data in the hotspot areas according to the indicators, and relay the data to the control team.

The control teams coordinate the indicator monitoring and response teams, manage the technical aspects of the network, and ensure that the alert messages are acted on. A control team includes data analysts, who confidentially receive the coded data and process it into information or intelligence, which is to be given only to authorized persons on the system list for response. The system developer continuously monitors the performance of the technical system (including the software) and keeps improving on it to meet emerging challenges.

The response team is coordinated through monthly meetings in which their members share reports and narrate experiences, which helps in forming bridges across adversarial groups (since the team has members from across ethnic divides, all suffering from the conflict). The response teams include security agencies, the administration, civil society organizations, community peace groups, and the Red Cross.

The state security agencies are responsible for responding to murder, robbery, cattle theft, and other crisis situations that threaten the public order. The local administrators such as the village chiefs (who are supported by village elders) are responsible for handling family conflicts, gender-based violence, alcoholism, and village crimes, which are discussed in community-based accountability meetings. The Red Cross handles all relief and humanitarian work and provides psychosocial support, including tracing lost community members and victims of violence. Then there are NGOs and faith-based organizations engaged with rights-based issues such as child abuse, domestic violence, and corruption, and which undertake mediation, advocacy, and reconciliation processes.

The EWERS depicted in Figure 8.1 had different interconnected components. The early warning coordination unit is the input mechanism of the field agents, who are equipped with phones with basic features that enable the receiving and sending of messages, and have adequate airtime and network coverage. Power banks or solar chargers provide backups to these agents. A key component of inputting are coded indicators that help identify potential acts of violence such as 'youths disappearing from their

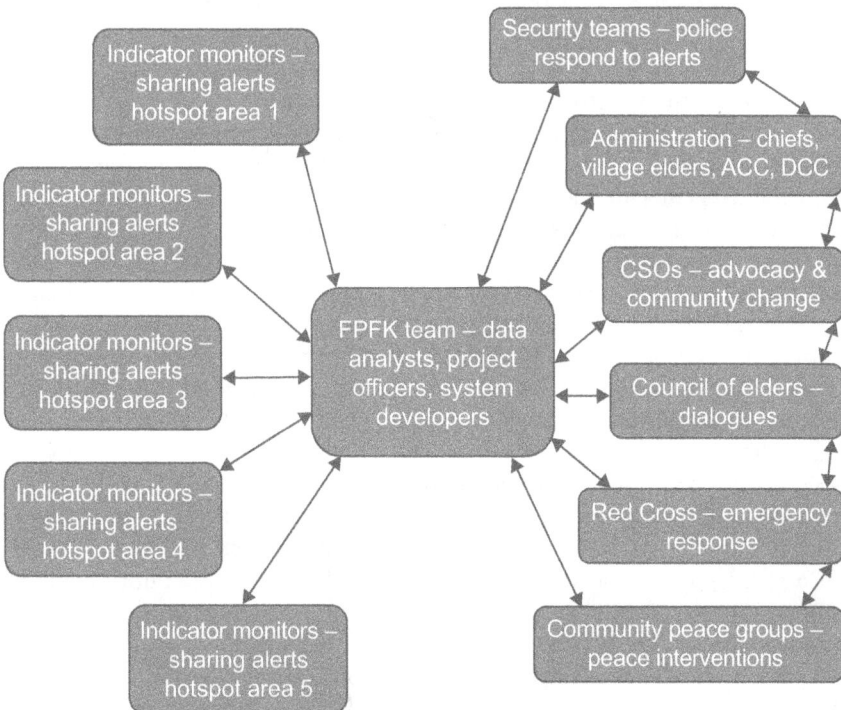

Figure 8.1 The Early Warning and Emergency Response System (EWERS)

homes', 'cattle theft', 'murder', or 'militia groups'. These indicators were formulated following intensive discussions with community members from a given conflict area.

The control unit comprises the computer and its accessories, a USB modem (from Safaricom), relevant software, and the analyst. The computer system is a branded Intel core i7 desktop with 16 GB RAM, 1 terabyte hard disk, and Windows 10 64-bit to run the EWERS application. This is connected to a printer, and is protected by antivirus software.

The user interface comprises a main dashboard, through which a user can search a given incident, and is guided by colours – for example, red at the top corner shows that the system is not working, green shows it is, while orange shows that the system is under repair. The message body is displayed in different colours: red depicts the highest level 3, calling for urgent action. The system forwards this message to the current user's phone automatically so that action can be initiated urgently. Various sub-dashboards provide more granular information, such as for Add Title/Image, send SMS, Codes, Graph Colour, and Office/Branch. On a sub-dashboard, the user can add as many groups or categories as possible, for example, chiefs, child abuse prevention organizations, and volunteers. Chiefs may handle family conflicts, while child abuse prevention organizations may handle only cases of child abuse. A chief in Waitaluk ward will receive cases only in that ward. But chiefs in border locations such as Nandi and Kisumu will receive information from both locations, so that if the Luo are planning to attack the Nandi, the two chiefs may together arrange a peace meeting for joint preventive action.

The contact details of field agents are captured from the sub-dashboard, where messages are routed only to contacts recognized by the system. One field agent can have several contacts, but a given contact belongs to only one agent because the system recognizes each contact as unique. Messages from other unrecognized contacts will be stored in the 'other messages' location within the database. Branches of the host organization are captured from this sub-dashboard: for example, the Kitale office, the Nairobi office, or the Muhoroni office, and administrators are assigned to these offices. An office or branch can have as many administrators as possible, but any given administrator will be attached to only one office.

Response coordination units are mandated to receive SMSs, and respond to information based on their geographical area of operation and to incidents they are interested in. Since the system sends messages to all the leaders of a given group of actors (e.g. the chief and the deputy county commissioner), there is visibility and accountability for action taken. The chief needs to act quickly, before the deputy county commissioner raises questions. The responders send feedback to the control unit on what action they are taking on a given incident. This feedback is later discussed in the review meetings. Figures 8.2 and 8.3 depict the cases of violence.

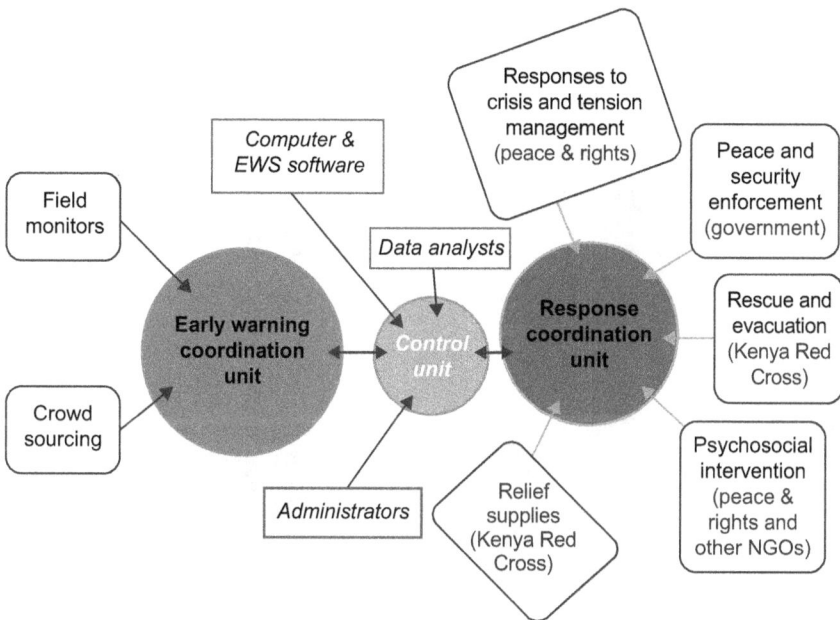

Figure 8.2 Categories and groups

Some observed results from the functioning of the EWERS

The anonymity provided by the EWERS and the visibility of actions taken enhanced the confidence of the field monitors. One agent told us:

> An Iteso family had sold many bags of maize and got lot of money. A group of Sabaot youths noted this and were planning to attack this family at night. It was also an opportunity to evict them from their land, which the Sabaot believed was theirs. A Sabaot who got a hint of the possible attack sent a message to the EWERS. The Iteso family got the alert and moved away that night. The security agencies kept a vigil on the home and arrested the youths who had come to attack.

The EWERS helped make visible acts of violence that were reported through community participation and information shared with security agencies. While the increase in cases reported cannot be attributed to the EWERS alone, as there were many other factors in play, we can, however, argue, that it played an important role, particularly in anonymizing the senders.

A policeman said:

> The system helped to improve the image of the police, as we sat together and shared challenges with the community leaders. The interaction of security teams at public meetings and community dialogues enhanced understanding among the parties. Through these meetings, more light was shed on best way of reporting. As a result, the senior officers

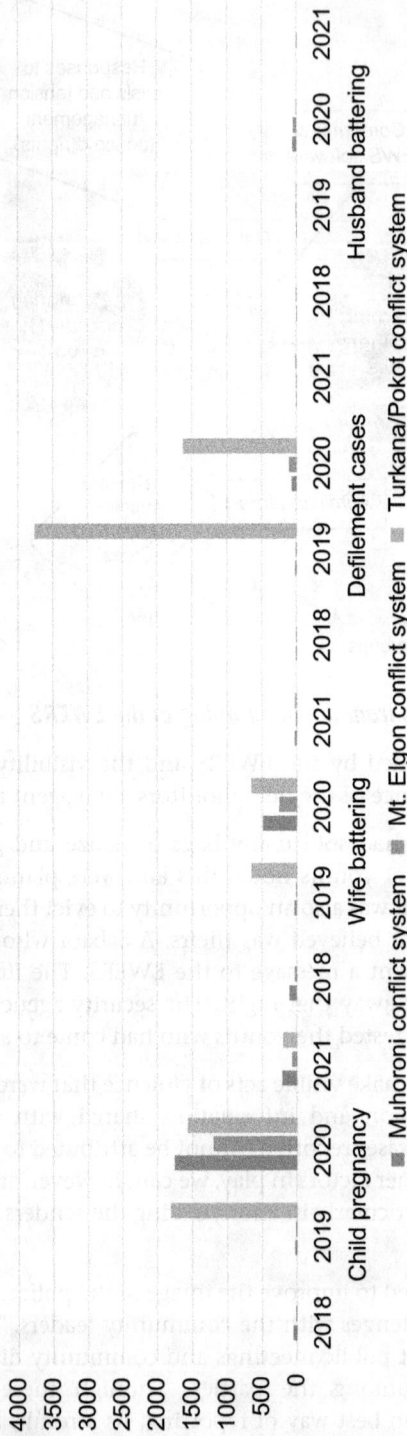

Figure 8.3 Cases of violence

agreed to share their numbers for reporting and further interaction with members of the community. I was a policeman in Mount Elgon before retirement, and it used to be rough due to the absence of technology. Any information that was not IT-based was being leaked. Indeed, the area chief was killed due to absence of confidentiality. The EWERS enabled proactivity from the security agencies, which results in quick action and apprehension of criminals. The killings in Matungu constituency in Kakamega County almost extended to the Bumula constituency in Bungoma County, but for reports in the EWERS revealing actors behind the threatening leaflets. While working as a policeman in Mount Elgon, I was threatened by criminals several times, but the relay of information through the EWERS system always saved me.

Evaluation studies (Otieno, 2013, TAABCO Research and Development Consultants, 2020 – an internal document accessed at FPFK) indicated a marked reduction in cattle rustling, raids, and bandit attacks due to the more widespread and rapid reporting and speedy response.

There are also various challenges, spanning technology, resources, local culture, and relating to incentives and payments. The EWERS system cannot, by itself, address these issues, but can possibly help develop awareness of them. Some key challenges are:

- *Scale of operation*. The geographical area in which violence takes place is vast, while the peace monitors operate in more limited spaces. Consequently, many cases go unreported, raising the challenge of expanding the scale of operations.
- *Poor network coverage*. The EWERS is dependent on a well-functioning mobile telephony network, which, in most conflict-prone areas, is not sufficiently developed. As a result, monitors and responders often struggle to send and receive messages, and action is delayed. This is particularly relevant in some areas of Turkana, Pokot, and Mount Elgon. Stronger advocacy efforts are required from the government to improve the networks.
- *Lack of reliable phones*. This limits the reporting of cases by peace monitors. Security agencies occasionally demand evidence such as images and photos on critical and sensitive cases. However, the lack of gadgets with appropriate functionalities places constraints on action. Addressing this is a matter of more resources.
- *Inadequate literacy*. In most volatile areas such as in Turkana and Pokot, levels of illiteracy are high, and this creates challenges in reading and sending messages. Some monitors end up asking other people to write on their behalf. In Pokot, for example, the chief asks a local teacher to read and interpret the alerts. This compromises their anonymity and can potentially be life threatening.
- *Absence of financial incentives*. Using the system calls for self-driven commitment, without monetary benefits. This is, however, a deterrent

for many, as their expectations are shaped by the money some NGOs pay for involvement in their programmes.

- *Staff turnover.* Security personnel are regularly transferred, which is an issue because the list of responders assigned to specific areas needs to be updated frequently to ensure effective response. Sometimes, those taking over may not exhibit the same passion as their predecessors. The FPFK provides continuous training to newcomers to meet the skill gaps.

- *Political interference.* Instead of apprehending them, some chiefs are known to have shared information with the perpetrators of violence to enable them to escape arrest. Some state security agencies, beholden to the politicians or the community in which they are working, fail to take appropriate action. To mitigate the consequences of such compromises, the EWERS has inbuilt mechanisms of accountability. When a case is reported, the control unit transfers the message to various levels of the hierarchy. A junior functionary is aware that a superior is keeping note of whether or not there has been effective action.

- *Inadequate budgets for training.* Projects require several training sessions and follow-ups by monitors, responders, and community representatives. Security is a fluid process of recurrent unplanned events. It is resource-intensive, and NGOs, being extremely resource-strapped, are circumscribed in their response.

- *Cultural practices.* Indicators of violence speak to the traditions and cultural practices of targeted communities. For instance, in some cultures, sexual and gender-based violence, child marriage, and female genital mutilation would be considered normal. This leads to members being reluctant to report such cases.

- *Positive reinforcement of violence.* There exist both perpetrators and beneficiaries of violence in communities in which conflicts are a norm. Over time, some communities that replenish lost animals through cattle rustling are motivated to continue their violence, since their livelihoods depend on it. Projects are, thus, resisted, often in the name of preserving local cultures and traditions.

How are ICTs contributing to a better world?

The ends the case description seeks to describe is how conflict mitigation is achieved. There are two key means in play: one, the peace networks in action; and, two, the EWERS. Two sets of processes convert the means to the ends: 1) the formation of counter networks; and 2) the leveraging of social capital.

The formation of counter networks

Our analysis brings us to Castells' theory of networks (Castells, 2009, 2011), where he argues that counter-power is exercised in networks to mirror the efforts of disrupting the switches that reflect dominant interests and replace them with alternative switches. In the network society, resistance through 'counter networks' (Mosse and Sahay, 2003) is powered by ICTs (Castells, 2011), which help to form alternative networks (which we call 'peace networks') that challenge those in power. Networks enable linkages with values and interests that people see as valuable, while disconnecting all that is not valuable, simultaneously leading to inclusion and exclusion in networks, and redefining the architecture of network relationships. Resistance to power can play a key role in forming or strengthening the peace networks that work against the networks that advance violent conflicts.

In reality, not all can easily become members of the network society, for reasons that range from access to ICTs, prior experience, and social and political discrimination. Including those marginalized groups in ICT-enabled networks is a non-trivial challenge. This is drawn from Mosse and Sahay's (2003) study of the deployment of health information systems in the marginalized regions of northern Mozambique. Joining the networks is not a matter of 'plug and play' but requires sustained and long-term efforts, often ably supported by ICTs. Given the invisibility of information about the challenges these marginalized groups face, there is an absence of advocacy leading to continued and systematic marginalization. Building informational capacity, both at the structural and the personal levels, becomes crucial in mobilizing these counter networks for advocacy. Our case highlights how community groups, often victims of violence, use the EWERS to become active participants in peace mitigation efforts. However, ICTs on their own can do little, and need to draw upon and build social capital in these networks.

Leveraging social capital

ICTs have to be supported and deployed within the context of a community's shared norms, values, solidarity, and desire to engage with peacebuilding efforts. The idea of social capital helps to understand the relationship between ICTs and peacebuilding. The role of social capital has been studied in various disciplines such as public policy, political science, economics, community development, sociology, anthropology, and education (Gaved and Anderson, 2006). Information systems researchers have also been engaged with the use of social capital as a lens to study technology development and knowledge sharing processes (Yang et al., 2009) by enabling access to useful value and resources to facilitate certain actions within the networks (Bourdieu, 1986; Coleman, 1990; Putnam, 1995).

Social capital is an essential ingredient of the civil society that forms important structures and resources in peacebuilding. It is simply the networks of social relations characterized by the norms of trust and reciprocity. Thus, social capital can serve as a resource for enabling communitarian action that can lead to either violent conflict or to peaceful coexistence. For collective action to bring the desired results to the community, members need to effectively participate in the social networks. Our case helps to understand the values and beliefs that motivate individuals to join or form networks that champion peace and against those that engage in conflict enterprises. Apart from values and beliefs, with mushrooming technologies, digital literacy plays an important determining factor in participation and/or inclusion in these peace networks. There are various enabling and constraining factors related to ICT that influence inclusion and participation in peace networks, and in fostering reciprocity and accountability. Trust as a key ingredient of social capital is fundamental in sustaining peace networks, provided members in these networks show a willingness to take risks for pursuing peace across the divides. However, there are often breaches of trust, for example, when a chief informs would-be perpetrators of crimes that they have been detected. Building trust has to constantly contend with such breaches, and to patch them up through discussion and dialogue.

New peace networks emerge with the increase in social capital resources. The EWERS created a platform for community members to connect with administrations and security agencies to respond to conditions of insecurity. These form social capital linkages that, in turn, form networks of trusting relationships between people interacting across explicit, formal, or institutionalized power or authority structures in society. These emerging networks are characterized by trust and reciprocity, key features of social capital developed through bottom-up approaches that linked with formal security structures. The use of ICTs encourages positive synergies towards transformations in peacebuilding and the cultivation of a culture of reconciliation. These linking mechanisms enable the creation of values of accountability, transparency, responsiveness, and tolerance, all of which are fundamental in mitigating ethnic violence. The ICTs enable effective communication among a range of entities, which help better coordinate response efforts.

The integration of ICTs has connected the warring communities, previously polarized and locked in violence. These communities were largely inward-looking and self-centred. A reduction in ethnic bonding worked in favour of peace and welfare of the majority. ICTs helped create links among people across the divide with common business interests, such as milk sellers, horticultural farmers, poultry farmers, livestock traders, and motorcycle dealers. The network not only improved their economic lives but also helped them realize that peace made their businesses thrive.

Previously, the dominant community used bonding to prevent the minority from being appointed to leadership positions. However, the EWERS provided a platform for those who supported the minority to gain a larger voice. The othering of those belonging to a different ethnic group led to discrimination and social exclusion. The resultant stigma fostered feelings of guilt, helplessness, incompetence, and reduced communal worth.

Economic bridges. Bridging economic relationships were created when markets opened up to accommodate members from across ethnic divides who had earlier been denied this access. Within the bonding framework, individuals and communities had restricted the freedom to interact with other community members because of norms, values, and cultural practices. Freedom of choice is an intrinsic human right that needs to be respected and promoted even when it is not exercised in rational or virtuous ways. By unlocking the freedoms, the use of the ICTs has helped develop trusting relationships, with the concomitant growth of inter-ethnic economic partnerships.

Increase in tolerance of diversity. Tolerance of diversity is fundamental to peaceful coexistence. The integration of EWERS in violence prevention and diversity of contact contributed to an increase in tolerance and acceptance of differences, values, and beliefs. This enhanced level of tolerance and acceptance followed the increased flow of information between communities and external stakeholders.

Reciprocity as a key to reconciliation. The act of returning stolen animals to their rightful owners sometimes negated the value of cooperation, as those who survived on stolen animals felt betrayed. However, Bentham's principles of utility state that the morally right actions are those that produce the best overall consequences in the utility or welfare of all affected parties (Crimmins, 2019), which helps justify the use of the EWERS.

Conclusions

The ICT-enabled peace network has arguably contributed towards creating a better world and a more hopeful future for the residents of the study areas. Noteworthy in this case narrative, particularly for ICT4D scholars, is how the EWERS was designed and evolved to produce actionable information and the mechanisms that linked the community members both to each other and with formal security structures. This helps to theoretically understand both the structure (who are included and why) and the (informational) processes underlying the counter network which promotes intermediation, conceptualized through the linking aspect of social capital theorization. The information flows enable mediators with particular characteristics to emerge from bottom-up counter networks and initiate from existing power bases. We discuss some key enabling roles of information flows in these networks.

ICTs as a platform for sharing sensitive information

The introduction and use of ICTs helped community members, particularly peace actors in Mount Elgon, to overcome conditions that constrained the flow of information between communities, leading to better social relationships and improved mobilization of community resources. The EWERS, with its inbuilt anonymization of the sender, motivated field agents to share sensitive information with one another, thereby saving lives and properties. This information sharing helped strengthen bridging relationships that protected members by pre-empting potential attacks. Prior to the introduction of the EWERS, this went unreported, because community members feared being victimized by the security agencies and were unwilling to take the risk of being embroiled in long-drawn and resource-consuming legal cases.

ICTs as a medium of minority empowerment

The EWERS was a medium for minority groups to raise their voices and be included in peacebuilding. The flow of information empowered the minority to challenge the deeply entrenched power structures of the majority. Where the exclusion of the minorities had sustained the violence, their inclusion contributed to increasing justice. The EWERS enabled leadership opportunities for women, in that they participated in responses to message alerts on gender-based violence, corruption, and small arms and light weapons proliferation. Equally, opportunities for youth empowerment increased, and regular interactions between the chiefs and the young from the affected communities led to the sensitization of the elders to the economic plight of the youth. Some chiefs began sensitizing the youth to the importance of peace and respect for the rule of law, and to focus on developing entrepreneurial skills.

ICTs as facilitating access to markets

The EWERS helped open up market spaces that had earlier been closed by ethnic divisions. These connections led to new economic opportunities and business partnerships. Communities in Mount Elgon formed *chamas* (informal cooperative societies that pool together and invest savings) and business groups in Saboti. The Sabaot harvest milk, honey, and firewood, and supply to the Bukusu, who, in return, supply maize, cooking oil, sugar, and soap. A high degree of polarization had prevented this from happening earlier. The Luo and the Kalenjin, which have been responding to alerts related to cattle theft, started to freely interact in the Sondu market, leading to joint business ventures.

ICTs as a driver of community conversations for peace

The EWERS messages made visible the polarization between the Abagusii and the Marakwet in Trans-Nzoia County. The persistence of these messages drew the attention of national level government leaders, who responded swiftly by forming community-based dialogue groups and enabling reconciliation efforts. After peace was achieved, the communities made a social contract to solve their issues amicably. The *simatwet* tree (*Curroria volubilis*) became their symbol for peace. Following regular conversations, many people who had been earlier displaced were recalled by their communities. In the Muhoroni cluster, in particular, and along the Kisumu and Kericho borders, the EWERS facilitated the timely reporting of thievery and the consequent recovery of stolen goods and animals.

ICTs enabling networking and collaboration to support governance

ICTs facilitated the creation of strong collaborative relations and informational trust between communities and security agencies, especially the police. A major factor was anonymization, as were messaging speed and quickness of joint response by the police and other security agencies. Also, police officers bridged the conflict divide to network and jointly respond to alerts. The EWERS catalysed a transformation in security management: the police started attending community forums such as church functions, organized seminars, and organized get-togethers to interact directly with the public. They also invited members of the public to give motivational talks to the police force. Police officers began educating the community on case reporting, investigation processes, and roles and responsibilities. The relaying of information to the constabulary as well as to their superiors led to enhanced accountability and better governance. The chiefs and their assistants began regularly holding consultative meetings with community leaders, which led to more transparency in how cases of violence were addressed.

Acknowledgements

The authors sincerely and deeply acknowledge the primary empirical work carried out by Festus Mukoya on this project both as a part of his PhD studies and as a long-standing member of FPFK, where he has for more than a decade been engaged with trying to bring peace to some regions of conflict in Kenya. We also acknowledge support of the EU Horizon 2020 project on 'ICTs for Community Oriented Policing in Post-Conflict Countries', which included Kenya. Arunima Mukherjee was the Technology Work Package leader on this project.

References

Berman, E., Felter, J.H., Shapiro, J.N. and McIntyre, V. (2018) *Small Wars, Big Data: The Information Revolution in Modern Conflict*, Princeton University Press, Princeton, NJ [online] <https://doi.org/10.1080/09546553.2019.169 3779> [accessed 26 August 2021].

Bourdieu, P. (1986) 'The forms of capital', in J.G. Richardson (ed.), *Handbook of Theory and Research for the Sociology of Education*, pp. 241–58, Greenwood Press, New York [online] <https://www.socialcapitalgateway.org/sites/social capitalgateway.org/files/data/paper/2016/10/18/rbasicsbourdieu1986-theformsofcapital.pdf> [accessed 26 August 2021].

Castells, M. (2009) *Communication Power*, Oxford University Press, Oxford.

Castells, M. (2011) 'A network theory of power', *International Journal of Communication* 5: 773–87 <https://ijoc.org/index.php/ijoc/article/view/1136/553> [accessed 26 August 2021].

Coleman, J.S. (1990) 'Social capital in the creation of human capital', *American Journal of Sociology* 94: S95–S120 <https://doi.org/10.1086/228943 >.

Convergne, E. and Snyder, M.R. (2015) 'Making maps to make peace: geospatial technology as a tool for UN peacekeeping', *International Peacekeeping* 22(5): 565–86 <https://doi.org/10.1080/13533312.2015.1094193>.

Crimmins, J.E. (2019) 'Jeremy Bentham', in E.N. Zalta (ed.), *The Stanford Encyclopedia of Philosophy*, Metaphysics Research Lab Centre for the Study of Language and Information, Stanford University, CA [online] <https://plato.stanford.edu/entries/bentham/> [accessed 26 August 2021].

Dowd, C. and Raleigh, C. (2013) *ACLED Country Report: Kenya*, Armed Conflict Location and Event Data Project (ACLED), USA.

Elfversson, E. and Brosché, J. (2012) 'Communal conflict, civil war, and the state: complexities, connections, and the case of Sudan', *African Journal on Conflict Resolution* 12(1) <https://www.ajol.info/index.php/ajcr/article/view/78700> [accessed 26 August 2021].

Gaved, M. and Anderson, B. (2006) *The Impact of Local ICT Initiatives on Social Capital and Quality of Life* [online], Chimera Working Paper Number: 2006-06, University of Essex, Ipswich <http://citeseerx.ist.psu.edu/viewdoc/download?doi=10.1.1.99.5524&rep=rep1&type=pdf> [accessed 9 March 2022].

Horowitz, D.L. (2000) *The Deadly Ethnic Riot*, University of California Press, Berkeley and Los Angeles [online] <https://www.researchgate.net/publication/247825866_The_Deadly_Ethnic_Riots> [accessed 26 August 2021].

Human Rights Watch (2008) *World Report 2008*, New York [online] <https://www.hrw.org/legacy/wr2k8/pdfs/wr2k8_web.pdf> [accessed 26 August 2021].

Kelly, L. (2019) *Uses of Digital Technologies in Managing and Preventing Conflict* [online], K4D Helpdesk Report, Institute of Development Studies, Brighton, UK <https://assets.publishing.service.gov.uk/media/5d0cecb640f0b62006e1f4ef/600_ICTs_in_conflict.pdf> [accessed 26 August 2021].

Mbugua, J.K. (2013) *Inter-communal Conflicts in Kenya: The Real Issues at Stake in the Tana Delta*, Issues Briefs No. 1, International Peace Support Training Centre, Nairobi.

Mosse, E.L. and Sahay, S. (2003) 'Counter networks, communication and health information systems: a case study from Mozambique', in M. Korpela, R. Montealegre, and A. Poulymenakou (eds), *Organizational Information Systems in the Context of Globalization*, pp. 35–51, The International Federation for Information Processing, Springer, Boston, MA [online] <https://www.researchgate.net/publication/220985061_Counter_Networks_Communication_and_Health_Information_Systems_A_Case_Study_from_Mozambique> [accessed 26 August 2021].

Mukherjee, A.S. and Mukoya, F. (2019) 'ICT enabled peace network: case study of conflict early warning system in Kenya', in H.K. Kiimaro and P. Nielsen (eds), *Proceedings of IFIP 9.4 Conference on Information and Communication Technologies for Development. Strengthening Southern-Driven Cooperation as a Catalyst for ICT4D, Dar es Salaam, Tanzania, 1–3 May*, pp. 127–39.

Mukoya, F. (2020) 'ICTs as enablers of resilient social capital for ethnic peace', paper presented at *COMPASS '20: ACM SIGCAS Conference on Computing and Sustainable Societies, 15–17 June 2020, Ecuador* [online] <https://www. researchgate.net/publication/342621108_ICTs_as_Enablers_of_Resilient_ Social_Capital_for_Ethnic_Peace> [accessed 26 August 2021].

Otieno, S. (2013) *Evaluation Report for Violence Prevention and Emergency Response Project*, FPFK, Kenya (internal document of FPFK, not publicly available).

Perera, S. (2017) 'To boldly know: knowledge, peacekeeping and remote data gathering in conflict-affected states', *International Peacekeeping* 24(1): 1–20 <http://dx.doi.org/10.1080/13533312.2017.1383566>.

Pierskalla, J. and Hollenbach, F.M. (2013) 'Technology and collective action: the effect of cell phone coverage on political violence in Africa', *American Political Science Review* 107(2): 207–24 <https://doi.org/10.1017/ S0003055413000075>.

Putnam, R.D. (1995) 'Bowling alone: America's declining social capital', *Journal of Democracy* 6(1): 65–78 <https://doi.org/10.1353/jod.1995.0002>.

Rohwerder, B. (2015) *Conflict Analysis of Kenya*, Governance and Social Development Resource Centre (GSDRC), University of Birmingham, UK [online] <http://www.gsdrc.org/wp-content/uploads/2015/12/KenyaConflict Analysis.pdf> [accessed 26 August 2021].

TAABCO Research and Development (2013) *FPFK Peace and Rights Programme: End of Term Evaluation*, Nairobi, Kenya [online] <https://www.norad.no/ globalassets/publikasjoner/publikasjoner-2015-/ngo-evaluations/fpfk-peace-and-rights-program-end-of-term-evaluation.pdf> [accessed 26 August 2021].

Torbjörnsson, D. (2016) *Managing Communal Conflict in Africa: Assessing the Role of the UN in Communal Conflict Management*, Totalförsvarets Forskningsinstitut (Swedish Defence Research Agency), Report no. FOI-R--4226--SE [online] <https://www.asclibrary.nl/docs/406779430. pdf> [accessed 26 August 2021].

Weidmann, N.B. (2015) 'Communication networks and the transnational spread of ethnic conflict', *Journal of Peace Research* 52(3): 285–96 <https:// doi.org/10.1177/0022343314554670>.

Yang, S., Lee, H. and Kurnia, S. (2009) 'Social capital in information and communications technology research: past, present, and future', *Communications of the Association for Information Systems* 25: 23 <https:// doi.org/10.17705/1CAIS.02523>.

CHAPTER 9

Enabling spaces for conversation: Engaging with violence against women in Guatemala

Arunima Mukherjee and Sundeep Sahay

This chapter describes a process of design and use of a digital intervention to engage with the problem of violence against women (VAW) in Guatemala. VAW is a historically existing problem in the country, manifesting in different ways, with particularly adverse consequences for indigenous women. There are multiple institutions in the country which are each addressing particular concerns, such as legal, economic, and police interventions and protection. However, there is limited data sharing and coordination among these institutions, which makes it very exhausting and resource-consuming for the victims of violence to access consolidated and holistic justice. With this background, the project sought to meet the following objectives: 1) to understand the process by which victims of violence accessed justice, the process they followed, and the challenges experienced; and 2) to use this understanding to design a digital intervention, which could create a unified database containing inter-institutional data and relevant visualizations of data as outputs. This would 'enable space for inter-institutional conversation' that could serve as a basis for more effective collective action, and hope for VAW to be transformed to a more peaceful future.

Understanding violence against women

We provide below three (potentially disturbing) excerpts depicting violence against women (VAW) in Guatemala, narrated to us.

> *Lupita grew up watching her father violently assault her mother. His attacks were both verbal and physical, often telling Lupita and her mother that they were useless women. This violence resulted in Lupita's mother experiencing several miscarriages. It was seeing her mother experience this loss at the hands of her father that marked her for life.*

> *Estrellita, a young 28-year old mother of three, gets beaten by her husband every time he returns drunk, which is three–four times a week. But for Estrellita, the most hurtful is she and her children being publicly mocked each time they step out. Her children have stopped going to school in fear of humiliation and shaming.*

Alondra went into labour and proceeded to the closest health centre to have her baby. As a two-time rape survivor, upon arrival she asked staff to be gentle with her and ask permission/explain before doing any procedures during birth. The attending midwife walked in, grabbed a stick and told to me, 'spread your legs.' The look of disgust on her face ... I don't think I've ever seen a look like that, like I was the most disgusting thing she had ever seen and she didn't want to touch me. Through the labour I was told shut-up, no sound, how 'raped woman' like me deserved more pain.

These stories capture how gender-based violence results in significant consequences for the cultural, social, and economic wellbeing of women. Violence against women is one of the most prevalent human rights violations in the world, with an estimated one in three women experiencing abuse in their lifetime, inflicted in public or in private. It also includes threats of violence, coercion, and manipulation. This violence takes diverse forms including intimate partner violence, sexual violence, child marriage, female genital mutilation, and 'honour crimes'. Victims of sexual violence experience various adverse consequences including forced and unwanted pregnancies, unsafe abortions, traumatic fistula, sexually transmitted infections including HIV, and even death.

The Convention on the Elimination of All Forms of Discrimination against Women (CEDAW) (United Nations Human Rights Office of the High Commissioner, n.d.) defines violence against women as: 'violence directed against a woman because she is a woman or which affects a woman disproportionately; including physical, mental or sexual harm or suffering, threats of such acts, coercion and other deprivations of liberty'.

The UN Declaration on the Elimination of Violence Against Women (VAW) (UN General Assembly, 1993) states that, 'Violence against women is a manifestation of historically unequal power relations between men and women' and that 'violence against women is one of the crucial social mechanisms by which women are forced into a subordinate position compared with men'.

The term VAW is subsumed within the broader term of gender-based violence, which also includes violence against men and those who are transgender. This term is broader than physical harm and includes aspects of emotional and financial stress, with adverse consequences. VAW is a violation of women's fundamental human rights, and deeply rooted in power imbalances and structural inequalities, between women and men in society. Some global declarations to address this violence include the Declaration on the Elimination of Violence against Women (UN General Assembly, 1993), and the Beijing Declaration and Platform for Action (UN Women, 1995).

Gender-based violence undermines the health, dignity, security, and autonomy of its victims, yet it remains shrouded in a culture of silence in society. According to the World Health Organization (WHO) (2013), one in every three women has been beaten, coerced into sex or abused in some other way – most often by someone she knows. One in five women are sexually abused as a child, and these women are 16 per cent more likely to have a low-birth-weight baby, twice as likely to have an abortion, and 50 per cent more likely to acquire HIV (UNAIDS, 2013).

While great expectations have been placed on ICTs to help engage with such acts of violence against women, relatively little is known about how, when, and why such transformations can be made possible. While there is literature on institutional and societal measures being taken to address VAW (Avis, 2017), the role of the digital has remained largely invisible. Technology mirrors the societies that create it and 'existing power relations in society determine the enjoyment of benefits from ICTs; hence these technologies are not gender neutral' (Gurumurthy, 2004: 1). Digital tools and methodologies need to be fit for the purpose of challenging and ending the inequalities for which they are designed (Cummings and O'Neil, 2015), and not reinforce structures of inequality. It is within this context that we describe an ICT-based research initiative to engage with the widespread phenomenon of VAW in Guatemala.

The context of violence against women in Guatemala

Guatemala suffered from almost four decades of armed conflict, ending with a peace accord in 1997, in which more than 200,000 people were killed or disappeared, mostly civilians and 83 per cent indigenous people. The legacy of this violence continues today with social relationships, particularly involving women, which are characterized by aggression and violence. The country ranks 127th out of 189 in the 2020 United Nations Human Development Report, with half the population living in poverty or extreme poverty (UNDP, 2020).

Indigenous people, who make up 42 per cent of the population, are considered second-class citizens and face severe discrimination and abuse, with 75 per cent living in poverty, compared with 38 per cent of the non-indigenous populations. Illiteracy among this population is 48 per cent (65 per cent for women), compared with 30 per cent for the non-indigenous population (National Statistics Institute, 2006). Guatemala has a Gender Inequality Index value of 0.523, ranking it 112 out of 149 countries in the 2013 index. Only 13.3 per cent of parliamentary seats are held by women, and 21.9 per cent of adult women have reached at least a secondary level of education compared with 23.2 per cent of their male counterparts. For every 100,000 live births, 120.0 women die from pregnancy-related causes, the adolescent birth rate is 97.2 births per 1,000 live births, and women's participation in the labour market is 49.1 per cent compared with 88.2 per cent for men (UN Women, 2014). Guatemala has the highest rate of homicides of women in the Americas and the fifth in the world. Every two days a young woman is murdered, 2 per cent of them aged under 5 years, and between 2000 and 2007, almost 4,000 women were murdered, often after rape and sexual assault, and bodies disposed of in desolate places and often in the victim's own home (Oxfam, 2015). These statistics are reflective of deep-rooted structural inequalities and violence against women in Guatemalan society.

Although the country has a legal framework of 14 documents specifying the protection of women's rights, the societal belief in the superiority of men over women, coupled with traditional social practices, lead to many injustices and human-rights violations against women, especially indigenous women. In Guatemala, there are various institutions directly involved in addressing violence against indigenous women, including the Office (national and regional) for the Défense of Indigenous Women (DEMI), local municipalities, civil police, the Human Rights Ombudsperson's Office, the Attorney General's Office (PGN), and Population Council. DEMI, created in 1999, is a nodal government institution that offers women psychological, legal, and health assistance. DEMI has published a series of three reports, in 2003, 2007, and 2013, on the social situation of indigenous women based on data from January to October of the respective years. This was a first in the country, covering both the national and the six regional levels.

Assessing the current social situation of indigenous women in Guatemala and their access to justice is a challenging task, as not all statistical data collected is systematically disaggregated by sex and ethnicity, often rendering indigenous women invisible. Further, DEMI is limited in both financial and human resources, constraining their capability to undertake effective action. In the 2003 and 2007 reports, DEMI characterized and analysed indigenous women's access to justice, while the 2013 report profiled the social situation of DEMI's users. These different reports established that at least 58 per cent of the country's population was indigenous, with 20 per cent of them living in rural areas and experiencing high levels of social exclusion and poverty.

Underreporting of incidents of violence serves as a serious deterrent for indigenous women to access justice. Surveys conducted by the United Nations Development Programme and Towards a Policy of Citizen Security Project showed that, in 2004, about 79 per cent of cases of violence went unreported. The most frequent complaint raised by indigenous women was domestic violence (DEMI, 2007), which was often unreported because of the women's limited economic resources, inadequate infrastructure to allow travel to the offices and institutions, lack of services in their language, a weak justice system, and the fear of victimization. Laws regarding criminal matters are weak and do not allow for certain cases to be classified as offences or crimes to be prosecuted. In 2005, 77.5 per cent of domestic violence cases reported could not be classified as crimes or misdemeanours. In 2005, the nine main types of crime included: injuries and threats, injuries in concurrence with threats, coercion, aggression, rape and rape in concurrence with other crimes and misdemeanours. DEMI notes that most often cases of discrimination and racism are not reported, making indigenous women and their children very vulnerable to systematic violence.

Stories from the field: digital intervention to engage with VAW

To understand the role of ICTs in the fight with VAW, within the context of a larger EU Horizon 2020 project on ICT4COP (ICTs for Community Oriented Policing), Guatemala was selected as a country of empirical focus. A research team was created with a researcher at Oslo who coordinated a group of field researchers with a background in anthropology and a technology development team based in India. The local team in Guatemala was further expanded to include victims of violence to conduct field research and also bring in their 'life stories' as a form of empirical understanding. After constituting the research team, a pilot study was conducted during 2019–2020 to understand how a process of dialogue could be initiated among the institutions dealing with VAW, so as to promote collective action. The study had the following components: first, to conduct a qualitative analysis by discussing with victims of violence how they accessed help through the different institutions available to them. The second component was to design a digital intervention to help share inter-institutional data with the aim of creating spaces for conversations between the different institutions involved, as a basis to strengthen collective action towards mitigating violence against women.

Understanding attention seeking routes of victims of violence

The aim was to firstly identify relevant institutions engaged with VAW and, secondly, to develop attention seeking routes of victims of violence as they sought justice. Once DEMI was on board with the conceptual idea for the pilot study, we jointly identified two empirical sites, Santa Rosa and Sololá, based on the status of gender violence in these areas. Following this, we identified the multiple institutions responsible for providing support to victims of violence (see Table 9.1).

Table 9.1 Institutions responsible for providing support to victims of violence

Institution	English translation
Pastoral Social Cáritas	Caritas Social Ministry
Oficina de Derechos Humanos del Arzobispado de Guatemala (ODHAG)	Human Rights Office of the Archbishop of Guatemala
Policía Nacional Civil	National Police
Ministerio de Agricultura, Ganadería y Alimentación (MAGA)	Ministry of Agriculture, Livestock and Food
Instituto Nacional de Ciencias Forenses (INACIF)	National Institute of Forensic Sciences
Secretaría Contra la Violencia Sexual, Explotación y Trata de Personas (SVET)	Secretariat against Sexual Violence, Exploitation and Human Trafficking
Procuraduría General de la Nación (PGN)	Attorney General's Office
Dirección Municipal de la Mujer (DMM)	Municipal Office for Women's Affairs

(Continued)

Table 9.1 Continued

Institution	English translation
Ministerio de Trabajo	Ministry of Labour
Asociación Pro Bienestar de la Familia (APROFAM)	Association for the Well-Being of the Family
Secretaría Presidencial de la Mujer (SEPREM)	Presidential Secretariat for Women's Affairs
Instituto Experimental Básico 'Juan José Arévalo Bermejo'	Experimental Junior High School 'Juan José Arévalo Bermejo'
Mujeres de Cambio de Santa Rosa (AMUCASA)	Women of Change in Santa Rosa
Ministerio de Educación	Ministry of Education
Grupo M. Solid	Grupo M. Solid
Asociación Santo Hermano Pedro	Holy Brother Peter Association
Dirección Área de Salud	Health Section Directorate
Ministerio Público	Public Prosecutor's Office
Centro de Investigación para la Prevención de la Violencia en Centroamérica (CIPREVICA)	Prevention Against Violence Research Center in Central America
Registro Nacional de las Personas (RENAP)	National Registry of Persons
Escuela Normal Intercultural	Intercultural Training School
Hospital de Cuilapa, Clínica de violencia sexual	Sexual Violence Clinic, Cuilapa Hospital
Defensoría de la Mujer Indígena	Office for the Defence of Indigenous Women (DEMI)
Procuraduría de los Derechos Humanos	Office of the Human Rights Ombudsman
Juzgado de Familia	Family Court
Hospital departamental de Sololá	Sololá Hospital

Next we sought to reconstruct attention seeking paths of justice with 13 victims of violence through in-depth interviews to map out the routes the victims followed, and through this process 'building their life-stories'. This included identifying the first contact where the women went for help, and their subsequent steps before they decided to approach DEMI. At each step, we identified the reasons behind each decision and their resulting experiences. Each victim took different paths, but with some common themes: for example the Family Court (in five cases) and the National Civil Police (in three cases) were visited before approaching DEMI. This reconstruction process, depicted schematically as 'attention routes' (see Figure 9.1), helped us to understand which institutions' victims were referred to in dealing with different forms of violence. On average, DEMI was the fourth or fifth institution that the victims attended of the available seven institutions visited.

Five of the women approached DEMI after being referred by someone close to them, such as family or friends, who knew of the existence of the DEMI and the services it provides. Three of these close people knew about

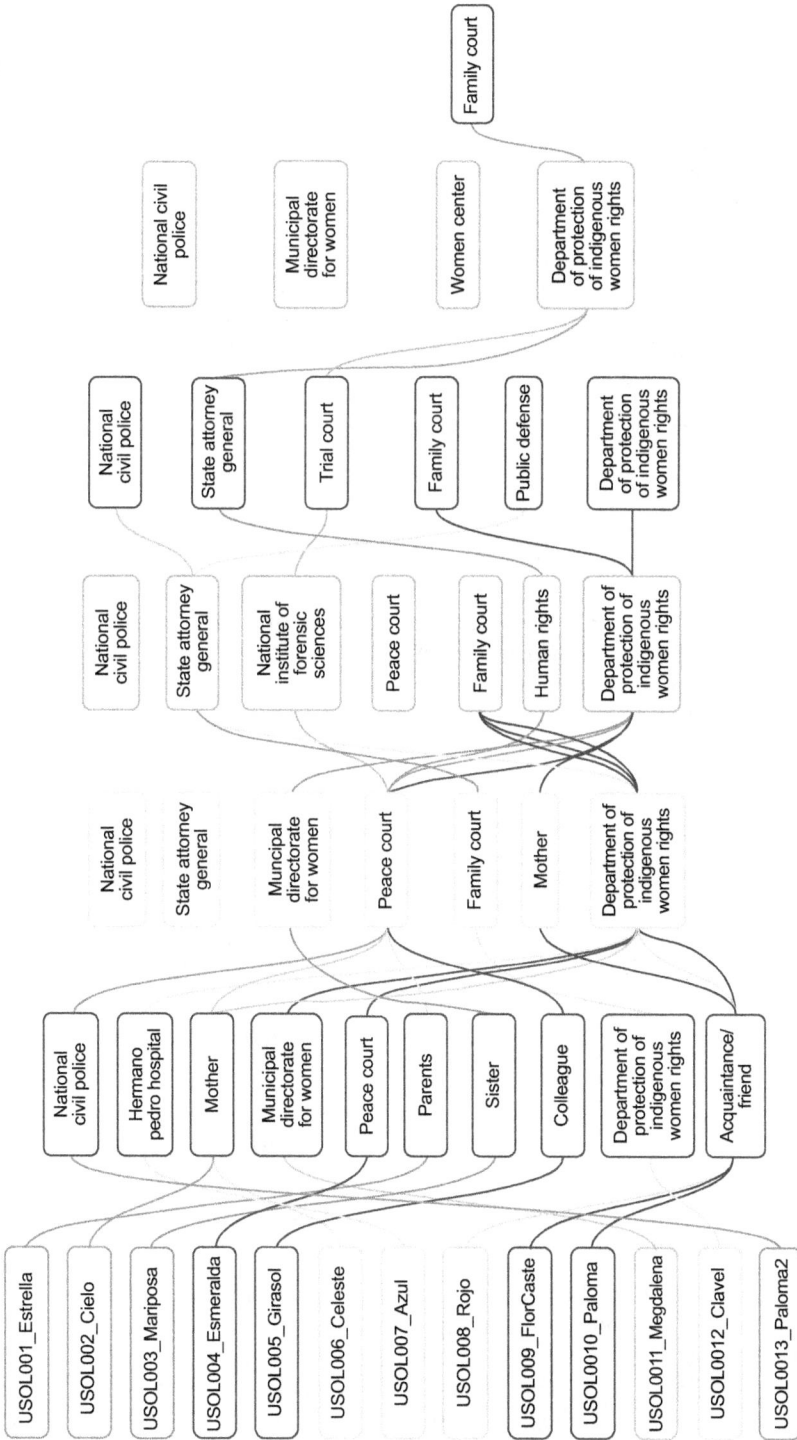

Figure 9.1 Mapping of attention routes in accessing justice

DEMI because they lived or worked nearby or themselves had experience of going to DEMI for their own psychological help. In Santa Rosa, the majority (14 out of 20) approached DEMI following violence against them by their partners and sought alimony and custody of their children. Since DEMI is not an institution that receives legal reports or complaints, this then required further visits to the courts and police. Some visited DEMI due to lack of financial resources for hiring private attorneys.

> After that I went to the family court, I had legal problems with the children's father; So they told me that we were going to go to trial, but I don't have money to pay a lawyer, so the family court officials told me to come to DEMI, that here they were going to give me legal advice. The secretary of the family court recommended it (a victim of violence).

> [I went to DEMI] because it was free, it had no cost (another victim).

> I went to DEMI because I had no money to sue this man legally (another victim).

DEMI encouraged their staff to identify other areas or situations where they could offer assistance. An example is the process of 'conciliation', which is a process that the social unit implements that allows users to seek extra-judicial consensus instead of only resorting to court processes that took more time and resources. A victim said: 'They made us sign an agreement to see how much money he had to give me [alimony] and in what ways he had to help with the kids.'

Other victims shared their experience:

> The thing is that I suffered with my husband who beat me a lot for many years now, he humiliated me, hit my children and I didn't want to go through those sorrows because he treated us very badly.

> We were going with the children to walk on a street next to the highway to El Salvador and he was drunk. He took the children from me and took them to the middle of the street with the cars passing by. Thank goodness we were able to take them back from him. He threw my boy on the street, he wanted to take the girl away from me and we struggled.

> The father of my daughters mistreated us. He hit me frequently. He would grab me by the feet and hit me. My daughters witnessed that and the oldest one is behind on her studies. She helped me when he was drunk and that's why she is behind in her studies. They were greatly affected by their dad's attitude.

The accounts of the victims emphasized that physical violence is often combined with other expressions of violence, particularly emotional and psychological, which had implications also for children, who lived in constant fear and had lower grades at school. While some women waited 3–6 years before seeking help, others waited even 20 to 30 years. What was common was that none reported abuse as they were experiencing it; they waited till they felt an irretrievable sense of weariness:

> *I just couldn't take it anymore. My oldest daughter told me not to suffer anymore, that this was an ordeal that I had and that I should not suffer, she told me to report it. She went with me to the police. And that's when we got him to leave the house.*

> *Because I thought to myself I have three children and if INACIF says that I am not crazy, that I do not have that disability, then I am going to seek help to defend my women's rights. I want to continue studying, I want to have a job of my own and I want to be well.*

> *Because when he saw me on the street he harassed me, he humiliated me, he wanted to take the baby from me and he didn't pay alimony. I didn't know what to do because I couldn't ask for help because sometimes you ask for help and they don't give it to you. So I came here to DEMI and they offered me support, I feel like I was at home and I was telling my family.*

> *I was going to leave him because it was already unbearable as he was. Then, on March 19, I did it, I got out of there, without money, without clothes, without anything. Only the essentials and I came with my parents. Thank God they accepted me back in the house (Lupita).*

> *I was waiting for him to change, because people can change, but he has no will to stop insulting me. Now that my son is 22-years I thought about disappearing, I had planned to get out of there but the house is mine ... but for me it feels like a prison.*

The kind of assistance and instructions women received varied depending on the type of violence they reported and the institution they went to before and were asked to go to subsequently. For all these women, the attention path involved several institutions, each prescribing a different set of paperwork and procedures. Different information needed to be furnished, such as photographic documentation of bruises and physical harm when visible, physical and psychological evaluation, medical certifications and notarial deeds to secure preventive measures such as restraining orders, police surveillance, or to get an arrest warrant against the attacker or to receive police protection.

> *I filed the report that day with the police. The attention at the victim's unit was great and they did all the paperwork. I was in the hospital, where they took x-rays and I got out at 3:00 AM to go to the Public Prosecutor's Office. There I gave my depositions they took photographs of the injuries because my arm was badly hurt and after that they sent me to the National Institute of Forensic Sciences to get some tests and get photographs taken.*

Navigating the different legal and institutional requirements was complicated and time- and resource-consuming for women, who would often consult experts to figure out whether they should continue.

> *I was interested in getting preventive measures, I felt it was the only way to prevent him from entering the house because he was separated from me, he wanted to be with other women, but he also wanted to have access to the house. One time he even made a copy of the keys to the door and he would go in to go through my things. I gave the papers to a secretary and she told me they would call me. She only received the papers that the Public Prosecutor's Office had given me, I just kept the copies and I gave the other papers to her. I felt relieved because I thought I would soon get preventive measures and that's as far as the process would go. I knew that if he bothered me once I had gotten the preventive measures, it would be easier for the police to come and to detain him and take him away. I wasn't afraid anymore by that time.*

In some cases, protective measures were violated by the attackers and women often felt compelled to accept these violations out of fear of retribution.

> *[At the magistrate's court] they filled out a form and the papers said that he can no longer get close to us and cannot touch anything in the house, because he wanted to take everything and I told him no sir, you cannot take anything. I felt supported because it was the only way to get the fear to go away. They told him he was out of our lives, and if he ever came back, I should call them (the court). After that I never returned, later the judge told me 'we got your husband [out of the house] and now you have him back there'. But that's because he didn't want to leave and kept asking his children for help, he said he would just sleep there until he found a place to go, but then he just played dumb.*

Often the women had inadequate knowledge of their rights, which left them unsure about the fairness of the actions and decisions taken by the pertinent authorities. In such situations, trust in the institution became important in the women agreeing to share their ordeal with the institutional staff. For building this trust, they mostly relied on word of mouth from others who had previously used their services. Distrust often led to fear, as expressed by two women who believed that their cases would not get any attention at the Public Prosecutor's Office because of the power and resources their abusers had. Often cases were deliberately delayed, and the women did not have the energy and resources to pursue their cases. Some women expressed distrust towards the police because they felt they had failed to protect them when requested for help, by not showing up or coming too late. To build this trust, the women suggested the need to sensitize the staff to be sympathetic towards them and avoid revictimizing them in the process of providing help.

Designing the digital intervention

A first step in this process was to build acceptance of the institution to share the data collected by them on gender violence with the others. For this, the research team held joint partner workshops to get to know each other, their respective mandates towards VAW, and what data they were collecting. We started with smaller workshops with 5 partners each, and then extended it to 10 and finally with all partners together. We did eight such workshops, which had a key focus on 'data', to develop illustrative examples of data visualizations on cases of violence. Initially, the partners were very 'possessive' and 'protective' of their data and they insisted that the 'problem lies elsewhere'. However, with time, slowly the discourse started to change and there was growing agreement to share and discuss data.

Once there was an overall agreement on sharing data, we started approaching institutions to share monthly aggregated data they collected/recorded on gender violence for 2019 and 2020. Primary data was appropriately anonymized and aggregated. Through this process, we realized that some of the institutions did have the capacity to collect data but lacked the time and the technical capacities to systematize data collection and analysis. After receiving data from the institutions, we started building the unified database. Each institution used their own classification methods, including how they classified age-ranges, types of violence against women, and even how they registered the events geographically. While some institutions did not include information on the exact village where the violent act occurred, others captured that information. Initially we considered a detailed standardization of data, but on assessing the state of readiness of the partner institutions, we decided to only standardize the age and ethnic groups, and would do further standardization, including addressing the political and technical concerns around it, at a later point when ownership and data acceptance was more integral.

Building the digital intervention included the following steps: 1) designing the database and required analytics; 2) importing the data in the database and creating the required analytics and visualizations; and 3) enabling processes, such as partner workshops, for the institutions to look at each other's data and start conversations on how improved collective action strategies could be developed. Given the time frame of the project, while we could effectively do the first two steps, the third needed more time and effort, which the project did not have.

The digital platform required for building the application needed to be open-source and easy to use, to enable ordinary users to be able to comfortably use it. Further, there were two functional needs. First, it should serve as a 'data warehouse' which could collect data in different formats and periodicities into one unified database. Second, it should have the ability to develop attractive and easy to use data visualizations which could allow for effective conversations to take place between the different institutions who were sharing data into the system. Given these identified platform requirements, the research team selected the DHIS2, which was open-source, designed to serve as a data warehouse, and with a strong analytical engine to create attractive visualizations of maps, charts, graphs, and tables, which could be easily shared across the different partners. Furthermore, the research team, which was coordinated by the University of Oslo, Norway, had strong existing technical expertise from working with DHIS2, and were confident of building the required Guatemala application on it.

In creating the application, the first step was to define the organizations, the hierarchy of reporting in the system, what data would be compiled, and for what time period. Data was to be compiled for the following institutions who had agreed to share data in the municipalities of Sololá and Santa Rosa, which were the pilot sites for the research: 1) Attorney General's Office, Sololá; 2) Ministry of Health; 3) Ministry of Interior; 4) National Institute of Forensic Sciences; 5) National Police, Sololá; and 6) Presidential Secretariat for Women's Affairs. Aggregate data from these institutions was made available for the years 2016, 2017, 2018, 2019 (January to July). The administrative hierarchy for supporting data flows was Nation level, Department, Municipalities, Towns/Villages, Communities.

To our surprise, institutions willingly shared data from 2016 onwards, which allowed the creation of a database with all this data which could be presented in different forms of visualization in graphs and charts and shared across partners. The legacy data shared by the institutions had different types of disaggregation for age groups and ethnicities. For example, the National Institute of Forensic Sciences captured data for cause of death and place where the corpse was found while similar information was not captured by other institutes. Similarly, the Presidential Secretariat for Women's Affairs captured data for violence based on gender for both men and women unlike other institutes. Given these variations in disaggregation, separate data entry screens were designed to capture data from particular institutions, as shown in Figure 9.2.

The Ministry of Interior captured data on VAW based on different typologies including Homicides, Injuries, Thefts, Crimes against Property, and so on, with different disaggregation (Table 9.2). An example of the raw data shared, and the corresponding data entry screens is shown in Figure 9.3.

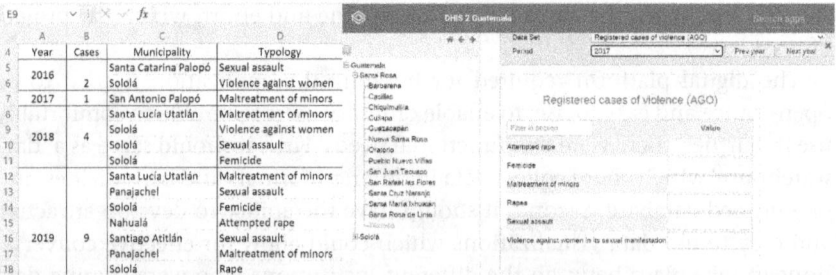

Figure 9.2 Data from attorney general's office and corresponding data entry screen in DHIS2

Table 9.2 Data captured by Ministry of Interior

Crimes committed against women registered in the department of Santa Rosa, during the year, disaggregated by municipality and typology

Crimes	Cuilapa	Barberena	Santa Rosa de Lima	Casillas	San Rafael las Flores	Oratorio	San Juan Tecuaco	Chiquimulilla	Taxisco	Ixhuatan	Guazacapan	Santa Cruz Naranjo	Pueblo Nuevo Viñas	Nueva Santa Rosa	Total
Homicide by															
Firearms	2	0	2	0	0	0	1	2	1	1	1	0	1	1	12
Bladed weapons	0	0	0	0	1	0	0	0	1	0	0	0	0	1	3
Blunt weapons	1	0	0	1	0	0	0	0	0	0	0	0	0	0	2
Explosive artifacts	0	0	0	0	0	0	0	0	0	0	0	0	0	0	0
Strangulation	0	0	0	0	0	0	0	1	0	0	0	0	0	0	1
Lynching	0	0	0	0	0	0	0	0	0	0	0	0	0	0	0
Total	3	0	2	1	1	0	1	3	2	1	1	0	1	2	18
Injured by															
Firearms	3	2	0	0	0	0	0	1	0	0	0	0	4	0	10
Bladed weapons	1	0	0	0	0	0	0	3	1	0	0	0	1	0	6
Blunt weapons	2	0	0	0	1	0	0	0	0	0	0	0	0	0	3
Explosive artifacts	0	0	0	0	0	0	0	0	0	0	0	0	0	0	0
Lynching	0	0	0	0	0	0	0	0	0	0	0	0	0	0	0
Total	6	2	0	0	1	0	0	4	1	0	0	0	5	0	19
Against property															
Burglaries of residences	1	2	1	0	0	0	0	0	0	0	0	2	0	0	6
Burglaries of businesses	0	0	0	0	0	0	0	0	0	0	0	0	1	0	1
Car theft	1	0	2	0	0	0	0	0	0	0	0	0	0	0	3
Motorcycle theft	3	5	1	0	0	0	0	1	0	0	0	0	0	1	11
Robbery of firearms	0	0	2	0	0	0	0	0	0	0	0	0	0	0	2
Robbery against foreigners	0	0	0	0	0	0	0	0	0	0	0	0	0	0	0
Personal robbery	1	4	1	0	1	2	0	2	1	0	1	0	3	1	17

DHIS 2 Pivot Tables

About Home

Table · Chart · «

>>> Update · Favorites · Layout · Options · Download · Embed ·

Typology of crimes committed against women

Period	2016		2017		2018		2019		Total
Data / Organisation unit	Santa Rosa	Sololá	Santa Rosa	Sololá	Santa Rosa	Sololá	Santa Rosa	Sololá	Total
Aggression por otros medios especificados, in unspecified place				1					1
Assault by bodily force	1	3	1						5
Assault by bodily force, in dwelling					1	7		7	15
Assault by bodily force, in other specified place					1	2			3
Assault by bodily force, in trade and service area								3	3
Assault by bodily force, in unspecified place		1				8	1		10
Assault by bodily force, on streets and highways						9		6	15
Assault by crashing motor vehicle, on streets and highways	1	1	1		1	6			10
Assault by crashing of motor vehicle, in unspecified place							1		1
Assault by drowning and submersion			2						2
Assault by drugs, medicaments and biological substances, in unspecified place							1	4	5
Assault by handgun discharge	1								1
Assault by other and unspecified firearm and gun discharge	4		8		3				15
Assault by other and unspecified firearm and gun discharge, in dwelling			9		6			1	16
Assault by other and unspecified firearm and gun discharge, in sports and athletics areas			1						1

Figure 9.3 Dashboard with analysed data

Table 9.3 Number of cases of violence against women in Santa Rosa by year

2016	2017	2018	2019
212	343	514	759

Source: Own elaboration with data from the Ministry of Health

Table 9.4 Crimes committed against women in 2016 by age group

Age group	<1 y	1–4 y	5–9 y	10–14 y	15–19 y	20–24 y	25–29 y	30–39 y	40–49 y	50–59 y	60–69 y	70+ y	Total
Number	4	7	24	80	40	22	7	9	7	6	3	3	212
Percentage	1.9	3.3	11.3	37.7	18.9	10.4	3.3	4.3	3.3	2.8	1.4	1.4	100

Source: Own elaboration with data from the Ministry of Health

Given the diversity of data shared from the different institutions, a standardization of age and ethnic groups was done by using similar category types. Indicators were then designed based on the standardized disaggregation groups to compare data across institutions. Designing for interoperability to enable data sharing across systems, is indeed a fundamental challenge to be addressed when building such multi-institutional databases. This integration will typically be done by electronically importing data (such as through Application Programming Interfaces) across systems. However, this was not possible in this case because the individual systems were not digitally mature and also there was no agreement between the institutions on what data should be shared and unified, and neither were there agreed data standards. Data was received from six different institutes across two municipal authorities (Sololá and Santa Rosa), each collecting different variables which disaggregated in varying ways for age and ethnic groups and had different logics of collection and aggregation. For example, the National Institute of Forensic Sciences captured data for cause of death and place where the corpse was found while this information was not captured by other institutes. Similarly, the Presidential Secretariat for Women's Affairs captured data for violence based on gender for both men and women, while others only captured violence against women. To address these variations, we designed individual data entry screens for the different institutes, so that in the first place all data could be compiled, this could then be shared and compared contributing to create a dialogue among the institutions on how data could be standardized and shared for building unified action.

Some consolidated analysis could now be developed, as shown in Table 9.3. Table 9.4 shows disaggregation by age of the victims.

Seeing this consolidated data, some basic analysis could be undertaken. For example, over one-third (37.7 per cent) of the cases registered by the Ministry of Health during 2016 were crimes committed against girls between the ages of 10 and 14 years, followed by girls aged 15 to 19 years (18.9 per cent). Other significantly affected age groups were 5–9 years (11.3 per cent), 20–24 years (10.4 per cent). Overall, 78.3 per cent of documented crimes against women were against underage girls and young women.

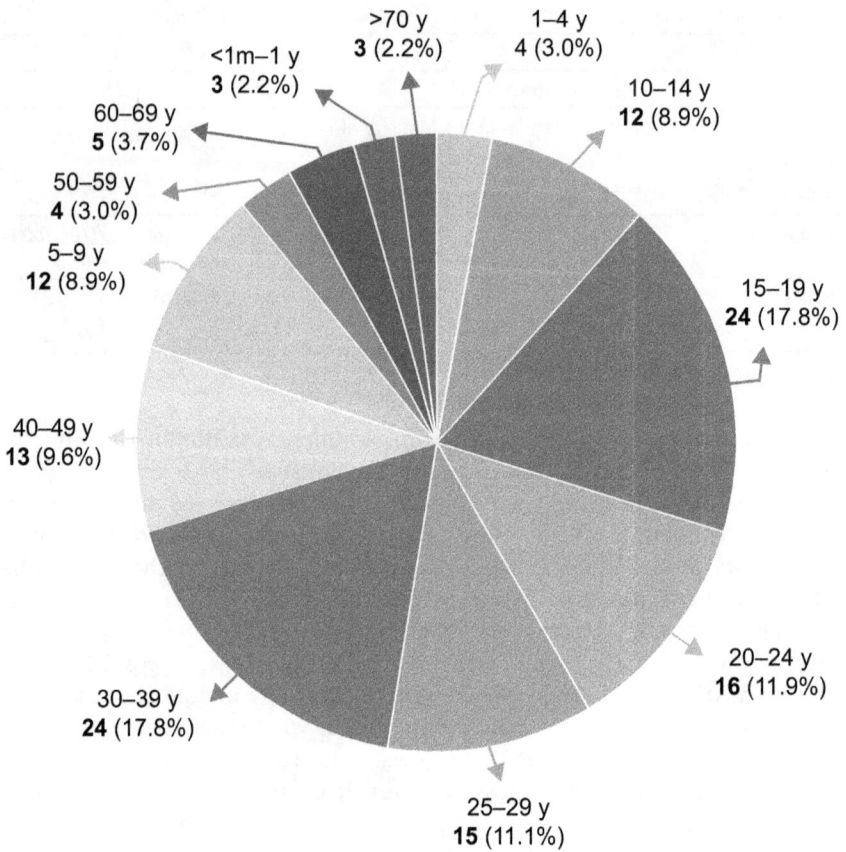

Figure 9.4 Crimes committed against women in 2017 by age group
Source: Own elaboration with data from the Ministry of Health

In 2017, the age groups most affected by VAW in Santa Rosa continued to be girls aged 10–14 years (24.8 per cent) and 15–19 years (27.4 per cent) (Figures 9.4, 9.5 and 9.6). This reflected an increase from the 2016 figures.

According to data collected (2016–2019) by the National Institute of Forensic Sciences, it was seen that the highest number of medical examinations performed due to sexual crimes was consistently on girls in the 10–14 and 15–19 age groups and was also high for 5 to 9 years in 2016 and 2018. This makes girls between 5 and 19 years old the group most subjected to medical examinations. The institutional participation in the data sharing workshops exponentially increased as we started sharing data visualizations of the combined institutional data and many new requests started to come from institutions for different types of visualizations.

The map in Figure 9.7 compares the percentage of cases of crimes against women reported for each municipality that were classified as intra-family

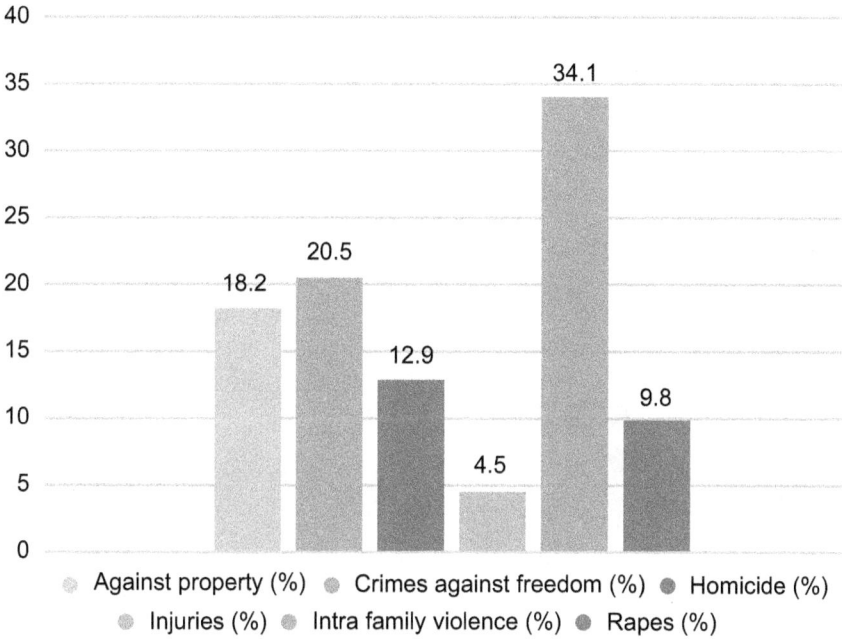

Figure 9.5 Crimes against women in 2018 by type
Source: Own elaboration with data provided by the Ministry of the Interior

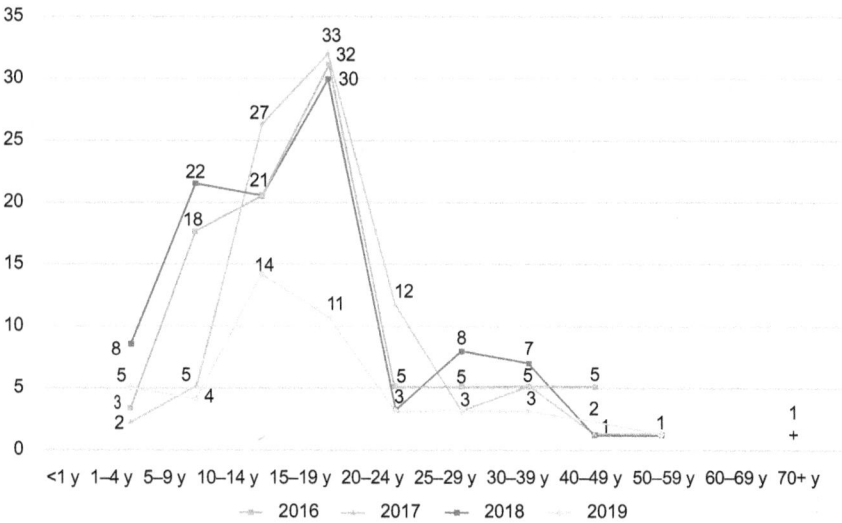

Figure 9.6 Medical examinations due to sexual crimes by age group and year
Source: Own elaboration with data from the National Institute of Forensic Sciences

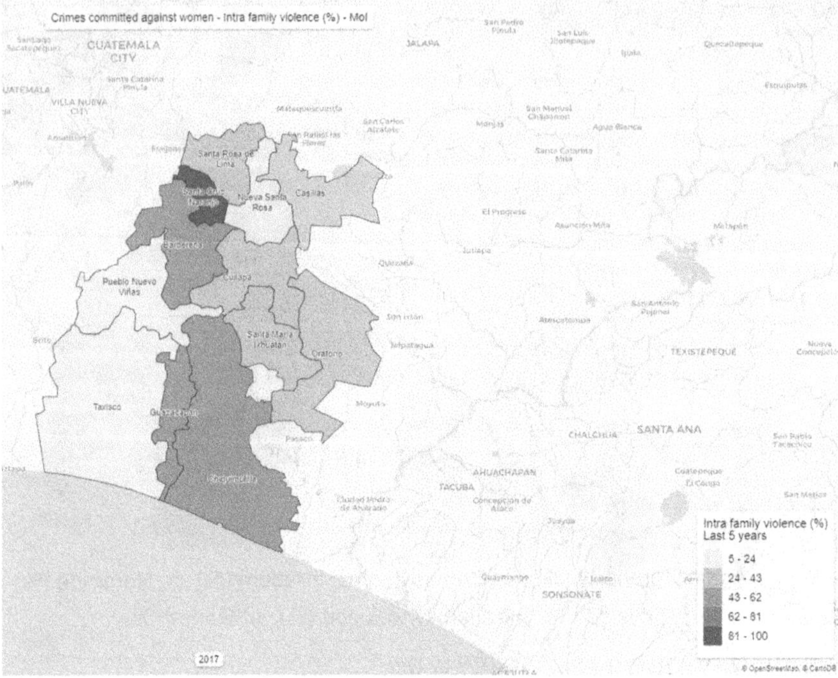

Figure 9.7 Intra-family violence rates in 2018 by municipality
Source: Own elaboration with data provided by the Ministry of the Interior

violence in 2018. The municipalities with the highest rates for that year were Guazacapán (69.2 per cent), Santa María Ixhuatán (66.7 per cent), and Casillas (66.7 per cent). Half of the cases of crimes against women registered in Chiquimulilla were identified as intra-family violence, which was also true for 45.5 per cent of cases in Santa Rosa de Lima, and one-third of cases in Pueblo Nuevo Viñas and Oratorio. In contrast, no cases of intra-family violence were registered for other municipalities, such as San Rafael Las Flores and San Juan Tecuaco. Such visualizations facilitated identification of municipalities in which there were higher rates of different types of violence, which was useful for institutions to plan for focused interventions (see for example Figure 9.8).

As institutional participation in data visualization workshops increased, there was greater discussion on the underlying social and institutional reasons contributing to this violence and how institutions could do better in addressing these issues. However, to institutionalize these processes of data sharing, generating outputs, and having discussions is a longer process than was available to us in the time frame of the project. However, arguably, an approach and methodology was created through the project on how spaces for inter-institutional conversations could be created.

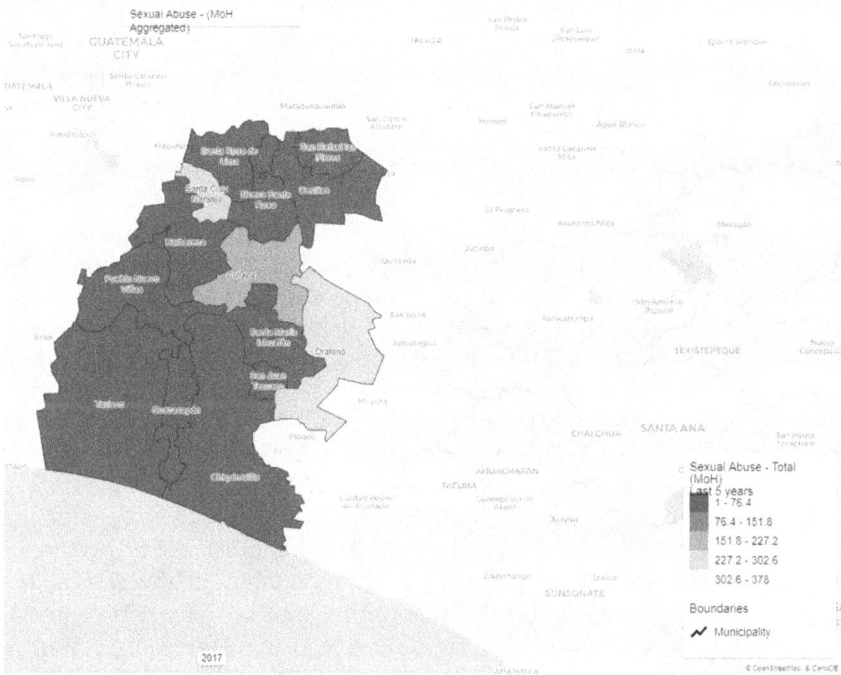

Figure 9.8 Mapping sites of violence

The role of information in creating hope

Johan Galtung, an eminent sociologist and credited with being the principal founder of the academic discipline of peace and conflict studies, has conceptually described violence and how it can be mitigated. He writes, the notion of peace is indisputable in policy initiatives, such as related to trade, health, tourism, and others, because it helps to project an image of harmony of interests. Discussing efforts for peace sounds more positive than expressions of violence and conflict. Since peace can be understood as the 'absence of violence', so, it becomes crucial to first understand violence. Galtung (1969) describes violence as being 'present when human beings are being influenced so that their actual physical and mental realizations are below their potential realizations'.

Violence then refers to the cause of the *difference* between the potential and actual, between *what could have been* and *what is*. The greater the difference between the *potential* and *the actual*, we can infer the greater the violence. Galtung gives the example that if a person died from tuberculosis in the 18th century it would be hard to conceive of this as violence since it might have been quite unavoidable, but if a person dies from it today, despite all the medical resources in the world, then violence is present. Similarly, a very low life expectancy (say of 30 years) would not reflect an expression of violence 300 years ago, but today it would be so. In the current context of the COVID-19 pandemic, if poor countries are deprived of vaccination shots because the richer countries are hoarding them, it would be seen as an act of violence.

According to this understanding, when the actual is unavoidable, then violence is not present even if the actual is at a very low level. However, when the actual is avoidable but not achieved due to different conditions, then it can be seen as the presence of violence. When knowledge or resources are mobilized by a group or class of people and used for other purposes which lead to the actual falling below the potential for certain groups, then violence is present in the system against those certain groups. However, while it may be relatively easy to understand achievement against physical targets (such as percentage of the population who have had a vaccination), it is far more complex to understand violence relating to mental trauma and stress.

In acts of violence, there will always be an *influencer* (who is inflicting violence), an *influence* (the object of violence), and a *mode of influencing* (the mechanism for inflicting violence). For example, in the case of the COVID-19 vaccination, the influencer can be seen as some rich countries that are hoarding the vaccines, the influence is the developing countries deprived of the vaccines, and the mode of influencing is hoarding, implying that countries use their resources to buy out the vaccine stocks. A person can be influenced not only by punishing them when they do what the influencer considers wrong, but also by rewarding them when they do what the influencer considers right.

Violence does not always involve someone doing overt and visible harm to another. Violence can be systemic and built into social and institutional structures creating unequal power relations with adverse consequences for certain groups. For example, the caste system in India ensures that resources are unevenly distributed, income distributions are heavily skewed, literacy levels are unevenly distributed, and medical services vary with geographical areas and population groups. The situation is aggravated further if the persons low on income are also low in education and health, which marginalize them further due to the magnified power asymmetries. This represents violence without a direct subject–object relationship and is built into structure, creating *social injustice*.

Personal violence will always be manifest to the person who experiences it. In contrast, structural violence is silent, it does not show, and is essentially static with a certain stability. While personal violence, which to a larger extent is seen as subject to the whims and wishes of individuals, should show less stability and will be more easily noticed. When there is bias built into the system for deciding guilt, this represents violence since the concept of guilt is tied more to intention, than to consequence. While ethical systems are directed against *intended* or manifest violence, they fail to capture structural or latent violence, which is not visible, yet might easily come about, when a certain event can act as a trigger for other and bigger acts of violence. This indicates a state of unstable *equilibrium*.

Peace could be understood as the 'absence of violence' and 'social injustice' representing constraints and restrictions to a person or system from achieving its potential. These constraints can act through both personal and structural mechanisms, which can be interrelated: for example, a person engaging in personal violence legitimizes it using expectations from the structure as an excuse. Illustrations of such violence include the caste system in India, racism, poverty, and country-based sanctions from rich countries imposed on Cuba and Iran.

Our case firstly helps us to understand the diversity in the acts of violence being experienced by women, particularly indigenous women, in Guatemala. The acts of violence come in different forms such as physical harm, sexual abuse, economic and social stigma, and various others. These acts of violence are both personal and structural with a variety of adverse consequences. Personal violence comes from the physical harm inflicted by the men in the house towards their spouses and children. However, there is a high degree of latent violence which also provides an enabling environment for personal violence to take place. For example, why do women wait for many years before they decide to report the acts of violence which they have been experiencing? They fear retribution from their attackers if they go public and also do not trust the institutions in place to provide them with justice. This existing fear and mistrust, which helps silence the women and provides confidence to the abusers that they can continue their acts of violence with impunity, represents a form of structural violence. The adverse consequences of these acts of violence are particularly experienced by indigenous women who tend to be economically and socially marginalized in the first place. This marginalization is heightened by the systematic acts of violence they experience, mostly silently, which severely limit them in reaching their social, economic, and cultural potential.

Given this complex situation of VAW, our project explored the question of what role (if any) can ICTs play in mitigating such violence. If violence is conceived when human beings are constrained from achieving or actualizing their potential, then can the role of ICTs be understood in terms of how it can help bridge the gap between the potential and the actual so as to help the victims of VAW to better achieve their potential? Or does it further expand the gap? For example, digital health comes with the potential of enhancing equity for people in accessing health services, but if they do not have access and capabilities to use the digital health tool, they may be further marginalized from accessing health services. The digital platform then can become a source of expanding violence. To mitigate this violence, the ICT needs to be 'sensitively' managed in terms of governance, infrastructure, capacity, and design. Whether ICTs can mitigate or expand violence, remains an empirical question.

Given this conceptualization of how to understand violence and approaches to its mitigation, our case demonstrates the role that ICTs can play in enabling conversations between different institutions involved in supporting efforts to mitigate violence against women. These different institutions, because of their varying mandates, capture both similar and different data on incidents of violence, but almost never share it with other institutions. Since these institutions do not share data among themselves, they lack a shared understanding of the problem, which impedes holistic and collective action, so urgently required in mitigating a problem with large-scale societal consequences. From the perspective of the victims of violence, this lack of institutional coordination means they have to traverse a long, difficult, expensive, and often traumatic path in reaching different institutions, as depicted through our attention path schematics. This expensive and time-consuming process constrains them from seeking justice, which contributes to silence on acts of violence, giving the perpetrators of violence the confidence that they will go scot-free.

Our project then was a very initial exercise of, firstly, making inter-institutional data visible and, secondly, providing a digital forum where these institutions can start to collectively look at the data and build a better shared understanding of the problem. Given the short time frame of the project (about 15 months), we did not have the opportunity to see how this shared understanding may lead to better coordinated institutional action and more solace and comfort for the victims of VAW. From Galtung's conceptual perspective, we can see digitally enabled information visibility and sharing can serve as tools to reduce the adverse effects of violence, by strengthening the agency of women to make visible to institutions their quest for justice, and for institutions to better respond through more coordinated collective action. Getting better justice would help the sufferers of VAW to achieve their potential, and in Galtung's conceptualization, to a reduction of violence and more peace and hope.

Acknowledgements

The authors sincerely and deeply acknowledge the insightful primary empirical work carried out by two anthropologists, Sophia Gabriella Dávila Díaz and Lucía Inés Jiménez Palmieri, based in Guatemala. We also acknowledge support of the EU Horizon 2020 project on 'ICTs for Community Oriented Policing in Post-Conflict Countries', which included Kenya. Arunima Mukherjee was the Technology Work Package leader on this project.

References

Avis, W.R. (2017) Digital tools and changing behaviour in relation to violence against women [online], Helpdesk Research Report <https://gsdrc.org/wp-content/uploads/2017/09/GSDRC-HDR-Digital-Tools-and-Behaviour-Change1.pdf> [accessed 11 March 2022].

Cummings, C. and O'Neil, T. (2015) *Do Digital Information and Communications Technologies Increase the Voice and Influence of Women and Girls? A Rapid Review of the Evidence*, Overseas Development Institute <https://odi.org/en/publications/do-digital-information-and-communications-technologies-increase-the-voice-and-influence-of-women-and-girls/> [accessed 11 March 2022].

Galtung, J. (1969) 'Violence, peace, and peace research', *Journal of Peace Research* 6(3): 167–91.

Gurumurthy, A. (2004) *Gender and ICTs: An Overview Report* [online], Bridge Development–Gender Institute of Development Studies <https://www.researchgate.net/publication/297737202_Gender_and_ICTs_Overview_Report> [accessed 11 March 2022].

National Statistics Institute, Guatemala (2006) GHDx [online] <http://ghdx.healthdata.org/organizations/national-statistics-institute-guatemala> [accessed 11 March 2022].

Oxfam (2015) 'Ten harmful beliefs that perpetuate violence against women and girls' [online] <https://www.oxfam.org/en/ten-harmful-beliefs-perpetuate-violence-against-women-and-girls> [accessed 25 January 2022].

United Nations General Assembly (1993) *Declaration on the Elimination of Violence against Women*, UN General Assembly.

United Nations Human Rights Office of the High Commissioner (no date) *Convention on the Elimination of All Forms of Discrimination against Women New York, 18 December 1979* [online] <https://www.ohchr.org/en/professional interest/pages/cedaw.aspx> [accessed 25 January 2022].

UN Women (1995) *Beijing Declaration and Platform for Action, Beijing+ 5 Political Declaration and Outcome* [online] <https://www.unwomen.org/en/digital-library/publications/2015/01/beijing-declaration> [accessed 11 March 2022].

UN Women (2014) *UNDP Human Development Report 2014: Sustaining Human Progress: Reducing Vulnerabilities and Building Resilience* [online] <https://www.unwomen.org/en/docs/2014/1/undp-human-development-report-2014#:~:text=The%202014%20Human%20Development%20Report,human%2Dinduced%20disasters%20and%20crises> [accessed 11 March 2022].

CHAPTER 10

Implications for theory, policy, and practice

Sundeep Sahay, Geoff Walsham, Thomas Hylland Eriksen, and Arunima Mukherjee

Building a synthesis across cases

In this book, we have presented eight case studies drawn from different domains of social development, including related to public health, pandemic management, refugees, mobile money, ethnic conflicts, and violence against women. These cases have been drawn from different geographical settings representing low-resource contexts. They include states in India, Kenya, Guatemala, Sri Lanka, and, with global implications, two smartphone-related cases. The cases also highlight the role of different kinds of digital interventions, including for health management information systems, hospital information systems, pandemic management systems, early warning and response systems, dashboards for facilitating inter-institutional dialogues, and smartphones that facilitate mobile money and host maps that support refugees. There is a rich diversity of cases, technologies, and social issues.

The cases have each been presented drawing upon a macro level means–process–ends framework that provides the basis for developing a cross-case synthesis. This framework is grounded in socio-technical thinking that represents an ontology of conceptualizing the phenomenon under study. It provides for a holistic approach to analysis that focuses on the interrelation of the constituent parts of the system, and how they each work over time and within the context of the larger system. Systems thinking provides a theoretical apparatus for conducting a holistic and systemic analysis that is necessary for engaging with the world's complex social problems. The COVID-19 pandemic is a case in point. It is not a health problem alone, but has interconnected economic, social, cultural, and travel-related consequences. These relationships are never static, but are continuously evolving and changing, as demonstrated by the speed at which the virus is mutating, creating unexpected consequences. In trying to understand these interconnections across time and space, we can analyse the sources of these unintended consequences.

Further, our analytical approach seeks to link the macro framework with micro concepts. Means–process–ends is by design a macro framework. It helps sensitize the researcher to the broad issues of importance. Each case is different. It varies with the context in which it unfolds, the particular social challenge being addressed, the digital interventions being attempted, and the available infrastructure and resources at hand. In order to understand how they interact in specific contexts, there is a need for more micro-level theoretical concepts that can be related to the macro framework. In this way, while acknowledging a certain broad pattern of how social problems play out, we also emphasize that the dynamics are situationally shaped and require more specific theoretical concepts. We seek to theoretically advance ICT4D research by explicitly focusing on the phenomenon in question while acknowledging the macro-level institutional context. From the information systems perspective, it reflects the 'situated practice' lens in terms of interpreting ICT4D interventions and how the actions of individuals and communities leads to incremental change and hope. The 'D' in ICT4D research is often positioned as a game changer through juxtaposing macro-narratives of ICT4D projects as game changers against prevailing deep-rooted development challenges. We emphasize the important and often understated claim that we should not lose sight of *locally grounded theories of change* reflected through middle-range concepts that help connect the macro and the micro. A significant qualifier, as emphasized in the long time horizon on nearly all the empirical cases, is that ICT4D initiatives blossom over extended periods. A long time horizon never only implicates ICT initiatives and from a policy and practice perspective, raising the real challenge of knowing when to foreground the technology and when not to.

While adopting the macro framework for analysis, the cases in this book are linked with micro-level contexts such as empowerment, agility, counter networks, and trust. Another important element in our analysis is the understanding of the specific materiality afforded by the digital intervention, and how it mediates the means–process–ends relationship. This analytical focus helps in unpacking the black box of technology, and understanding its role, both good and bad, in shaping social processes and consequences. This allows for the possibility of using more diverse and multidisciplinary theoretical approaches to study social phenomena and how they are mediated through digital interventions. A common 'ends' that the chapters seek to understand is that of hope, and what manner of means and processes can help reach it more meaningfully. The various cases provide combinations of means and processes that help generate narratives of hope, such as related to empowerment, violence mitigation, collective action to engage with violence against women, and increasing the trust of public health systems.

Case studies seen through the means–process–ends framework

Chapter 2 is concerned with the Mother and Child Tracking System (MCTS) in India. The context is the relatively poor mother and child health indicators India is facing, and the faith placed in digital interventions to bring in improvements. The means are conceptualized as pan-India digital intervention through the MCTS system. The process concerns the tactics and approaches adopted by the state to implement the MCTS, such as building digital capacities, providing the required infrastructure, and, most importantly, building the buy-in of the health staff to adopt the MCTS. The desired ends of the MCTS was improved maternal and child health indicators. The specific materiality of the MCTS, as a web-based deployment, helped achieve data coverage on the national scale. The MCTS was designed to collect personal data of pregnant woman and children for immunization, which, coupled with web-based deployment, allowed for the creation of individual-level data in centralized databases. This centralization enabled the strengthening of the gaze of the central authorities on the everyday work of health workers. While the MCTS in its existing form can be seen as a failure, we identify unintended consequences in terms of invisible learning and empowerment of the health workers – the micro concepts in our analysis. Furthermore, the initiative helped establish a national level digital infrastructure that would be leveraged for future digital efforts. The extended temporal scope of the analysis helped us discern this story of hope.

Chapter 3 is an analysis of how smartphones are used by refugees as they are displaced across time and space. The context of this displacement is conflict and strife in their home countries. The dangerous methods of their escape take them to unknown and often unwelcoming lands. The means in this case is the smartphones they carry during their displacement. The process is how refugees use their phones for both personal purposes, such as accessing photographs from their past, and to support them in their engagement with the authorities where they seek refuge, such as accessing relevant information and filling forms. The desired ends in this case concerns providing refugees with a sense of connectedness and identity with their social and official worlds during the complex process of displacement. An important materiality of the smartphone is that, being mobile and stored in the pocket or bag of the refugee, it also makes the journey along with its owner. Furthermore, the smartphone, with its multifaceted features – storing images, voice transmission, and ability to communicate across different media – helps provide refugees with a museum of memories that keeps them connected with their past and their homeland while also enabling avenues for future opportunities.

Chapter 4 concerns building the digital response to the COVID-19 pandemic in Sri Lanka. The context is the strong public health and education systems in the country and its long-term investments in strengthening the digital capacities of medical doctors working in the health ministry. The robust public health system and its strong health informatics capacity were leveraged during the pandemic to develop various new modules and functionalities to both maintain the existing systems and respond to the new informational needs. An important means to building the response was the use of the DHIS2 digital platform on which the country had extensive prior experience, and which was malleable enough to respond to the different information needs of the pandemic. This ability to both 'bounce back' and 'bounce forward' signified the resilience of the digital and health systems, which was a desired end. Two conditions contributed to the process of translating the means to the desired ends: one was agility in governance, systems design, and development that allowed the means to be rapidly processed, which led to improved policy support; and the second was the platform features of the DHIS2, which allowed for agility in systems development, as nothing was needed to be built from scratch. Agility and platform features helped us to understand how resilience could be developed and applied.

Chapter 5 is the case of a state in India seeking to build, deploy, and sustain its health management information system (HMIS) for more than a decade. The state, which is resource-constrained and has a high proportion of tribal population, has taken progressive steps to strengthen its health systems. The means in this case is the use of a flexible, open-source digital platform (the DHIS2) to build its HMIS. The affordances provided by the DHIS2 made it easily state-owned and malleable enough to meet state-specific information requirements while simultaneously complying with the national demands of reporting. Supporting the actualization of the potential offered by the DHIS2 were consistent processes of governance, through which the state made long-term investments in stabilizing the DHIS2. The state shaped the processes of data quality improvements, which combined existing practices, such as relating to the responsibilities of the validation committees, with the new capabilities offered by DHIS2, such as identifying data quality errors. This hybrid approach mitigated the health staff's perception that they were dealing with something completely new and alien. The state developed the desired ends of sustainability qualifiers for the HMIS, which was deeply rooted in the health system and was simultaneously capable of evolving with changing needs. This capability would give the state the confidence to use digital technologies to improve the delivery of health services.

Chapter 6 studies the design, development, implementation, and evolution of an integrated hospital information system within a network of secondary and tertiary hospitals in the northern Indian state of Himachal Pradesh. It is a progressive state that has, over time, developed a strong public health system supported by innovative digital interventions. The key means in this case is an integrated, open-source-based hospital information system scaled across all state public hospitals. The processes involved include a decentralized approach in which individual hospitals have an important say in defining the vision of the system, and the enrolment of a strong technical partner comprising local actors who built strong relationships of trust with the state. The materiality afforded by the OpenMRS platform was easy customizability that evolved through competent users without the need for specialist programmers. The digital interventions contributed to the ends of building the citizens' trust in the hospital systems by providing them with superior patient experience, better documentation of their health encounters, and a forum to voice their suggestions and concerns. Improved citizens' trust is an incentive to states to continuously strengthen the public health systems.

Chapter 7 documented the everyday experiences of people in their use of the smartphone for various aspects of their social, cultural, and economic activities. What we focus on is how new apps are continuously produced and fit into the smartphone ecosystem, and how they become part of everyday use. The materiality offered by the smartphone is primarily concerned with ownership, leaving individuals the choice on what apps to use and for what purposes. In the form of a smartphone, the digital becomes integral to the lives of citizens, and enables new choices on how they want to live. In the event, some previously existing choices are closed off. While the positive ends achieved vary from person to person, they include more economic activity, opportunities for dating and marriage, transfer of money, and opportunities in the informal economy.

Chapter 8 is a study of the creation and evolution of an ICT-enabled peace network in Kenya. The context is the historically existing conditions of ethnic violence, and the efforts of a faith-based organization to mitigate them. A key resource is the use of a digital intervention, an Early Warning and Emergency Response System (EWERS). The constituent parts of this peace network include: 1) the peace monitors who draw upon the EWERS to provide inputs in the form of SMSs that warn of potential or ongoing acts of violence (the inputs or the means); 2) messages that come to the control unit, where they are processed to verify authenticity and then distributed to different responders who are expected to take action to diffuse the violence (the throughput or process); and 3) actions taken, which could be in the form of police action or mediation meetings that, hopefully, reduce the ethnic violence (the outputs or the ends). The role of the digital is fundamental. EWERS, for example, provides anonymity to the peace monitors, which encourages them to provide their inputs with confidence and without fear. Further, the control unit, an infrastructure of computers, servers, and networks, allows for the same message to be transmitted to different responders – for example a police officer and his or her superior. This visibility of information helps create accountability and transparency, providing an impetus to prompt and timely action. The ends achieved through the peace networks are reduced violence and the development of a model of digital intervention that can be scaled to other regions that are also experiencing ethnic violence.

Chapter 9 describes efforts towards mitigating violence against women (VAW) in Guatemala. VAW is a long-standing problem in the country. While various state institutions are involved in the fight against this violence, their efforts are fragmented. Consequently, victims of violence rarely trust the system to provide them the necessary relief. The DHIS2 has been employed as a central repository for various institutions to share the data they are collecting on the topic. The aim was to enable these institutions to view one another's data, presented in easy to comprehend charts and graphs, and help open up spaces for conversations that could provide the basis for unified action.

In each of the cases, a key argument is that the digital is becoming an integral component of complex social systems, and its materiality (for example, providing anonymity or simultaneity in the transmission of messages in Kenya) influences the relations between the system components, leading to new types of behaviour. By influencing these relationships in a positive manner, the digital contributes to desirable outcomes that we refer to as 'stories of hope'. This theoretical apparatus of means–process–ends also has implications for policy and practice.

Implications for theory, policy, and practice

The book has implications for scholars from the field of ICT4D, information systems scholars, given the increasing special issues and panels devoted to LMIC interventions, as well as for students from media and communications and social policy/anthropology. Policymakers undertaking reforms using ICT will find relevant implications, for example, health officials at state and sub-state levels will find it useful to learn about how earlier interventions have played out on the ground. At the same time, as tech start-ups and hubs in LMICs pilot new applications to address local priorities, they may find the narratives useful in terms of showcasing the 'twists and turns' in technology adoption and evolution. We discuss three themes as implications.

Designing with frugality in mind. Designing with frugality in mind is a theoretical implication evident across the cases. The underlying principles of frugality are about 'doing more with less' and 'build once and use multiple times'. It has also been pointed out that frugal innovations are not only about the technological artefacts but require the technology, the institution, and the social to intersect with each other (Bhatti, 2014). Frugal innovation combines characteristics of affordability, accessibility, simplicity, sustainability, quality, and purpose. Bhatti et al. (2018) write that 'to solve the wicked problems confronting humanity and the planet, we need frugal innovators – wise problem solvers who operate with a business mind, social heart and ecological soul'. The notion of frugality plays out as an underlying principle in all aspects of the means–process–ends framework.

The use of free and open-source digital platforms is a common theme across the cases presented in this book. The DHIS2 platform was used in Sri Lanka, Odisha, Kenya, and Guatemala, and the OpenMRS platform was used for the Himachal Pradesh hospital system. The materiality of these platforms in terms of being available without licensing restrictions, and their ability to be customized and configured in an agile manner for a variety of cases (such as health management, pandemic response, and early warning for peace), without high levels of programming expertise, makes them a solid base on which to develop digital innovations frugally. More importantly, these systems, which can largely be managed and sustained by the user organization (in our case the state) itself, with minimal external technical support, helps to make the effort more sustainable and scalable. These characteristics of being low cost, self-managed, sustainable, and scalable are crucial to the promoting of social development in LMICs.

Frugality has to be designed. The pandemic response information system initially built in and for Sri Lanka was subsequently made more generic by the core Oslo team, which enabled its adoption in more than 40 countries, including in Norway itself. While fulfilling the frugal design principle of building once and using multiple times, the digital platform also provides the basis for creating reverse innovations that are built in an LMIC setting and exported to richer countries in the West. This process challenges traditional technology transfer models where knowledge is assumed to be generated in the North and diffused to the South, which is positioned as a passive recipient of knowledge. Another important feature of these digital platforms is their ability to promote collective action based on mutuality and reciprocity. Developers and users work together, even as they are distributed in time and space, on the same digital platform to build apps. They, too, have a stake in using an app under development, and share pride in their achievements with the global community.

The theory of designing for frugality has definite implications for both policy and practice. Making the use of free and open-source platforms mandatory to build public systems, as countries such as India and Brazil have done, is important. Releasing these systems as global public goods, making them non-rivalrous and non-exclusive, is another policy implication. Various practices need to be enabled to ensure the full value of these policy steps. For instance, governments need to modify their procurement practices, which tend to traditionally support proprietary and licensed systems. Often, there are inadequate incentives and not strong enough disincentives to ensure effective implementation of these policy directions. These need to be designed and gradually deployed and reinforced through everyday use.

Barking up the wrong tree. The history of ICT4D projects is replete with stories of new technologies coming in with renewed promises of addressing institutional and social challenges. In the 1980s, the technologies under discussion were desktop computers, web-based systems, and mobile technologies, stretching to the current discussions around artificial intelligence and machine learning. Unfortunately, the focus is limited to the technology, and the institutional challenges that need to be addressed fade into the background. A case in point are contemporary discussions around digital transformations, where the digital is expected to bring about transformation. As our cases have emphasized, focusing primarily on technology is akin to barking up the wrong tree.

The means–process–ends framework emphasizes that we need much more than the digital to create positive outcomes. In most cases, the digital is a necessary condition for bringing about relevant change, but it is surely not sufficient. Our cases have highlighted various other means and elements of the process that need to be mobilized. For example, in Sri Lanka, while the DHIS2 was a very important means, it was successful because it was situated in a country where the government had prioritized public health and education, and there were ongoing processes of building health informatics in the country.

Take the case of the ICT-enabled peace network in Kenya, where the EWERS played a crucial role in enabling coordinated action between different stakeholder groups in the network. A precondition for the digital to be relevant was the prior existence of the peace network, which comprised stakeholders (peace monitors and responders, among others) who, being victims of violence, were innately motivated to engage in violence mitigation efforts. Without this social setting, and minus review meetings, consultations, counselling, and discussions in public forums, the digital would have had minimal effect.

Thus, it is theoretically important to understand the role of technology within the broader means–process–ends framework, and how it can be best deployed to bring about positive social outcomes. For example, to mitigate the fear the peace monitors felt in transmitting messages of potential or ongoing violence, they needed to be anonymized. This was achieved using the SMS technology and in the manner of its transmission and processing. The temptation to use the novel features of the mobile phone to send videos and voice messages would have compromised anonymity, the need for which was fundamental. Policy implications would involve defining the roles and responsibilities of the different stakeholders, making technology choices, and defining the indicators to be monitored. The implications for practice would entail identifying the mechanisms for counselling, mediation meetings, and reviews, and how, where, and when they should be carried out.

Long temporal horizon for ICT-enabled change. The evaluation initiatives of ICT projects take a snapshot view to understand their impacts. Such an approach is inadequate to understand the dynamics of ICT projects, which have their own ebb and flows. A perceived failure could blossom into a success later. A classic example of such changes was the study by Madon (2006) in which she traced the evolution over 17 years of the Computerised Rural Information System Project (CRISP) in Indian public administration. As the nature of reforms changed in the state government, the relation between the front and the backend of the initiatives varied, leading to different trajectories of CRISP. More recently, Sahay et al. (2013), who traced the growth over the DHIS2 over nearly 15 years, argued that the growth reflected a pattern of 'same, same, but different', where the new and the old got intertwined and became part of the evolution trajectory. Taking a long-term temporal perspective provides rich insights into the evolution of the means, processes, and ends, which are not possible to glean through the snapshot approach.

A number of cases have drawn upon a temporal perspective extending more than 10 years. Sri Lanka is an outstanding example where investments in 2009–10 in strengthening health informatics capabilities at university and ministry levels showed results in 2020 when the pandemic arrived in the country. In the intervening decade, there were processes of nurturing and evolving the digital and institutional capabilities for mutual trust to develop, and resilience of the digital and health systems to develop. Similarly, the HMIS in Odisha started its development in 2008. In 2020, when the systems were studied, we found significant improvements in data entry and data quality, but there was still a long way to go in strengthening the processes of use. The evolution of these systems follows large-scale efforts to build information infrastructure, rather than isolated systems. Research has emphasized that large-scale information infrastructure development is typically a long-term effort with no definite start and end dates, and developing as 'a shared, evolving, open, standardized, and hetero-geneous installed base' (Hanseth and Lyytinen, 2004). The existing installed base becomes an important determinant of the future trajectory of an infrastructure.

A key theoretical implication of a long temporal perspective is the analytical understanding of how historical conditions shape the development and use of systems, and also that systems can never be designed from scratch. Further changing of the means–process–ends conditions will require the response of information systems to be continuously adjusted and reconfigured. An under-standing of history is imperative while making future plans.

Conclusions

We have tried to focus this book on generating narratives of hope, on how the digital can possibly contribute to positive social outcomes. Such a focus can be aspirational, and can allow individuals and organizations to imagine positive futures without getting shackled to the past. These are typified by stories of digital interventions that did not work. Building hope is a complex effort that takes time. It involves a plethora of means and processes to achieve positive outcomes in different domains. While our analytical focus has been broadly on the domains of health and social development, the ideas can be generalized to fit other domains such as rural development, forestry, and education. As the world becomes more complex and social challenges more interconnected, systems thinking becomes a useful approach in the generation of stories of hope.

References

Bhatti, Y. (2014) '"Reverse Innovation: Create Far from Home, Win Everywhere", book review', *South Asian Journal of Global Business Research* 3(1): 102–4 <https://doi.org/10.1108/SAJGBR-03-2013-0023>.
Bhatti, Y.A., Basu, R.R., Barron, D. and Ventresca, M.J. (2018) *Frugal Innovation: Models, Means, Methods*, Cambridge University Press, Cambridge.

Hanseth, O. and Lyytinen, K. (2004) 'Theorizing about the design of information infrastructures: design kernel theories and principles', *Sprouts: Working Papers on Information Environments, Systems and Organizations* 4(12) [online] <https://www.uio.no/studier/emner/jus/afin/FINF4001/h16/hanseth-and-lyytinen-2004.pdf> [accessed 29 August 2021].

Madon, S. (2006) 'IT-based government reform initiatives in the Indian state of Gujarat', *Journal of International Development* 18(6): 877–88 <https://doi.org/10.1002/jid.1320>.

Sahay, S., Sæbø, J. and Braa, J. (2013) 'Scaling of HIS in a global context: same, same, but different', *Information and Organization* 23(4): 294–323 <https://doi.org/10.1016/j.infoandorg.2013.08.002>.

www.ingramcontent.com/pod-product-compliance
Lightning Source LLC
Chambersburg PA
CBHW070932030426
42336CB00014BA/2645